# BIRDS OF THE CORNISH COAST

Oystercatchers

# BIRDS of the CORNISH COAST

## INCLUDING THE ISLES OF SCILLY

R. D. Penhallurick B.A.

D. BRADFORD BARTON LTD.

© R. D. Penhallurick 1969

*Printed in Great Britain by Wordens of Cornwall Ltd., Penzance*
*and bound by Robert Hartnoll Ltd., Bodmin for the publishers*
D. Bradford Barton Ltd · Truro

Greenshank

Ringed plovers

*to Colin P. Rees*
*who introduced me to*
*ornithology in the Vale of Glamorgan*

# CONTENTS

# ILLUSTRATIONS

'The Island' at St Ives from Porthkidney beach, the foremost headland for watching sea-birds in Cornwall

# MAPS

The following maps shew the distribution and numbers of breeding birds in late May or early June 1967. This census was prompted by the pollution of oil and detergent that followed the wreck of the *Torrey Canyon* on 18 March 1967 on the Seven Stones reef between Land's End and the Isles of Scilly.

with sixty drawings in the text by the author

# INTRODUCTION

"Upon the utmost end of Cornwall's furrowing beak,
Where Bresan from the land the tilting waves doth break;
The shore let her transcend the promont to descry,
And view about the point th' unnumbered fowl that fly;
Some rising like a storm from the troubled sand,
Seem in their hov'ring flight to shadow all the land;
Some sitting on the beach to prune their painted breasts,
As if both earth and air they only did possess;"

Michael Drayton's *Poly-Olbion*, 1622.

The much quoted sentiment that some beloved spot has an individuality and charm of its own, is nowhere in England more justly applicable than to Cornwall which lies in grand isolation, almost aloof and certainly distinct from the rest of the country. Cornwall is a cartographer's dream outlined for the greater part by nature's most natural frontier—the sea—while its eastern boundary with Devon is traced by the Tamar which rises in Morwenstow parish only three and a half miles from the cliffs at Marsland Mouth. Such a self-contained natural region is perfect for study. No other part of Britain has invited more attention from students of human and natural history than Cornwall. Interest is particularly strong in such fields as geology, botany, and marine-biology, where much can be investigated that is rare or absent elsewhere.

Cornwall may not be able, as Scotland may, to boast of birds peculiar to itself. Indeed, species like the nightingale and common redstart, which are well known in other parts of England, are conspicuous by their absence or rarity. Nevertheless, the county has acquired an impressive check-list of birds as a result of its geographical position. It straddles the flight line of the migration route along the west coast of Britain; its proximity to the Continent provides a useful landing-stage and point of departure for migrants; its winters, normally tempered to "languid springs", offer a refuge to fugitives from less genial quarters, while its westerly position offers a welcome landfall to trans-Atlantic travellers.

Sea-birds more than anything else typify Cornwall's avifauna. Over 320 miles of coastline—more than in any other English county—one hundred of them delineating the intricacies of long estuaries, attract most attention from bird-watchers so that no excuse is needed for presenting a book that deals only with sea-birds, water-fowl, and waders. Inevitably this has allowed a few apparent inconsistencies to appear in the text. The woodcock, as a wader, is included even

13

though it is hardly a water bird, when such species as the chough and peregrine
falcon, emblematic denizens of the rockier shores in days past if not at present,
have been excluded along with all passerines and raptors.

Cornwall's fame—'notoriety' is perhaps more appropriate—as an ornithological
*El Dorado* has increased during the past ten years by an amount that mushrooms
annually. A new subspecies of bird-watcher, the unswerving rarity-hunter,
invades Cornwall and the Isles of Scilly, especially during the autumn, in the near
certainty of glimpsing one of the rarities that the elements and passing ships cast
upon our shores. It is now considered almost disastrous if at least one new species
is not added annually to the European, British or, at very least, the county list.
In this volume all occurrences of rare birds are listed, either from the earliest
reference or, if this would result in too cumbersome a catalogue, from 1900 or
even later. In so doing it is not intended to over-emphasise 'rarity-mania' to the
exclusion of other aspects of the growing hobby of ornithology. In preparing this
volume, the lack of attention paid to the commonest birds which, after all, are the
ones which matter most, has become very apparent. Writing of the oystercatcher,
P. J. Dare made a statement that applies equally well to many other familiar
species—

> In general the amount of data available is inversely proportional to oystercatcher abundance.
> Thus, for many counties where the species breeds less plentifully a reliable indication of local
> population size is usually obtainable . . . Where, however, oystercatchers are much more
> numerous . . . published records are usually so inadequate that estimates have had to be based
> largely on other sources of information.
>
> (*Fishery Investigations*, Series II, Vol. xxv, No. 5. H.M.S.O.)

It is hoped that this volume will encourage more observers to enlarge on the
scanty knowledge of the commonest species, particularly those nesting in the
county. Of the 171 species contained in the following pages, only the 44 listed
below are known to have nested at any time. Those breeding annually are given
in capital letters.

| *Species* | *Cornwall* | *Isles of Scilly* |
|---|---|---|
| Great crested grebe | Once in 1930 | — |
| LITTLE GREBE | Widespread | — |
| MANX SHEARWATER | Probably extinct | Common, especially on Annet |
| STORM PETREL | Gulland Rock, doubtfully still elsewhere | Common at certain colonies |
| FULMAR PETREL | Common | Common |
| Gannet | Mediæval colony at Gulland Rock | — |
| CORMORANT | Widespread on the north coast | Small numbers |
| SHAG | Common | Common |
| COMMON HERON | Small scattered colonies | — |
| MUTE SWAN | Widespread | A few on Tresco |

| | | |
|---|---|---|
| SHELDUCK | Widespread – increased since 1900 | About twelve pairs on Sampson and Eastern Isles |
| MALLARD | Widespread | On several islands |
| TEAL | Very sporadic records | A few annually |
| SHOVELER | — | Annually since 1958 |
| Garganey | First authenticated in 1968 | A few records |
| Tufted duck | A few records | — |
| GADWALL | — | Annually on Tresco |
| Corncrake | Rare but perhaps still annual | Sporadic records |
| WATER RAIL | Widespread but local | Apparently only on Tresco |
| Spotted crake | Formerly bred, present status uncertain | No definite records |
| MOORHEN | Widespread and common | Mainly on Tresco |
| COOT | Widespread but rather local | Tresco and St Mary's |
| OYSTERCATCHER | Mainly on the north coast | Widespread |
| RINGED PLOVER | Formerly common, now probably extinct | Widespread |
| LAPWING | Widespread in small numbers | — |
| Dunlin | A few pairs, perhaps annually | — |
| Redshank | In 1903 and probably in 1968 | — |
| Common sandpiper | No records since 1910 | — |
| CURLEW | Mainly on Bodmin Moor, some further west | — |
| Woodcock | Exceptionally | — |
| COMMON SNIPE | Mainly on Bodmin Moor | — |
| Black-headed gull | Exceptionally | Regularly until mid-19th century, exceptionally since |
| LESSER BLACK-BACKED GULL | Small numbers | Numerous |
| GREAT BLACK-BACKED GULL | Widespread | Numerous |
| HERRING GULL | Widespread and common | Numerous |
| KITTIWAKE | Some large colonies especially at St Agnes | Several colonies |
| Sandwich tern | — | Extinct since 1903 |
| COMMON TERN | No certain record | Common |
| Arctic tern | — | Formerly annual, now sporadic |
| ROSEATE TERN | — | Became temporarily extinct c. 1900, now a few annually |
| Little tern | Extinct since about 1910 but older records probably untrustworthy | Extinct |
| RAZORBILL | Mainly on north coast | Small numbers |
| GUILLEMOT | Mainly on north coast | More common than razorbill |
| PUFFIN | Several dwindling colonies | Good numbers only on Annet |

All known details of the past history and present distribution of breeding birds are given in the text and on the accompanying maps, so that it is sufficient to make only a few general points here. The more rugged northern coasts from the Lizard to Boscastle, with abundant off-shore stacks and small islands, contain far more breeding birds than the gentler southern coast where only Gull Rock (or The Gray) in Veryan Bay is important. The reason for the sparsity of breeding birds from Boscastle to the Devon border is geological. Although the highest sheer cliffs in the county are found here, the rocks of well-banded shales and sandstones (Culm Measures) are tilted to near vertical strata for many miles or contorted into such complex folds as in the famous "zig-zags" at Millook Haven. This results in few and small ledges inhabitable by little apart from a few herring gulls. In the Land's End peninsula the contrast between breeding numbers on the north and south coasts is partly geological. The southern side is principally of granite, which weathers to a characteristic "castellated" formation with "mural jointing" and provides fewer suitably isolated ledges for nesting colonies than do the harder "greenstones" (altered rocks of mostly diorite type) which outcrop extensively on the northern shore. The Lizard complex of serpentines, hornblende schists and other metamorphosed or igneous rocks, mainly attracts birds to its western shore and islands where schists are particularly extensive. This makes the area one of the most thickly colonized parts of the county. Few birds nest in the eastern part of the Lizard where gabbro and primary serpentine are commonest. The Isles of Scilly, entirely of granite, support large colonies of birds, especially on the isolated stacks like Menavawr and Rosevear. Many areas in Cornwall, apparently suitable for breeding birds, are empty. This may not always have been the case. The ringed plover was certainly driven from shingle beaches on the mainland by human disturbance and remain widespread only at Scilly. The influence of man and other factors, such as the piratical attacks of gulls on razorbills being a possible reason for the latter's habit of nesting under granite boulders on Scilly, mask the real influence of geology and the whole subject remains to be properly studied.

Apart from herons and shelducks, few birds covered in this volume nest in the vicinity of estuaries which are essentially feeding, not breeding, habitats. The merits of the various estuaries, sheltered bays, and stretches of freshwater need not

A small creek off the Tamar above Cargreen where the avocets may be seen in winter

be detailed here as they soon become apparent on reading through such species as great northern diver, wigeon, and redshank. Suffice to say that the most important estuaries are the Tamar-Lynher complex, the Camel, the Ruan stretch of the Fal, and the Hayle. The Camel estuary is made especially attractive by the recently constructed hide near Burniere Point below Trewornan Bridge over the Amble river (open only to key-holding members of the Cornwall Bird-Watching and Preservation Society), and the long-established Walmsley Sanctuary between Trewornan Bridge and Chapel Amble—a winter refuge for the only flock of white-fronted geese regularly to visit the south-west outside Gloucestershire.

Much of the information on the numbers of wintering wildfowl is taken from the National Wildfowl Counts organised by the Wildfowl Trust. In Devon counts began in the winter of 1954–55 and include two areas covered here—Tamar Lake and the Tamar estuary. In Cornwall the first counts were organised in 1959–60 and most of the major waters, apart from the Fal at Ruan, are now covered. The following dates refer to the first winter count in each area. River Lynher, 1959–60; St John's Lake, 1965–66; Looe River, 1965–66; Par beach, 1959–60 to 1964–65; Tresillian River, 1962–63; Truro River with Calenick Creek and Lambe Creek, 1966–67; Restronguet Creek, 1962–63; Stithians reservoir, 1965–66; Loe Pool, 1959–60; Marazion Marsh, 1960–61; Drift reservoir, 1967–68; Hayle estuary, 1959–60; Camel estuary and Walmsley sanctuary, 1959–60. Other waters were visited but found to contain too few birds to merit continued counting— The Gannel, Melancoose reservoir near Newquay, and Helford River. Counts take place between September and March inclusive about the middle of each month. At the time of writing the latest available Wildfowl Trust figures were for the 1966–67 season. The information from these counts has proved very encouraging and the British Trust for Ornithology is now (1969) organising a similar census dealing with other species, principally waders and gulls, which eventually will probably be conducted throughout the year. A pilot scheme to count godwits in the winter of 1968–69 produced encouraging results.

The Wildfowl Trust's census of breeding birds commenced in Cornwall in the summer of 1965, but few records have so far been received. Far more ambitious is the projected *Bird Atlas of Britain and Ireland* in which the distribution of all

*Where the River Amble meets the Camel is the best locality for watching birds on the estuary. This is the view at low tide from the observation hide built at this point in 1967.*

breeding birds will be plotted on the 10-kilometre squares of the national grid found on Ordnance Survey maps. The initial season's work for this was in 1968.

The records of ringed birds were abstracted from the record cards at the headquarters of the British Trust for Ornithology at Tring, Hertfordshire, in November 1968.

*Probus, Cornwall, 1969*                         R. D. PENHALLURICK

" Green sandpiper "

# BIBLIOGRAPHY

## GENERAL ORNITHOLOGY

The following are the most frequently consulted works; others are given full reference in the text.

BANNERMAN D. A. *The Birds of the British Isles*, 12 vols. 1953–63.

PARSLOW J. L. F. Changes in status among breeding birds in Britain and Ireland, *British Birds*, eight monthly issues from January 1967 to June 1968.

VOOUS K. H. *Atlas of European Birds*, 1960.

WITHERBY *et al. The Handbook of British Birds*, 1948 impression.

YARRELL W. *A History of British Birds*, 2nd ed. 1845 and revised 4th ed. 1871–74.

## CORNISH & DIALECT NAMES

NANCE R. M. *A Glossary of Cornish Seawords*, published posthumously for the Federation of Old Cornwall Societies, 1963.

NANCE R. M. Celtic bird names of Cornwall, *Old Cornwall*, 1965 (posthumous).

SWAINSON C. *The Folk-lore and Provincial Names of British Birds*, 1886.

WRIGHT J. (editor) *The English Dialect Dictionary*, 1896–1905.

## CORNISH ORNITHOLOGY

The following list is chronological—naturally there is some overlap. For the earliest references to Cornwall see under gannet and puffin.

CAREW R. *The Survey of Cornwall*, 1602. This was quoted from extensively by later authors, as in Childrey's *Britannica Baconica*, 1660.

RAY J. *The Ornithology of Francis Willughby*, 1678 (Latin ed. 1676). Both visited Cornwall in 1662 and Ray came alone in 1667. For an account of their journeys see the *Memorials of John Ray with his Itineraries*, 1846, for the Ray Society.

TONKIN T. & MOYLE W. At the County Museum, Truro is a MS entitled—*The Natural History of Cornwall of Thomas Tonkin of Trevaunance* [St Agnes near Truro] and below written *Lambriggan* 1700, evidently the date he began his history. Most of the observations on birds were copied from the MS of Walter Moyle (1672–1721) of Bake near Looe, the foremost local naturalist of his day. He recognised several "gross errors" in Willughby's *Ornithology*, and would have corrected these but for his untimely death. Much of his collection of birds dated from 1715 to 1717. His letters to Dr Tandred Robinson and Dr Sherard were published in *The Works of Walter Moyle Esq.*, 1726. Those of ornithological interest were reprinted in Rodd's *Birds of Cornwall* (1880). Some of Tonkin's notes were added to the De Dunstanville edition of Carew's *Survey*, 1811.

BORLASE W. *Natural History of Cornwall*, 1758. More interested in geology than ornithology, this author lists rather than details most species of birds. Additions to his *History* were published in the *Journal of the Royal Institution of Cornwall* for 1864, 1865 and 1866. These are taken mostly from Tonkin and Moyle.

19

JAMES F. The Literary Repository of Cornwall and Devon, Quadrupeds, Birds, and Fishes, *Monthly Magazine*, December 1808, by Francis James (anonymously) of Manaccan who died at Helston in 1849. He briefly comments on 132 species.

MONTAGU G. *Ornithological Dictionary of British Birds*, 1802 with supplement in 1913.

MOORE E. M. On the Ornithology of South Devon, *Transactions of the Plymouth Institution*, 1830.

COUCH J. *A Cornish Fauna*, published for the Royal Institution of Cornwall, Part I, 1838. The 1878 edition revised by E. H. Rodd is mostly a copy of the latter's own *List* of 1864.

COCKS W. P. Contributions to the Fauna of Falmouth, by William Pennington Cocks (1791–1878) in *The Naturalist*, 1851.

At the County Museum, Truro, is a MS list of British birds observed between 1844 and February 1849 and found 'a' in the county, and 'b' in Falmouth and neighbourhood. The list is of limited value and contains several errors—notably the inclusion of hooded merganser and great auk under 'a'.

BULLMORE W. K. Cornish Fauna, *Royal Cornwall Polytechnic Society*, 1866. This deals mainly with the Falmouth area.

RODD E. H. Edward Hearle Rodd (1810–80) was the giant of nineteenth century ornithology. He was a regular contributor to *The Zoologist* from 1843. Other works are a list of birds in the *Penzance Natural History and Antiquarian Society* for 1850, which was expanded into *A List of British Birds* (principally to the Land's End district) in 1864—the copy at the County Museum, Truro contains marginalia by his nephew F. R. Rodd made not later than about 1871 and referring to birds at Scilly and Trebartha Hall (now destroyed) near Launceston. Rodd's major work, *The Birds of Cornwall and the Scilly Islands*, 1880, was completed after his death by James Edmund Harting, editor of *The Zoologist*. F. R. Rodd added further notes from his "Journal of a Sportsman and Naturalist in the Scilly Islands", and appended a list of the birds seen there. E. H. Rodd supplied information for many guide books including— *A Week in the Isles of Scilly*, L. H. Courtney. Five editions appeared up to 1897 and was itself based on Revd. J. W. North's book of the same name in 1850.

*A Guide to Penzance*, L. H. Courtney, 1845.

*A Week at the Land's End*, T. J. Blight, 1861. The 1876 edition contains engravings of birds from Rodd's collection, most of which had been set up by the Penzance taxidermist W. S. Vingoe.

JOHNS C. A. *A Week in the Lizard*, 1848. Birds are scarcely mentioned, but the 1874 edition contains a catalogue of birds by F. V. Hill, of Helston.

D'URBAN W. S. M. & MATHEW M. A. *The Birds of Devon*, 1892 with supplement in 1895. This contains more useful information on Cornwall than its title would suggest.

CLARK J. Dr James Clark was Cornwall's most brilliant naturalist at the turn of the present century. After being Professor of Agriculture at Leeds in 1897, he became Principal of the Central Technical Schools for Cornwall, at Truro until his appointment as Rector of Kilmarnock Academy in 1908. His most important contribution was the bulk of the zoological papers, including *Birds*, in *The Victoria County History of Cornwall*, Vol. I., ed. W. Page, 1906. His other papers are—

The Birds of Cornwall, *Journal of the Royal Institution of Cornwall*, 1902.

Notes on Cornish Birds, *Ibid*, 1906.

American Birds in Cornwall, *Ibid*, 1907.

Bird Migration in Cornwall, *Ibid*, 1908.

The Birds of Scilly, written jointly with F. R. Rodd, *The Zoologist*, 1906.

Recent Occurrences of Rare Birds in Cornwall, *Ibid*, 1907. His only other contribution appears to be MS letters written to C. J. King on birds seen at Scilly since mid-summer 1906, and dated 9 and 25 October 1923.

1909 to 1931 are the years most lacking in ornithological information. Short notes appeared in *British Birds* by such contributors as A. W. H. and G. H. Harvey, A. W. Boyd, and for Scilly by H. W. Robinson and H. M. Wallis.

HARVEY A. W. H. Wrote a chapter in *The Homeland Handbooks Series*, Penzance and the Land's End District, *c.* 1915. This is one of the most reliable 'popular' guides.

KING C. J. *Some notes on Wild Nature in Scillonia*, 1924. This deals with the common sea-birds and seals.

RYVES B. H. 1931 was an important year with the foundation of the Cornwall Bird-Watching and Preservation Society by Lt.-Col. B. H. Ryves (1875–1961). He remained an editor of the Society's journal until 1959. As well as contributions to *British Birds*, dealing mostly with aspects of breeding biology, he published jointly with Miss H. Quick an account of the status of birds breeding in Cornwall and Scilly, *British Birds*, 1946. His main work, *Bird Life in Cornwall*, 1948, is in two parts—the first contains monographs on the chough, raven, peregrine falcon, buzzard, and Montagu's harrier; the second part is a check-list of birds compiled from the annual reports of the Society's journal from 1931 to 1945 inclusive.

QUICK H. M. *Birds of the Scilly Isles*, 1964. This deals mostly with the present status of the islands' birds in general terms.

# ABBREVIATIONS

| | |
|---|---|
| **AR** | Abbey Record Book, Tresco, Scilly (information *per* J. L. F. Parslow). The Abbey collection of birds is now in the Isles of Scilly Museum. |
| **BB** | *British Birds*, 1907 to present. In references in the text, the year is given only if the record is published in a year subsequent to the one in which the observation was made. Clearly, however, a record in late autumn may not appear until the following spring. The same applies to *The Zoologist*. |
| **BS** | *Bird Study*, 1954 to present. |
| **CBWPS** | Cornwall Bird-Watching and Preservation Society. So much material has been gleaned from the reports of this society that all information since 1931 which appears without any references can be assumed to have been taken from them. There are no references given to the few reports taken from *St Agnes Bird Observatory Reports*, 1957–1962, which are not duplicated in CBWPS publications. |
| **D & M** | D'Urban and Mathew, *The Birds of Devon*, 1892. |
| **F. R. RODD (MS)** | Pencilled notes in E. H. Rodd's *List* of 1864. |
| **G** | *Royal Cornwall Gazette*. |
| **N** | *The Naturalist*, 1851–1854. |
| **P** | *Royal Cornwall Polytechnic Society*. |
| **PI** | *Transactions of the Plymouth Institution*. |
| **PZ** | *Transactions of the Penzance Natural History and Antiquarian Society*, in three, short separate runs between 1845 and 1895. Important papers not mentioned in the bibliography are by N. Hare of Liskeard in 1849, and by Smart on the birds of Scilly in 1885–86. |
| **R** | Recent records of rare birds known to have been accepted by the Rare Birds Committee are followed by (R). |
| **RI** | *Report* or *Journal of the Royal Institution of Cornwall*. |
| **W** | *Wildfowl in Great Britain*, ed. G. L. Atkinson-Willes, H.M.S.O., 1963. |
| **WLE** | *Week at the Land's End*, T. J. Blight, 1876 *ed.* |
| **WLZ** | *A Week in the Lizard*, C. A. Johns, 1874 *ed.* |
| **Z** | *The Zoologist*, 1843–1916 (incorporated with *British Birds* from January 1917). See note given under *British Birds*. |
| **1** | Recent information followed by a name marked [1] indicates that the present author received that information from the person concerned in writing or verbally. |

Note that St Agnes, unless stated to the contrary, always refers to the island at Scilly and not the mainland parish.

# ACKNOWLEDGEMENTS

The author gratefully thanks the army of enthusiastic field-workers whose records were published in the annual reports of the Cornwall Bird-Watching and Preservation Society and appear here without individual acknowledgement.

A special debt of gratitude is owed to J. L. F. Parslow, founder of the St Agnes Bird Observatory, who unhesitatingly handed over his personal note books containing much unpublished material on the birds of Scilly. The maps have been drawn from information collected for the British Trust for Ornithology in June 1967 following the wreck of the *Torrey Canyon*. J. L. F. Parslow organised the count on the Isles of Scilly while N. R. Phillips and R. J. O'Connor were principal organisers on the mainland.

S. C. Madge of Torpoint contributed much useful information from the comparatively little-watched coastline between Looe and the Tamar estuary. A. G. Parsons of Redruth, Lt.-Col. W. E. Almond of St Breward, and R. J. Salmon of Lanivet also contributed a great deal of information on many aspects. Also deserving special mention are Dr G. Allsop, Revd. J. E. Beckerlegge, R. M. Bere, A. T. Beswetherick, R. J. Beswetherick, Major S. Bolitho, J. B. Bottomley, Dr C. J. F. Coombs, Dr P. J. Dare, Major J. S. Fortescue, Miss C. Hawkridge, D. P. Holmes, D. Hunt, C. P. Jarvis, R. Khan, T. Langford, Lord St Levan, Mrs F. E. Lott, P. Marriott, H. Millington, T. P. Morrissey, D. F. Musson, C. Noall, Miss H. Quick, D. Rundle, J. W. V. Sheldon, F. R. Smith, C. J. Stevens, P. A. Taylor, Professor A. C. Thomas, R. B. Treleaven, Dr F. A. Turk, F. Wardle, Mrs R. P. Weeks, Commander A. Williams, L. W. Williams.

Organisations that have kindly allowed publication of their material are The Wildfowl Trust, The British Trust for Ornithology, and the Royal Society for the Protection of Birds.

Finally, the production of the MS owes much to Miss Susan Dawe and Miss Angela Broome for translating frequently abominable handwriting into a presentable typescript; to H. L. Douch, my senior colleague at the Royal Institution of Cornwall, for general help and encouragement in its production; and to my publisher D. B. Barton who originally suggested its writing.

# NOMENCLATURE

The nomenclature of the species is that of the Check-list of the Birds of Great Britain and Ireland published by the British Ornithologists' Union in 1952 with subsequent amendments. Latin binomials only are used except where subspecies are referred to.

Curlew

# ISLES of SCILLY

ROUND ISLAND

MENAVAWR

WHITE ISLAND

ST HELENS

PLUMB IS.

Shipman Head

Hangman Is.

Gimble Porth

TEAN

Norwethel

Hedge Rock

ST MARTIN'S

SCILLY ROCK

BRYHER

Old Grimsby

TRESCO

Gweal

New Grimsby

Pool

GREAT POOL

Great Cheese Rock

HANJAGUE

Maiden Bower

Merrick Is.

Guther's Is.

Nor-Nour

Great Ganilly

Little Innisvouls

EASTERN ISLES

Little Ganilly

Great Ganinick

Great Innisvouls

Illiswilgig

ABBEY POOL

Pentle Bay

Castle Bryher

Skirt Island

Little Ganinick

Great Arthur

MINCARLO

White Island

SAMSON

Green Island

Bar Point

MENAWETHAN

Newford

ST MARY'S

Porthloo

Higher Moors

Porth Hellick Pool

The Garrison

Hugh Town

AIRPORT

Porth Hellick

N

Peninnis Head

ANNET

ST AGNES

GUGH

GREAT CREBAWETHAN

BISHOP ROCK

WESTERN ROCKS

MELLEDGAN

0        1   MILES   2        3

ROSVEAR

ROSVEAN

GORREGAN

R.D.P. del. 1969

## ST AGNES

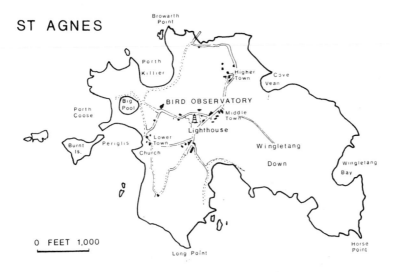

Browarth Point

Porth Killier

Higher Town

Cove Vean

Big Pool

BIRD OBSERVATORY

Porth Coose

Middle Town

Burnt Is.

Periglis

Lower Town

Lighthouse

Church

Wingletang Down

Wingletang Bay

Long Point

Horse Point

0  FEET  1,000

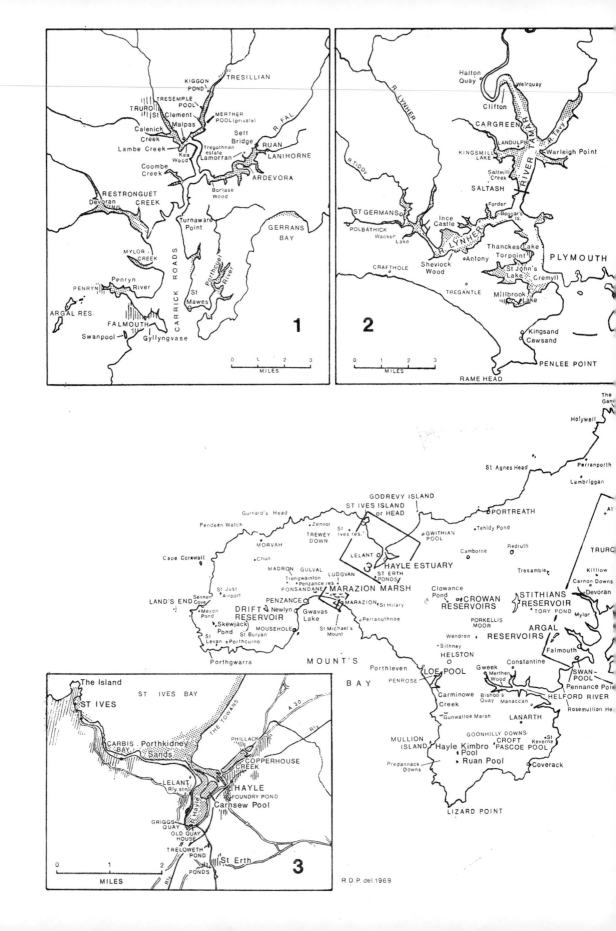

# CORNWALL

Localities mentioned in the text
ADDITIONAL COASTAL LOCALITIES ARE INDICATED
ON THE MAPS OF BREEDING BIRDS

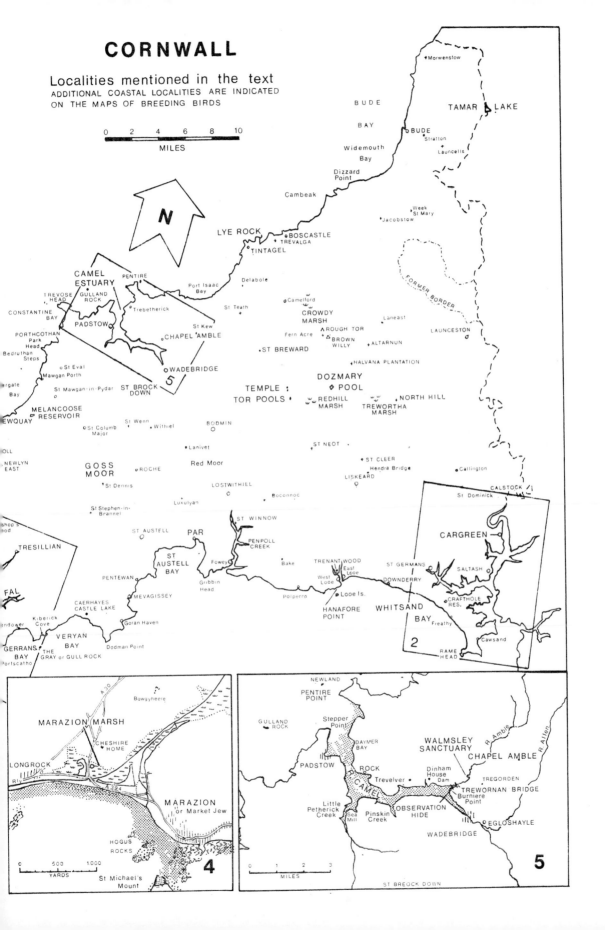

## BLACK-THROATED DIVER
*Gavia arctica*

The breeding distribution of the black-throated diver is almost circumpolar; only the north Atlantic seaboard is largely devoid of this bird, although it is a scarce resident in Scotland.

In Cornwall it is a far less common winter visitor than the great northern diver, but has been recorded annually since 1960. Its status has probably changed little since the nineteenth century, the lack of records prior to the 1950's probably being the result of insufficient careful watching for recent observations shew the black-throated diver is more inclined to stay further away from the shore than other members of the family. Records of birds entering harbours are rare (as St Ives, January 1957, and Padstow, December 1965); also unusual was one at Carnsew Pool, Hayle in January 1961.

Most black-throated divers are reported from sheltered bays, notably Mount's Bay and St Ives Bay and less regularly at the mouth of the Camel estuary. Autumn passage has been noted at St Ives as early as 10 and 11 October in 1965, but few appear before the end of November. Over 50 per cent of winter records comprise single birds, with 30 per cent as parties of two to four. As many as ten were off St Ives in the severe weather of February 1963, seven off Marazion on 17 December the same year, and eleven in Mount's Bay on 16 April 1967.

Despite the predominance of records from west Cornwall, the south coast between Gerrans Bay and the Tamar would repay greater attention, especially in the spring when Scandinavian birds—some of which winter off Portugal and beyond—

move north. The main movement is well to the east, but its effects are more apparent off Cornwall than published records suggest. Off south-east Cornwall few are seen except at migration time from late February to early May, the main movement being from late April (Madge[1]). Indeed, more have been reported in April than in any other month. Ten were seen off Portholland on 3 April 1965, and as many as 25 in breeding plumage in Veryan Bay on 16 April 1960, where a fleet of about a score were reported in April 1938. The latest record is of two birds off Tregantle, Antony on 2 June 1965. Unusual was one off Cawsand on 29 August 1966.

Records from Scilly are rare. Clark and Rodd (z, 1906) did not know of a single occurrence although King probably saw one in January 1904 and one was seen off Tresco from 8 to 19 March 1929 (BB). Since 1951 the only published records are of single birds at migration time—

| | |
|---|---|
| 1951 | Found dead on 5 October. |
| 1952 | Off St Mary's on 21 April. |
| 1957 | Off St Agnes from 31 March to 10 April. |
| 1965 | Off St Mary's on 10 and 11 November. |
| 1967 | Off Bryher on 7 April and another off St Agnes on 11 October. |

## GREAT NORTHERN DIVER
*Gavia immer*

The great northern diver, largest and commonest member of the family in Cornish waters, is essentially a bird of North America. It may have nested in the Shetland Isles but does not definitely do so any nearer than Iceland from whence it is assumed that most of our visitors come.

The great northern diver was first re-

ported from Cornwall by Walter Moyle
(Tonkin MS) who obtained a 'greater
speckled Diver or Loon' in the winter of
1715–16. The species may have become
more common since then for Rodd (1880)
wrote that it appeared to be more common
than earlier in the nineteenth century,
although still not so plentiful as the red-
throated diver. At the present time it is
certainly far more common than the latter
species, while the maximum numbers
quoted by Rodd are less than half the size
of the largest parties reported in recent
winters. Great northerns were unusually
numerous in the winter of 1874–75; a dozen
or more were reported in one day within
a mile and a half of Mevagissey. Similar
numbers were recorded from south-east
Cornwall and south Devon by Gatcombe
(z) in January, February, and October 1877.
By contrast, such numbers are by no means
rare nowadays, and as many as 35 were seen
in St Ives Bay during the hard winter of
1963. Early autumn arrivals may be in
breeding plumage, as were most of the nine
off Porthminster, St Ives as late as 11
November 1960.

The great northern diver has been seen off
the Cornish coast in every month of the
year. Records from June to mid-September
are rare and presumably represent non-
breeding birds which have remained in
southern waters—a habit common enough
off northern Scotland. Two birds, in winter
or immature plumage, remained off St
Michael's Mount throughout the summer of
1961.

Great-northern diver

Autumn migrants first appear off west
Cornwall normally in late October. Early
dates include one off St Ives in breeding
plumage on 31 August 1958; four flew past
St Ives Island and another off Newquay on
29 September 1963, and one off Godrevy on
30 September 1964. In south-east Cornwall
they have not been recorded before the end
of October and remain rare until the end of
November. In west Cornwall the largest
parties are sometimes seen in late November,
consisting of passage migrants on a temporary stay and winter residents soon to
disperse around the coast. As many as 30
flew past St Ives during a morning watch on
27 November 1960 while during single days
in 1965 there were fourteen on 27 November and eighteen on the 28th.

The peak numbers occur in January or
February and are evidently related to the
severity of the weather. Thus, exceptional
numbers were reported early in 1963 and
include 35 in St Ives Bay on 15 February,
and fifteen there and in Mount's Bay on
3 March. The winter of 1965–66 saw great
northern divers at most of their usual haunts
in greater than average numbers. On the
north coast they were seen on the Camel
estuary—their favourite sector being between Rock and Trebetherick, off Newquay, and in St Ives Bay with a maximum
of eleven on 2 January. Divers are rarely
reported elsewhere on the north coast but
a flock of eighteen to twenty sheltered under
the cliffs at Widemouth Bay on 25 January
1963. In 1965–66, Mount's Bay contained a
maximum of fifteen on 29 January. Most of
the coast around the Land's End and Lizard
peninsulas affords little shelter for divers but
they have been seen at Sennen and Kennack.
On the south coast birds were reported from
Helford Passage; Falmouth Bay with up to
nineteen in December 1965; off Gribben
Head; Mevagissey; Looe with 30 on 6 February 1966; Porthallow with thirteen on
24 March 1966; Millbrook Lake; St John's
Lake and the Lynher. In most years birds
frequent the sheltered bays at Par, Gerrans,

and Veryan. Only in the last few years have some of the south coast localities been watched with the same intensity long given to west Cornwall. Divers are more common at places like Veryan Bay than published records suggest; winter numbers probably equal if not surpass those found in Mount's Bay. S. C. Madge[1] wrote that the sheltered waters between Looe Island and Hannafore are very attractive to them, and at least 30 have been counted there after south-westerly gales in January and February.

Spring passage is not so well reported as that in autumn, but returning birds are seen from the end of January and account for many of the small parties seen particularly in April. Latest records are eleven off St Ives on 11 May 1963 and one off Marazion on 2 June 1964.

While the great northern diver is not infrequently reported on the Hayle estuary or Carnsew Pool, it rarely ventures up estuaries far inland—only once has a bird been reported from the Tresillian river. However, the species is much more an inshore bird than the black-throated diver and it is considered a 'bad year' if a few have not been seen within Newlyn or Penzance harbours where they shew little fear of man, swimming close under the quayside. Indeed, their inquisitive nature gave rise to many stories of divers falling foul of fishermen's nets from which, according to Rodd (1880), they tried to wrench ensnared fish.

In contrast to the mainland, the great northern diver is an uncommon although regular visitor to Scilly, but apparently less common than formerly. Clark (z, 1906) wrote that it was to be seen in autumn and winter both singly and in small flocks, and occasionally in late spring. During the winter of 1901–2 it was quite common in flocks of six to ten. King (1924) stated that they were to be seen between October and May "in flocks of five to six—rarely ever in larger numbers. In winter one can seldom make a passage between any of the islands without seeing one or more of these birds,

and during the early months of the year two or three are constantly fishing in St Mary's Pool". More recent records are less common, although since 1957 at least they have been seen annually, but only singly or in twos. Most have occurred in March and April and were probably birds on passage or possibly moulting. Several have remained until late May. In 1947 one was seen off St Mary's on 29 July.

## WHITE-BILLED DIVER
*Gavia adamsii*

A number of these vagrants to eastern Britain from northern Finland and Siberia have been reported in Cornish waters—one off Toll's Island, Scilly in April 1925 (King MS) and two at Scilly in February 1965, but the only authenticated bird is that seen off Marazion from 11 to 19 April 1967 (R).

## RED-THROATED DIVER
*Gavia stellata*

The breeding range of the red-throated diver is similar to that of the black-throated, but more widespread. It has increased in this country following a decrease in the last century. Birds now nest in Scotland, including the Northern and Western Isles, and in County Donegal, Ireland.

During the nineteenth century the red-throated diver was held to be the commonest diver in Cornish waters, a position since unsurped by the great northern. Gatcombe (z, 1878) noted that the species had become scarce in the past few years, but there is no real evidence that it is any less common now than formerly. Its position relative to that of the great northern seems entirely dependent upon an increase in the latter's numbers.

The red-throated diver is less shy than the black-throated and is commonly seen close inshore; indeed, it is the only member of the family to be seen on freshwater. Since 1960 it has occurred at Tamar Lake, Argal and Crowan reservoirs, and Marazion Marsh. These records are unusual, but in seven years since 1955 it has been seen at Loe Pool or just off the Bar. Three were reported there in 1955 and 1966, five on 17 March 1956, and a similar number in February and March 1963 during very cold weather. It may be found in all the sheltered bays and estuary mouths listed under the great northern diver. The red-throated will, however, venture further up estuaries than its larger relative. One was swimming in Lambe Creek near Truro on 12 November 1967, and they are frequently found well up the Tamar. Most are recorded in ones or twos. The largest numbers are at least ten in Newquay Bay on 22 January 1966, ten in Par Bay on 4 May 1962, and six at Mawgan Porth in April 1953. The latter is an unusual locality, although the Padstow-Constantine-Trebetherick area is a favourite haunt, one or two being reported here annually. The only record further east is of a single bird at Crackington Haven in July 1965, the only summer record for the county.

Passage migrants are occasionally reported in September, the earliest dates being in 1967 when two in breeding plumage flew west past St Ives Island on 3 September and another flew into St Ives Bay on the 6th. Most divers are seen from the end of October until mid-April. Off the south coast of Cornwall there is certainly a spring passage; in fact birds are rare here in autumn. Spring records for the latter half of April and May are almost annual, and include birds in full or partial breeding dress. Latest records are of one at St John's Lake on 17 May 1965, and one in Mount's Bay from 24 to 29 May 1967.

The red-throated diver is a rare visitor to Scilly. Rodd (1880) noted its occurrence in autumn and winter, but the only specimen traced by Clark and Rodd (z, 1906) was one shot by David Smith in spring 1894 and presumably the bird now in the Tresco Abbey collection. In recent years it has proved to be equally rare. The only reports for this century are—

1958  One off Gugh on 16 October.
1963  One found dead on St Mary's on 1 February.
1965  One off St Mary's on 17 October.
1967  At St Agnes, an oiled bird on 29 March and another on 17 October. Off St Mary's one was seen on 15 and 17 October.

Two were seen somewhere between Land's End and the Scillies on 4 September 1961. Why the species should be so rare in the Scillies, when it is an annual visitor to the mainland, remains a mystery.

## GREAT CRESTED GREBE
*Podiceps cristatus*

The great crested grebe is a widespread breeding species throughout most of Europe. The lack of large stretches of open water surrounded by a sufficient cover of reeds, makes Cornwall one of the few English counties where it does not nest. There is only one record of it having done so; the 1931 enquiry (BB, 1932–33) stated that a pair reared three young at Tamar Lake in 1930 but not in the year of the census. In recent years nesting has occurred in south-east England at seemingly unsuitable sites such as abandoned gravel pits, but no increase is thought likely in the south-west.

This grebe is a winter visitor to Cornwall, mostly recorded from November until mid-March. Unusually early was one at Tamar Lake from 15 August to early September 1962. In some years, especially off the south coast, records are more frequent between mid-February and late March, suggesting an early spring passage movement. The latest date is one on the River Lynher on 14 April 1967.

Since the early years of this century, the great crested grebe has decreased in numbers. Clark (VCH) described it as not uncommon in flocks of twelve to fifteen, while today it is usually seen singly except in south-east Cornwall where up to four are not uncommon in the Lynher-Tamar-St John's Lake area. Uncommonly large numbers were reported during the cold weather early in 1963; nine on the Lynher on 10 March; six on the Tamar on 31 January; three in Falmouth Bay on 12 February and 28 March; six in Penzance harbour on 23 March; three in St Ives Bay in early March; and five on the Camel estuary in mid-February. While flocks of several hundred are not uncommon in eastern Britain, nineteen at Restronguet Creek in March 1937 is the largest party yet recorded in the county. The above localities give a good indication of the distribution of this species; away from the south coast it is rarely seen except at Mount's Bay, St Ives Bay, and the mouth of the Camel estuary. During the nineteenth century, this grebe was not infrequent on freshwater pools in the Land's End peninsula (Rodd, 1880), but the only inland locality where it is now seen with any degree of regularity is Tamar Lake, and here it is not annual. One was seen at the new Stithians reservoir on 24 January 1966 and another on 30 November 1967.

At Scilly, it is a rare visitor, unknown to Clark and Rodd (z, 1906) although Tresco Abbey records refer to one shot on 14 February 1895. The only records since then are of single birds off Plumb island in Tean Sound on 16 September 1953 (AR), and off St Agnes on 5 February 1956.

# RED-NECKED GREBE
*Podiceps grisegena*

In Europe the red-necked grebe breeds mainly east of a line from Denmark to the Balkans and excluding most of Scandinavia. Not surprisingly, therefore, most birds wintering in Britain do so off the east coast.

Statements by Rodd, Couch, and Bullmore, in the nineteenth century, inferring that this grebe was almost as common as the great crested grebe—itself more common than at present—were regarded with scepticism by later writers. D'Urban and Mathew (1892) called Rodd's remark "singular", and Clark described the species as "usually scarce", noting in 1908 (RI) that it was unknown at Scilly. The only records from the islands are one shot sometime between 1906 and 1923 (letter, 1923); one off Borough Beach, St Mary's, on 17 October 1965, and one off St Agnes on 9 October and 8 November 1966.

On the mainland the red-necked grebe is certainly the rarest of the family at the present time, although probably annual. It is almost always seen singly, mainly on the south and west coasts between early December and the beginning of March in those sheltered bays and estuaries visited by the great crested grebe. Exceptionally early was one at Dozmary Pool on 30 September 1965. The arctic conditions early in 1963 drove more than average numbers into Cornwall, notably seven into St Ives Bay in February, where three were still present

Tamar Lake,
constructed in 1819,
has been recognised as
a bird-sanctuary since 1949

as late as 31 March. Loe Pool is a favourite locality but it is apparently not seen there annually. In the south-east there were at least twelve individuals between early December 1965 and mid-March 1966 at St. John's Lake, Millbrook, River Lynher, Torpoint, Rame, and Looe. This may have been exceptional for the following winter only one was reported at Hannafore, Looe on 19 November. Recent reports suggest that one or two occur annually at the mouth of the Camel estuary, their only usual north coast haunt other than St Ives Bay. In 1967 one was seen off Newquay harbour from 28 October to 2 November.

## SLAVONIAN GREBE
*Podiceps auritus*

The slavonian grebe breeds in a belt extending from the northern Baltic to the Pacific, and in much of Canada. Within recent years it has colonised Scotland.

It was first reported as a British visitor by Montagu (1802) who described a male 'Sclavonian Grebe' killed at Truro on 4 May 1796. Rodd (1880), recording that the slavonian was not as rare as people supposed, wrote that it was far less common than either the great crested or red-necked grebes. At present it is certainly more common than either of these, while published records suggest it is also more common than the black-necked grebe, a view supported by the known increase of breeding birds in Britain and Scandinavia and the decrease of the black-necked even to the point of extinction in Ireland.

Most slavonian grebes are seen between late November and early March. Early arrivals include single birds at Tamar Lake on 16 October 1962, and at St Ives on 17 October 1961. Several have been reported in late April in recent years; exceptional was one in Mount's Bay on 21 May 1966, and another at Dozmary Pool on 26 June 1960. Records from freshwater localities are rare—in 1966 two were at

Stithians reservoir in January, one remaining until 18 April, and another from 7 to 20 October.

Slavonian grebes are normally seen in ones or twos, larger numbers being dependent upon weather conditions. In 1963 seventeen were in St Ives Bay on 15 February, and twelve in Mount's Bay on 3 March, eight of them remaining until 15 April. While most are reported from these two bays, they regularly occur on the lower reaches of the Camel where up to seven were seen in February 1966, in Falmouth Bay, off Looe, in the Tamar-Lynher area, and from other sheltered bays especially on the south coast.

On the Scillies the slavonian grebe has not been reported since 1902. Until then it was regarded as "an autumn and winter casual, chiefly on Tresco, and by no means rare" (z, 1906), but the only dated specimen is that at Tresco in November 1868.

## BLACK-NECKED GREBE
*Podiceps nigricollis*

The black-necked grebe in its European range nests further south than the slavonian. It is now extinct in Ireland, but small numbers nest in Britain, mostly in the north.

In Cornwall it is only a winter visitor, apparently in smaller numbers than the slavonian grebe—a point elaborated under that species. Flocks of fifteen were reported, mainly on the Fal, in winter up to the mid-1940's with as many as 52 off Restronguet Point on 25 January 1948, more than twice the size of the largest flock of slavonian grebes. However, records since 1959 indicate that parties of more than four are now unusual, the largest comprising five in Mount's Bay on 21 March 1965 and six on the Lynher on 17 December 1963. Most reports are of single birds between November and early April. One was seen at Seaton on 16 April 1966 and another in St Ives Bay on 13 May 1967. At Loe Pool one was seen as early as 19 September 1960 and at

Stithians reservoir on 14 September 1967. The black-necked grebe frequents the same sheltered bays and estuaries as other grebes and divers. Records from freshwater localities such as Helston Park lake, Loe Pool, Stithians reservoir, and Dozmary Pool are very rare. In Cornwall the species seems to be as maritime as the slavonian grebe.

Published records from the Scillies are few—

1867   One seen in late November (z, 1906).
1895   One shot on Tresco on 14 February (z, 1906).
1947   Three shot on 2 September.
1949   Two in St Mary's harbour on 15 December.
1964   One seen at St Agnes from 22 to 24 December.

## LITTLE GREBE     *Podiceps ruficollis*

The little grebe or dabchick is a common breeding species throughout western Europe excluding most of Scandinavia and in this country is the most familiar member of the family.

During the past ten years breeding numbers are said to have increased in west Cornwall but the vague statements normally used to describe its status suggest a decrease since the last century. Rodd (PZ, 1850) inferred that they bred at Trengwainton Ponds, Madron, and Cocks (P, 1851) wrote that they nested at Swanpool, Falmouth, but by 1866 Bullmore reported that they had left due to disturbance from mining. Clark (VCH) stated that it was not uncommon on the estuaries and tidal rivers in the Tamar-Fowey districts and also records breeding at suitable localities in the Truro-Falmouth area, at Loe Pool, and at pools in the Land's End district. The only recent reports of breeding, usually one or two pairs at any locality, come from Tamar Lake, Helman Tor, Temple Tor, ponds and disused clay-pits in the St Austell area, Melancoose reservoir, Clowance Pond at Crowan, St Erth ponds, Marazion Marsh, and Stithians reservoir. Birds have been seen in summer in

south-east Cornwall at Crafthole reservoir and on a freshwater pool near East Looe, but breeding has not been proved (Madge[1]).

Between September and March the local population is augmented by an influx of winter visitors. The British population is predominantly sedentary only moving when local waters become ice-bound, so that Cornish immigrants may be largely of Continental origin. Estuaries and freshwaters near the coast are the typical wintering habitats, few occurring on inland waters. Few details have been published. About a dozen at the Hayle estuary is normal. Up to 30 have been counted on the Lynher, twenty at St John's Lake, and a dozen at Looe, whilst 21 were counted at Tresemple Pool near Tresillian in January 1967.

None breed on the Scillies and only two or three are seen on the larger islands in autumn and winter (Hunt[1]). The latest spring record is one at Tresco on 6 April 1967.

## ALBATROSS     *Diomedea* sp.

In recent years an increasing number of albatrosses, especially the black-browed (*Diomedea melanophris*), has been reported in British waters. None has been specifically identified off Cornwall, but a *diomedea* of indeterminable species was seen by J. B. Bottomley[1], his wife and a friend on 23 August 1964 over the shore-line between Penzance and Marazion (R). It was "like a very big fulmar with long, narrow, stiff, pointed wings and a 'glide-flap-flap-flap-glide' flight with wing-beats shallower than those of a gull. It was dark above, pale beneath, with a dark streak through the eye and a 'tube-nose' bill. When gliding it shewed an apparent anhedral white rump."

A probable albatross was seen off Camborne North Cliffs on 27 September 1962 by Dr. C. J. F. Coombs[1]. The bird, several miles out, was estimated to be the size of a gannet. It moved up channel banking on long, stiff wings just above the waves like an immense shearwater. Watched in very poor weather through x12 binoculars, its upper parts appeared as dark wings and mantle contrasting with a white head and white tail. From below it appeared all white except for a dark *trailing* edge to the wings.

An albatross is said to have been seen off Golden Bar, Scilly on 22 May 1921, but no further details are known (AR). Amusing is the newspaper report (G) of 9 September 1887 that "a splendid specimen of the albatross (the largest species of sea birds) alighted on the church tower at St Columb on Saturday evening [3rd] and was shot by Mr. Jonathan G. Colliver".

## WILSON'S PETREL
*Oceanites oceanicus*

Four geographically distinct races of the Wilson's petrel breed in the southern oceans—one group inhabiting the South Orkneys and South Shetlands. During the southern winter they wander into the north Atlantic, but Britain is beyond their normal range.

A bird picked up dead in a field near Polperro in mid-August 1838 after a week of continuous storms was reported by Couch (*Annals of Nat. Hist.* Vol. II.) and sent to Yarrell who made a drawing of it— the first authentic British specimen. The same year, Gould wrote after his journey to Australia that in May—

> Immediately off the Land's End, Wilson's Storm Petrel was seen in abundance, and continued to accompany the ship throughout the Bay. The little Storm Petrel was also seen, but in far less numbers; both species disappeared on approaching the latitude of Madeira..." (*Trans. Linn. Soc.* Vol. xviii).

Gould's account is regarded with scepticism, but 1838 could have been an exceptional year and the record would need reconsidering if the following account proved satisfactory. On 8 December 1948, following prolonged south-westerly gales, about fifteen petrels feeding close inshore off Lariggan, Penzance may have been this species. Too large to be storm petrels, with square tails and rounded wing-tips, they shewed many features characteristic of the Wilson's petrel.

A more recent record still awaits verification—a bird seen by three observers two miles north of Eddystone Lighthouse on 10 September 1967 (Madge[1]).

## LEACH'S (FORK-TAILED) PETREL
*Oceanodroma leucorhoa*

Unlike the storm petrel which is a bird of the Old World, the main breeding grounds of the Leach's petrel are in Newfoundland and New England. The isolated islands in the St Kilda to North Rona groups form its main British colonies.

Leach's petrels leave their breeding grounds in August but do not move into the open ocean as quickly as storm petrels so that birds are driven by bad weather onto the Cornish coast from September until well into November. Records are now annual, mostly from west Cornwall and between Land's End and Scilly. A few are recorded as early as August—as one on the 14th in 1967 and three on the 17th in 1963 at St Ives. Parties of five or more may occur after severe weather from mid-September. At St Ives, sixteen flew past the Island on 10 October 1964 and eighteen the following day.

At irregular intervals, after spells of particularly inhospitable weather, large 'wrecks' of American petrels occur around the coasts of Britain. The exertions and ultimate fate of many of these birds were graphically described by Bullmore in 1866 when a good many were picked up in Cornwall—

> During the prevalence of one of the gales of last winter a pair were observed at the mouth of Falmouth harbour, trying all they could to get up the river. In vain did they attempt to forge to windward, dipping from time to time in the trough of the sea, and as rapidly emerging from the hollow, just tipping the crest of the waves with their tiny feet. While thus occupied a

violent gust drove them both on board a fishing-smack that was working into the harbour. One struck against the mast and fell dead in the boat. The other struck the vessel's side and disappeared beneath the waves.

The largest recorded 'wreck' is undoubtedly that of 1952 carried by a small but extremely deep depression which sped across the Atlantic between 26 and 28 October. In England and Wales birds were picked up in every county except Rutland. The south-west of England was especially affected with a third of all casualties coming from Bridgwater Bay in Somerset. In Cornwall 34 were picked up dead and reported between 25 October and 23 November as well as one on 26 December, from all parts of the Cornish coast. Many live birds were also seen; at Bude nine on 29 October, fifteen at Widemouth Bay on the 30th, while at Newquay there were about 30 on 31 October and over 100 on 1 November. R. B. Treleaven[1] recalled seeing large numbers off Bude breakwater on the sea or attempting to fly into the wind—as soon as they rose more than a few feet above the surface of the water they were caught by the full violence of the storm and shot landward as if from a gun.

The year 1963 provided a large number of live birds in the St Ives area. 35 were counted on 2 October, and in the severe W.N.W. gale of 12 November there were 52.

Spring records are very rare. Single birds were seen at St Ives on 24 March 1966, at Towan Head, Newquay on 18 April 1965, and at St Ives on 30 April 1964. Inland records are rare, but more common than for the storm petrel. Birds have been picked up dead or dying as far inland as Bodmin Moor, Launceston and Foxhole.

Apart from birds seen between the Scillies and Land's End, the only records from the islands themselves concern the following individuals found dead—

1869　At Tresco in the late Autumn (z, 1906).
1931　In October—presumably on Tresco (AR).
1952　25 October (Parslow[1]).
1955　22 December—one found by a cat.

1966　The first live birds are four reported from St Agnes observatory on 12 October and one the next day.
1967　Single birds seen off St Agnes from 4 to 12 October and two on the 16th.

## STORM PETREL
### *Hydrobates pelagicus*

The storm petrel nests in short tunnels on rocky coasts and islands from the Algerian coast to Iceland.

The first British naturalist to describe the species was Walter Moyle, who gave it the name of "Lesser Round-tail'd sea swallow" thinking it was a form of tern and not (as he first assumed) of "the Penguin-kind" (Tonkin MS). Moyle first saw one obtained near Launceston in 1714, and found another in September 1716 near Bake some three miles from the sea, where it had been driven by "the great storm of the 14th and 15th which made a terrible Havock in our County". In a letter dated 19 September 1716, Moyle wrote ". . . it is generally seen off at Sea, a good distance from the Land, is almost perpetually on the wing and rarely observ'd to alight anywhere, and scarce ever appears ashore. In misty Weather, it flies near the Fishermen's Boats, who sometimes knock it down with their Poles; and 'tis very difficult to take it any other time."

The storm petrel was known to the local fishermen as the storm-finch and as the 'pinnick'† a dialect name generally used for a puny child or a person of small appetite.

The storm petrel ranges far into the south Atlantic in the depths of our winter, returning to land only for the duration of the breeding season. The species has bred on the Cornish mainland. Bullmore wrote that during the summer of 1866 Mr. Gill took the eggs from a close-sitting female at Gull Rock, Falmouth (i.e. The Gray, off Veryan) and eventually obtained both adults and had them stuffed. This is the only record from the south coast. According to Clark (VCH) it bred at Godrevy rocks, the Logan Rock in

† Also applied to the wryneck, *Jynx torquilla*.

St Levan, and at Tintagel, but gave no dates. *Cornish Notes and Queries* (1906 p. 254) refers to breeding between Tintagel and Cambeak. Nesting certainly occurred on the north coast early in the nineteenth century, for Montagu (*Supplement*, 1813) wrote that he had received specimens taken off their eggs in June in north Cornwall and continued—

> We are also informed that some are annually seen [presumably at sea and not nesting] on the western part of the peninsula of Cornwall about Marazion or Penzance; in the former of which places we saw one that was taken.

Nearer the present day, a colony was recorded off the north coast in 1933, when on 15th June five birds were found sitting under boulders. Col. Ryves never revealed the locality but it seems certain to have been Gulland Rock where petrels nested in the 1920's (Weeks[1]) and still do. J. Morrissey (1968[1]), who has visited all the nesting localities along this coastline, has found storm petrels only on Gulland where "about six pairs nest every June, always occupying the same holes". Breeding is also possible at Carter's Rocks off Newquay where N. R. Phillips found an old egg in 1967. Eggs can survive in sheltered crevices for a considerable time, but relatively recent breeding at least seems indicated.

While the storm petrel is certainly very scarce as a mainland breeding species, the Isles of Scilly remain one of its main colonies. Since it nests on the remoter uninhabited islands and only comes to land at night, its distribution at Scilly has always been rather obscure. In the nineteenth century it was recorded only from some of the smaller Western Rocks, the most frequently mentioned being Rosvear where it was noted as fairly common prior to 1863, tolerably common a decade later (Rodd, 1880), but in greatly diminished numbers early this century (z, 1906).

Nesting on Annet was not reported until 1903, but must have been overlooked, perhaps for many years. Certainly in 1915

their numbers ran into thousands. Since then, all observers have reported it as common or abundant, and today the island is the species head-quarters. The main colonies are along the storm beaches, especially around the southern half of the island and on the Neck. Most birds nest on the bare shingle floor beneath the boulders several feet from the surface. A few pairs nest away from the shore in cracks and cavities in the granite outcrops. No proper estimate of the population has been made, but is probably at least two or three thousand pairs. Over 200 adults have been ringed in a single night. In all, over 600 were banded in 1958 and over 700 in 1960, in each case with very few re-traps indicating that only a small part of the population was marked. On the night of 24 June 1961, P. Z. MacKenzie made a count of the number of "crooning" birds on a boulder beach at the south end of the island by marking the position of the burrows with white paint. At dawn he found no less than 296 nests along 121 yards of storm beach.

Small numbers still breed on other islands (the date of the most recently published record is given after each locality)—

Rosevear (1962); Melledgan (1961); Castle Bryher (1961); Scilly Rock (1960); Menavawr (1960); Gorregan (1964); Rosevean (1948); and Round Island from about 1915

storm petrel

until at least 1951, but none were there in 1961 or 1962. Birds were suspected of breeding on the Garrison, St Mary's in 1947 and said to have nested on Peninnis in 1952. King (1924) wrote that a nest was found in a back-yard in Hugh Town, St Mary's, but gave no further details. Birds were thought to be present amongst boulders on Gugh in 1943 where they were again heard at night in 1950, but there has been none on either island in more recent years.

Limited information from Annet suggests that storm petrels begin to arrive and nest much earlier than on Skokholm, 130 miles to the north. First birds arrive at Annet about the first week of April compared with the last week at Skokholm. Thus over 100 were present on the night of 8 April 1958 when birds were not noticed at the Welsh colony until the 27th. Most eggs are laid in June at both localities, but a fresh egg was found on 20 May 1957 at Annet—eight days before the earliest date at Skokholm. Some chicks have been found still in the nest well into October. An apparent increase in the population at both colonies takes place in mid-summer, probably due to the arrival of non-breeding birds.

Adult storm petrels are being increasingly preyed upon by great black-backed gulls. In June 1963, over 100 castings comprised of individual petrels were found on Annet in two days.

In September and October most petrels have left their burrows but have not yet wandered far from British waters. This is the time when most of the storm driven birds appear off the Cornish coast. The largest parties reported in recent years consisted of 100 to 150 birds off Mevagissey harbour on 21 September 1953 and a similar number off St Ives Island on 5 September 1967—96 were seen there two days earlier. Also exceptional were 90 off St Ives Island during a strong W.N.W. gale on 12 November 1963 and over 40 on 31 October 1952. Most records consist of one or two birds at a time from St Ives Bay and Mount's

Bay—rarely are they reported from mid or east Cornwall. Between Land's End and the Scillies there are frequent records in summer and early autumn with occasional parties of 50 or more. The greatest number seen on a crossing comprised about 200 on 16 September 1966. Records after October are rare, but include one caught by hand in the dark on the quay at St Mary's on 14 November 1959, and one found freshly dead inland at St Mary's on 10 December the same year. Day sightings of storm petrels within the Isles are rare at any time. In the seven years from 1957 to 1963 there were only three records of single birds seen from St Agnes despite intensive watching and the close proximity of the large Annet colony. The latest mainland records are of one dead in a field by Mylor Creek on 10 December 1948, and seven battling over heavy seas off Par harbour the next day.

There are nine recovery records involving birds ringed at Annet and Skokholm. An adult ringed at Annet on 1 July 1965 was recovered in a breeding colony at Burhou, Alderney on 2 July 1966. Five others have been controlled at Skokholm, between May and June.

Recoveries within the county are—

| | Ringed | Recovered |
|---|---|---|
| Skokholm | 14.9.'55 | Found dead, Widemouth Bay 4.8.'56 |
| Skokholm | 16.6.'49 | On board a fishing vessel 47 miles W.N.W. of the Longships 1.7.'51 |
| Skokholm | 16.6.'49 | Found on a trawler 10 miles N.E. of the Wolf Rock 18.6.'52 |

## MANX SHEARWATER
### *Puffinus puffinus*

In Europe the Manx shearwater breeds mainly in the Mediterranean and around Britain at scattered colonies from the Isles of Scilly to north Shetland. Birds also nest off south Iceland and in Brittany.

With an important colony on Scilly, it is not surprising that the shearwater has been for centuries a familiar bird to Cornish fishermen who christened it 'skithen' or 'skidden', or frequently 'pilchard-bird'. Nance suggested 'skithen' is connected with Cornish *cudhon* and Welsh *ysguthan*, wood-pigeon, but it is more likely that the slender, dark upper-wings of the shearwater, brought into view by its characteristic banking-flight, recalled for the fishermen a *skethen*, Cornish for a long piece or a strip and used in dialect for any strip or tatter of cloth. Nance noted that for hake-fishing a whole pilchard was used cut into three parts—head, *skethen*, and point-piece.

Dialect names used at Scilly are 'cock-athodon' and 'crew', "both derived from the guttural melodies they pour forth as the spade approaches the end in which the egg is deposited. I once caught a pair in one burrow who were crooning a duet of this kind before we commenced operations" related Mitchell in an account sent to Yarrell in 1838, of a night's diversion on Annet.

The earliest written account of the 'skithen' was given to Thomas Tonkin on 10 July 1733 by Arthur Kemps of Rosteage in Gerrans (Tonkin MS) who was clearly very familiar with the birds—

> In the Months of March, April & May, they fly constantly westwards or out of the Channel in great flocks, pretty nigh the water & generally in Lines one after the other: I have seen, I believe, Ten thousand in a day, and all flying the same way, and in the same manner; and never saw one flying Eastwards. I have been told by the Old Fishermen, that one year, a long time Since, they lighted on the water (which is not usual) And dyed in great quantities: And in that year there were no Pilchards taken on the Coast.

While Kemps noted them from March to May, it is only between November and February that 'Manx' are rare in Cornish waters. How far south they fly in winter remains uncertain, but an increasing number of recoveries of birds ringed at Skokholm indicates that some at least winter off the coasts of Brazil and Argentina.

Shearwaters return to their nesting burrows on Annet about the third week in March—9 March 1961 on Gugh—and lay their eggs about the second week in May. An egg found on Round Island about to hatch on 5 June 1962 must have been laid about 15 April allowing for an incubation period of 51 to 54 days. Details of breeding numbers are very scanty (as with the storm petrel and for similar reasons) even though the main colony on Annet has been visited for many years by bird and egg collectors. Millet in 1826 (North, 1850) found them reposed on the waters at midday in numerous groups in St Mary's bay where they apparently always rested at that time of day.† Mitchell encountered in Smith's Sound one evening "a congregation of at least three thousand in the middle of the tideway, washing, dipping, preening feathers, and stretching wings, evidently just awake and making ready for the night's diversion".

During the breeding season and in the summer months they are occasionally seen in Broad Sound and about the Western Islands at dusk sitting on the water or flying in great clouds estimated to contain as many as 6,000 birds (Quick, 1964). King (1924) noted that they were very punctual leaving Annet, at 10.00 p.m. (G.M.T.) almost to the minute. By 10.30 or 10.45 the air was full of them and the noise deafening.

Nesting takes place in burrows, either dug themselves or by rabbits, which vary in length from only a few feet to nearly twenty feet, the intersecting passages honeycombing the ground. Despite the protection afforded by the burrows, large numbers are killed by great black-backed gulls which literally turn them inside-out. The shearwaters cannot walk properly and are compelled to shuffle on their feet, breasts and wings, until they find a suitable drop from which to launch themselves into space. In this position they are extremely vulnerable to the gulls' attacks and dozens of corpses

---

† This is an unusual observation for they do not normally venture out of their burrows until after dark. Miss Quick (1964) only once saw shearwaters at close range by daylight. They were sitting in St Mary's Sound in early September about mid-morning and allowed the boat to drift within a few yards before they took to flight.

litter Annet. Wallis thought there had been a decrease due to persecution in the 1920's. Hundreds were reported dead, with forty corpses within as many feet at the end of May 1924, but Miss Quick (1964) thinks that numbers are now being maintained.

This century shearwaters have spread from their main Annet colony. Eggs were found on Gugh in 1925 (BB), but it is not known whether the island has been occupied continuously since, although birds were present in 1953 and 1961. In June 1945 Buxton found proof of breeding on Tresco with a few pairs at two places on St Agnes, and Dorrien-Smith knew of breeding at several islands off the north end of Tresco early in the 1920's, probably including Round Island where in 1962 were seven accessible burrows and many more with signs of occupation. A. T. Beswetherick (1968[1]) estimates the breeding population on Round Island at about 50 pairs, but no more, which occupy all the coast except for the north face. A few nest on the surface of the ground under the thick carpet of kaffir fig (mesembryanthemum), *Carpobrotus edulis*. Manx shearwaters are also said to have bred recently on Bryher (Quick, 1964). The Manx shearwater has bred on the Cornish mainland. Clark (VCH) wrote that the only colony was near Newquay—perhaps on the stretch of coast between Porth Joke and Holywell Bay which Ryves and Quick (BB, 1946) said was honeycombed with rabbit burrows "which might conceivably have harboured shearwaters and puffins". J. C. Tregarthen mentioned nesting in "Perran Towans", perhaps the same locality (*Cornwall and its Wild Life*, 1923). A small colony at Kellan Head, St Endellion is believed to have become extinct about 1937, while in 1933 a young bird was seen on 15 June on the same island off the north coast where the storm petrel nests—Gulland Rock off Padstow. Dead birds (up to 21 at a time) have been collected on mainland cliffs, as at Pentire, where suitable nesting holes exist, but without the proof of young

birds, these corpses and the sound of birds calling from the cliffs on moonless nights, only support the view that petrels frequent cliffs in the breeding season where they do not raise young.

Throughout the spring and summer varying numbers of 'Manx' may be seen passing west along the north Cornish coast and heading south off the Land's End. Many of these birds are from Skokholm, travelling as far south as the north coasts of Iberia and Portugal, a distance of some 600 miles. One bird remains at the nest while the other is "on holiday" feeding and recuperating. There are many recoveries of ringed birds in the Bay of Biscay where the sardine-fishermen consider them a delicacy. Birds from Scilly make similar journeys (see ringing records at the end). Birds engaged on the flights to Biscay may be seen from many suitable promontories in west Cornwall. It is known that the shearwaters leave Skokholm as early as 2.30 a.m. and accounts for the large movements off Cornwall before noon. On 1 April 1962, some 15,000 were estimated to have headed west at St Ives between 9.00 a.m. and 11.30 a.m. The size of the shearwater movement visible from the shore depends quite obviously on how close the birds fly to land. Observations over many years have shewn that bad weather, especially strong winds from the

Manx shearwaters

northerly quarter, force birds close under such headlands as St Ives, Gurnard's Head, and the Land's End. These movements are sometimes accompanied by a circular, or "eddy" movement around Mount's Bay with the birds flying west past Mousehole and Porthgwarra in the direction of the Scillies. The size of the movements increases in the autumn. From the end of July until early October, the true migration of shearwaters from British breeding stations is under way and at its height in August and September movements of 9,000 birds an hour have been estimated in stormy weather. By the end of October most shearwaters are clear of our coasts.

Despite the huge southerly migration, movement in the opposite direction is rarely noticed, and then consists of only a few birds. Trahair Hartley commented on this; in four years of observations from 1932, only once did he see shearwaters flying north, and that was not from the mainland but six miles south-east of the Scillies on 25 August 1933. The only explanation appears to be that northward movements, both of birds returning to nesting sites in early spring and from feeding flights from Biscay, occur well to the west of the mainland and probably west of Scilly.

There are eight recoveries of birds ringed on Annet. Most have been controlled where they were ringed or found dead or exhausted on the Scillies and north Cornish coast, particularly in the autumn. Only one has been recovered from the south coast, a bird, apparently shot, on the Helford river. Recoveries from other parts of Britain are—Three from north Devon, and single birds from Maryport and Bootle, Cumberland; Fairbourne, Merioneth; Criccieth, Caernarvon; and Garrestown, Co. Cork. Abroad there have been three Spanish recoveries—

|  | Ringed as Adult | Recovered |
|---|---|---|
| Annet | 12.7.'52 | Grove, Pontevedra 16.9.'52 |
| Annet | 1.9.'60 | Cabo de Lastres 10.3.'66 |
| Annet | 27.4.'60 | Fuenterrabia, Guipuzoca Feb. '62 |

Fifteen have been recovered in west France,

mostly in autumn and winter—Manche, 1; Finistère, 6; Morbihan, 1; Vendée, 1; Loire Atlantique, 2; Loire Inférieure, 1; and Landes, 1.

Birds from St Agnes have been recovered from Hayle, 1; north Devon, 2; and in France single recoveries from Finistère, Charente Maritime, and Gironde.

Despite the number of Breton recoveries the only return visitor is an adult ringed at Phare du Creac'h, Ushant, Finistère, 30 July 1957 and controlled at Annet on 9 April 1958.

There are sixty-five recoveries of birds ringed at Skokholm. Most were found dead or exhausted on the north coast with a few at Scilly, mostly in September but some as early as June. Five have been recovered on Annet where they presumably nested. Four birds from Skomer were found on the north Cornish coast between late July and mid-September. A shearwater from Lundy Island was found dead in a falcon's eyrie at St Agnes (mainland) in July 1948, and another was controlled at Annet in June 1950.

## BALEARIC SHEARWATER
### Puffinus p. mauretanicus

Careful observations have shewn this sub-species of the Manx shearwater from the western Mediterranean to be a regular visitor to Cornish waters between July and November in flocks of migrating 'Manx'. Sometimes they are seen on their own, particularly in October. Especially large numbers were reported off west Cornwall in 1961; 300 to 400 massed off Bass Point east of the Lizard may all have been Balearic shearwaters, but conditions of light made identification difficult. At St Ives in the same year, when birds were seen between 14 July and 20 October, about 350 were estimated on 7 October with 150 on the 1st, while between the Scillies and Land's End, 100 to 150 were present on the 16th. These observations invalidate the view that Balearic shearwaters keep to the English Channel, and probably nearer to the French coast, and do not pass the Scillies or Land's End into the Irish Sea.

The Balearic and Levantine (*P. p. yelkouan*) races of manx shearwater were separated in 1924. A specimen in the British Museum, obtained in the English Channel somewhere south of Plymouth in 1868, and originally classified as Levantine, was subsequently referred to the Balearic form. The Levantine shearwater, which breeds in the eastern Mediterranean has not certainly been identified off the Cornish coast, although two birds thought to be of this race were reported off St Ives in the autumn of 1958.

## LITTLE SHEARWATER
### *Puffinus assimilis*

There are two races of little shearwater—the Madeiran *P. baroli baroli* which breeds in the Azores, Salvages, Madeiran islands, and the Canaries, and the Cape Verde form *P. baroli boydi*. There have been less than a dozen occurrences in the British Isles. One is said to have been seen off St Agnes, Scilly on 18 October 1967 but the record has not yet been confirmed.

## GREAT SHEARWATER
### *Puffinus gravis*

This, the largest of the shearwaters, has a breeding range restricted to the Tristan da Cunah group of islands in the south Atlantic, but ranges far to the north outside the breeding season occurring off the Cornish coast regularly, albeit in greatly fluctuating numbers. To the Isles of Scilly fishermen it was sufficiently well known to have earned itself the name of 'hackbolt'[†] the meaning is obscure but the word was also used in the Isle of Man and on the eastern coast of North America.

Occasional birds, usually singly, have been seen close inshore between July and late October after severe gales, but generally are to be found five or more miles out to sea, particularly off the Wolf Rock and the Scillies. Clark and Rodd (z, 1906) described the species as a regular autumn and winter visitor off the islands where several hundred were seen in autumn 1906 (AR). Few records were published in the nineteenth century. The specimens illustrated in Yarrell's *British Birds* were supplied by D. W. Mitchell of Penzance. One was taken to him alive in November 1839 by a man who said he had found it about mid-afternoon asleep in his boat moored a few hundred yards from the shore. "There were great numbers of this species off Mount's Bay at that time and I soon after had two more brought to me which had been taken by hooks."[†] 1874 was a notable autumn; both Rodd and Gatcombe (z) saw them for the first time in some years—two out of four were captured off Penzance on 8 November. The claim of Clement Jackson that they appeared in some thousands off Looe and Polperro in some autumns in the mid-nineteenth century, appears to be something of an exaggeration. Dr. Eagle Clark, in his pioneering studies of migration, spent a month at the Eddystone lighthouse from 19 September 1901 and saw them almost daily and "often in considerable numbers." Similarly Trahair Hartley saw about 40 here when trawling in September 1934.

The greatest numbers sighted within recent years have been in the far west with rafts of up to a hundred birds on several occasions—as between the Wolf Rock and the Seven Stones on 20 October 1953 and 50 or more on 22 September 1961. 1965 proved to be a good year when birds were recorded on many crossings to the Scillies

---

[†] As Newton rightly pointed out (*Dictionary of Birds*, 1893–96) the name would doubtless have been applied to any of the larger species of shearwater, "If indeed they recognised any distinction".

[†] The dark bird in the same illustration is the sooty shearwater as pointed out in later editions of Yarrell.

between 21 August and 10 October, the largest numbers were 123 or more on 21 August, up to 40 on the 28th, at least 125 on 10 September and 85 the following day, while on the 18th there were over 170 as well as another 100 large shearwaters too far away for specific identification. By contrast only one was reported from the M.V. *Scillonian* in 1966—on 13 September. Large numbers were again recorded in this area in 1967—including about 100 on 7 October, and 240 off St Mary's and St Agnes in mid-October.

Spring records are rare in the British Isles. Single birds were identified off St Agnes, on 8 May 1958, 18 April 1962, 17 April 1966, and at sea off St Mary's on 30 April 1962.

## CORY'S
## (OR NORTH ATLANTIC)
## SHEARWATER
### *Procellaria diomedea*

Cory's shearwater is the rarest of the genus found in Cornish waters. There are several geographically isolated groups indistinguishable in the field; the Mediterranean birds are thought to be resident and those visiting northern waters to be the form breeding off the coasts of Portugal, Madeira and in the Azores.

Since Wynne-Edwards saw parties of up to 60 between the Casquets and a position 23 miles south of Prawle Point, Devon in September 1933† the inference has been that Cory's shearwater, although rarely recorded until recently, is a regular autumn visitor as far as 50°N. and several were seen at this latitude between Land's End and the Scillies in August and September 1938. One reported at St Ives on 1 November 1965 (a very late date) was rejected by the Rare Birds Committee, but two seen there on 3 September 1967 were accepted. However, larger numbers have been seen, notably in

1965, off the Irish coast and even as far north as the Shetland Islands. In five of the nine years from 1959 to 1967, Cory's shearwaters were reported between Land's End and the Scillies especially near the Wolf Rock. In 1965, when more than usual were sighted in British waters, fourteen were recorded on three separate crossings on 21 August, and twelve near the Wolf on 18 September, as well as four on 4 September and single birds on the 16th and 17th. In August the St Agnes Observatory recorded maxima of seven on the 22nd and twelve on the 29th. Two on 1 November 1967 is the latest record from the Scillies.

Among the earliest dates is 13 August 1966 when three were seen in Mount's Bay off St Levan. Most unusual was one seen from M.V. *Scillonian* on 30 June 1962. Late August and September is certainly the most likely time to see Cory's shearwaters and if regular watching were practical seven or eight miles off the Cornish coast, the species would certainly shew itself to be an annual visitor.

## SOOTY SHEARWATER
### *Puffinus griseus*

Like the great shearwater, the sooty shearwater is a bird of the south Atlantic breeding, for example, in the Falkland and Cape Horn islands and dispersing far into the north Atlantic during our summer.

The sooty shearwater was formerly thought to be the young of the 'great' and was designated "cinerous shearwater". A bird given this name by Couch (1838) was taken alive to him in October 1833 having seized a fisherman's bait. There is little doubt that Couch had been presented with the sooty shearwater, but the first fully authenticated specimen was obtained by D. W. Mitchell in Mount's Bay in the autumn of 1838 and figured in the woodcut in Yarrell's *British Birds* as a young great shearwater—the mistake being rectified in the text of Saunders' revised edition (1884–85).

† He expressed doubts about his observation but H. F. Witherby considered it correct (BB, 1939–40).

There are very few early records of its appearance off Cornwall. Clark published only one (z, 1907)—a bird, which he identified, shot near Looe on 21 August 1899, but in his letter to King (25 October 1923) he wrote that enormous numbers had been seen between the Land's End and the Scillies on two occasions since 1906. Ryves (1948) knew of only one occurrence—a bird ten miles south of Newlyn on 7 June 1937, the earliest autumn record.

Recent observations have shewn the sooty shearwater to be a regular visitor. Most are reported from St Ives with smaller numbers between Mount's Bay and the Scillies. Records were fuller than usual in 1966 with up to six off St Ives on 13 September and five on the 15th, up to three in Mount's Bay off St Levan on 13 August and up to nine off West Pentire, Newquay on 13 September. Early records at St Ives include one on 16 July 1962 and one on 27 June 1966. Few are seen from late October, but include one on the 29th off St Ives in 1965 and two off Pendeen, St Just on the 26th in 1967.

The sooty shearwater is normally seen in ones or twos, so that it is rare compared with the 'Manx' comprising less than one per cent of total shearwater movements. A large visible passage occurred at St Ives on 22 August 1965 during a N.W. gale force 7–8. By 9.00 a.m. 'Manx' were passing west at the rate of about a thousand an hour. During the morning 21 'sooties' came into view—one of the largest numbers counted during a single watch. In 1962 at least twenty were seen off St Ives on 12 September.

Only since 1961 have there been regular reports from Scilly, mostly of ones or twos off St Agnes, but on 17 September 1965 twenty-four were seen. Extreme dates are 8 August 1961 and 18 October 1966. Unusual was one off St Agnes on 18 April 1965.

## FULMAR PETREL
### *Fulmarus glacialis*

The fulmar petrel is an Arctic colonizer from the Antarctic and one of the World's most northerly breeding birds. The best known and most impressive accounts of the changing distribution of any bird, is surely that supplied by this species. Until 1878 its only British breeding station was on St Kilda; today it all but encircles our islands, establishing in Cornwall its most southerly European breeding station until the recent colonization of Rouzic off the Brittany coast.

Fulmars

Until it spread to southern Britain, the fulmar was a rare vagrant to Cornwall being occasionally seen or picked up dead in winter. Couch (1838) referred to a "grey petrel" described to him by a fisherman which may have been of this species. By 1851 Cocks had reported birds from Falmouth harbour, Penryn river, Gyllingvase and Swanpool, while Rodd (PZ, 1850) already knew of single birds captured near Land's End and in Mount's Bay.

By 1931 the fulmar had spread south to Pembrokeshire and on 25 April of that year one was seen flying past Carn Lês Boel near Land's End, and on 4 June one was picked up dead at Penzance. The next reports were not until 1936—a Lowestoft trawler sighted a "St Kilda bird" 45 miles N.W. of Land's End, while on 28 April two were seen off Pentire Head. During the next two years

# FULMAR

## ESTIMATED BREEDING PAIRS — 1967

Figures probably not more than 75% accurate.
Many non-breeding birds present. Ideally
young should be counted in July
and August.

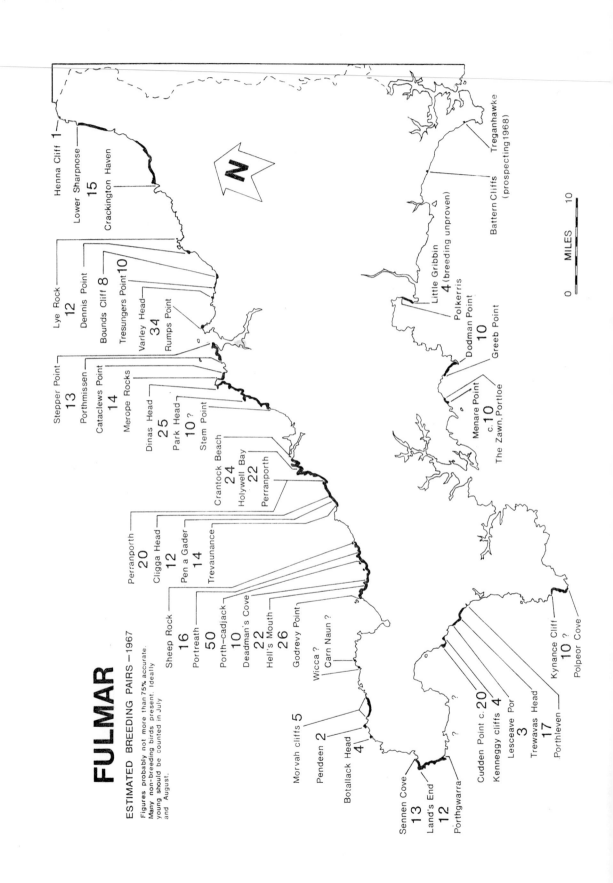

N

Henna Cliff 1
Lower Sharpnose 15
Crackington Haven

Lye Rock 12
Dennis Point
Bounds Cliff 8
Tresungers Point 10
Varley Head 34
Rumps Point

Stepper Point 13
Porthmissen
Cataclews Point 14
Merope Rocks
Dinas Head 25
Park Head 10 ?
Stem Point

Crantock Beach 24
Holywell Bay 22
Perranporth

Perranporth 20
Cligga Head 12
Pen a Gader 14
Trevaunance

Sheep Rock 16
Portreath 50
Porth-cadjack 10
Deadman's Cove 22
Hell's Mouth 26
Godrevy Point
Wicca ?
Carn Naun ?

Morvah cliffs 5
Pendeen 2
Botallack Head 4

Sennen Cove 13
Land's End 12
Porthgwarra

?
Cudden Point c. 20
Kenneggy cliffs 4
Lesceave Por 3
Trewavas Head 17
Porthleven

Kynance Cliff 10 ?
Polpeor Cove

Treganhawke
Battern Cliffs
(prospecting 1968)

Little Gribbin
4 (breeding unproven)
Polkerris
Dodman Point 10
Greeb Point

Menare Point
c. 10
The Zawn, Portloe

0    MILES    10

several birds were reported off the north coast, and in 1939 birds remained on the cliffs for the first time—up to 15 at Godrevy in late April. Breeding at new sites occurs only four to five years after the first 'landings'. Not surprisingly, therefore, no young were seen until 1944 when there were two pairs with chicks on the 'Marble Cliff' at Trevone. Non-breeding birds had increased with up to 30 on Camborne North Cliffs.

Breeding was reported from five or six sites in 1946, and at eleven sites in 1947 with another eleven being prospected. From 1948 progress slowed; 'new' colonies were sometimes the result of birds moving house a mile or two. The Mawgan Porth colony was established in 1950, and new sites were being prospected along the coast to Hartland in Devon in 1954.

The fulmar was slow to prospect the south coast; probably because the lower, less isolated cliffs, did not provide the security the species desired. The Lizard peninsula provides more suitable sites and a young bird was reared at Housel Bay in 1956. Prospecting around the Dodman took place in 1951 and led to the occupation of cliff ledges in subsequent years, but without any confirmed reports of breeding. Further spread around the Cornish coast seems likely only on a limited scale, but in 1967 two sites were being prospected at Battern Cliffs, a quarter mile east of Downderry, by up to four pairs, and one pair at Treganhawke.

The number of young successfully reared each year varies considerably at individual colonies. Thus, at Bedruthan there were 22 in 1955, but only eleven in 1956. The largest number so far reported is 33 from the same site in 1963, with another 5 reared 'next door' at High Cliff. 'Blue phase' fulmars, that is birds with a darker plumage on the back, become more common further north in their range. Few have been seen in Cornwall—one at Whipsiderry, Newquay on 8 April 1965 was probably the same bird as returned there on 23 March 1966 and

paired with a normal plumage bird. They did not, however, breed.

Fulmars arrive at their breeding sites in late December and January, but the chicks are not hatched before mid-July. These fly about 45 days later, in early September, to spend the next three or four years at sea. Adult birds leave the cliffs at this time, rarely making an appearance again until the end of the year.

On Scilly the fulmar was unknown until early this century. Clark knew of four records between 1906 and 1923, including one on 26 October 1916 (letter 1923), found injured after apparently striking wires on St Mary's. In 1937 a pair was seen about Menavawr and one on one of the Western Rocks. During the next decade several pairs were seen about the islands throughout the breeding season, but not until 1951 was breeding proved when a nest with one young was found at Shipman Head, Bryher. The following year three pairs were seen sitting high on Menavawr and two birds apparently sitting on Shipman Head, but no young were seen. The fortunes of these birds have fluctuated greatly; thus in 1957 and 1958 there was no evidence of any breeding. In 1954 there were three pairs each with an egg at Shipman Head, four pairs sitting on Menavawr, and one bird on Hanjague where they had first appeared the previous year. Two pairs reared single chicks on Shipman Head in 1955. Since 1959 the position can best be summarized as follows—

1959  Hanjague, one pair. Menavawr, two or three pairs.
1960  One pair successful on Menavawr.
1961  Two pairs (at least one successful) on Menavawr. One nest with an egg on Castle Bryher. Two nests with eggs on Hanjague.
1962  Round Island. A pair seen with nesting material in June but did not breed.
1963  Four pairs on Castle Bryher, three on nests on 26 May.
1964  At least eight pairs breeding on Menavawr, Castle Bryher and Hanjague.
1965  At least four pairs bred on Castle Bryher and three pairs on Hanjague.

1966   Two pairs nested on Hanjague. A pair bred for the first time on Round Island. (Six to eight pairs bred successfully throughout the islands).

1967   Two nests on Round Island. Three pairs bred successfully on Hanjague, and four pairs had eggs on Castle Bryher.

Little information has been published on the time of occupation and vacation of nesting sites. Fulmars are scarce or absent from the Scillies from October to February and in recent years birds have been seen off St Agnes in every month from March to September. Most records refer to one or two birds at any one time, but there is some indication of passage movements in May and September; the most reported during a single day being seven on 9 May 1958 and six on 2 May 1961.

# DALMATIAN PELICAN
*Pelecanus crispus*

The Dalmatian pelican breeds in scattered areas eastwards of the Balkans. It formerly occurred, possibly as a breeding species, in Britain, as sub-fossil bones have been found on archaeological sites of the Neolithic period in the Fenland, and the Iron Age at Glastonbury in Somerset.

Recent records have proved to be escaped birds. One at Marazion Marsh in April and May 1951 had escaped from Holland in February. A pelican, now known to have escaped from Colchester Zoo in October 1967, was later reported from other south coast localities before arriving at Falmouth on 11 December. From the 16th to the end of the year it remained at the Hayle estuary, finally moving to St Agnes and Tresco, Scilly, in January 1968.

# GANNET                    *Sula bassana*

The gannet is a north Atlantic species nesting in the Newfoundland area, but mostly on rocky coasts and island stacks from Brittany to Iceland. Over 75 per cent of birds breed at the thirteen British and Irish colonies, most of which have shewn great increases in breeding numbers since the end of the last century. The nearest colony to Cornwall is at Grassholm, Pembrokeshire, where less than 6,000 pairs nested in 1939 and about 15,000 in 1964. Other colonies in the south-west have long been extinct. Lundy, which boasted a colony at least as early as 1274, contained some seventy nests in 1890, but became extinct in 1909 after the eggs had been systematically taken for sale to tourists at a shilling each.

A gannetry existed in Cornwall in the mediæval period. William Bottoner (otherwise William of Worcester), the earliest traveller to leave a record of a journey to Cornwall (1478), wrote in his curious Latin that at Pentybers-rok "nest birds called ganettys, gullys, seemowys and other birds of the sea". This rock, "west of the port of Padstow, four miles from Tintagel Castle and one mile from the mainland" is quite obviously Gulland Rock. No details of this colony are known, but it may well have become extinct in the sixteenth century, for neither Carew (1602) nor subsequent writers refer to it. Carew only stated that the gannet "is a sea-fowl not eatable".

In Cornish the gannet was known as *saithor*. The late 12th century Cottonian MS translated this as "diver and plunger" which has been variously interpreted as cormorant and gull. Lhuyd (1660–1709), however, was undoubtedly right in equating the bird with the gannet, for the Cornish name must be derived from *saith* (or *saeth*) an arrow; most appropriate for the arching up of the gannet and its plunging flight.

From a bird "seen and described this March 1715", Walter Moyle of Bake shewed that Willughby made a gross error over the "Cornish Gannet". The species described under that name is evidently a skua (q.v. great skua). Why this mistake was made is difficult to understand for on their tour of Cornwall, Willughby and Ray learned of gannets from the inhabitants of Padstow (27 June 1662) who told them that the birds were "almost of the bigness of a goose, white, the tips of their wings black". This is exactly the bird described in Willughby's *Ornithology* as the Soland-Goose, a name long used for the gannet. They were also told of the curious method used for catching these birds—

> The Cornish gannet doth constantly accompany the shoals of Pilchards, still hovering over them in the air. It pursues and strikes at these fish with that violence that they catch it with a strange artiface. They fasten a Pilchard to a board, which they fix a little under the water. The Gannet espying the Pilchard, casts himself down from on high upon it with that vehemence, that he strikes his Bill clear through the board, and dashes out his brains against it, and so comes to be taken.

Borlase wrote that a gannet over Penzance dived at a plank in a fish-airing centre, and broke its neck. Such stories persisted until well into the nineteenth century; Bullmore in 1866 said the method was still employed at Falmouth while Gatcombe (z) wrote that in January and February 1877 many were obtained by the fishermen off Plymouth, either with a baited hook or the old plan of a board and fish.

According to Fisher and Lockley (*Sea Birds*, 1952) these stories are in the true fisherman's tradition of being without foundation on fact. Experiments shewed that the fish was always devoured by birds alighting beside the wood and, in any case, the gannet attacks the fish from underneath, seizing it in its *open* bill and usually swallowing it underwater.

More credible is the story that gannets could be caught by rod and line. The bird described in detail by Moyle and caught near Mevagissey about the end of January or beginning of February 1716–17, was obtained alive "by a hook baited with a Pilchard & fast'nd to a long line thrown off from a fisher-boat". The gannet was certainly very fond of pilchards . . .

> See where the bird of force
> The quick-eyed gannet marks the pilchard's
> course,
> Darts with the lightning's flight amid the shoal
> And fill with raptuous hope the fisher's Soul.
> Auspicious bird!
> Welcome, thrice welcome to our southern shore!
> (G, 24.7.1802).

Rodd (1880) recorded that fishermen would pick on a bird that had so gorged itself as to become incapable of flying, and pursue it until it disgorged itself, enabling

Gannets

them to form an impression of the fish present.

The pilchard may have deserted the Cornish coast, but the gannet is still with us throughout the year. Many come from the Grassholm gannetry, as shewn by the recovery of ringed birds. The first adults begin to disperse from the breeding colonies in July while the movement of immatures is from August to October. The latter eventually leave British waters, the migrating instinct being much stronger in birds two years old or less, and may urge them as far south as the west African coast. The very size of a gannet makes its migration especially conspicuous although it normally comprises only a few per cent of total seabird movements. The heaviest migration visible from such well-watched promontories as St Ives Island and West Pentire, Newquay, takes place in stormy weather. Movements of a thousand birds an hour are reported regularly from late August onwards. At St Ives 6,500 were estimated to have passed in five hours on 5 September 1965 and about 6,000 in three hours on 26 October 1967.

Unlike immature gannets, the adults largely remain in British waters during the winter months and fishing parties of fifty or so may be seen off the south and west coasts of the county from December to February. 150 were feeding off Looe on 27 December 1965 while three days later, 250 reported flying west past Looe is the largest movement so far recorded from south-east Cornwall; while large parties are seen in this area during the winter, the gannet is comparatively scarce here in the late summer and autumn (Madge[1]). Large feeding flocks are noted quite close inshore after gales at any time, for example, about 700 off Rame Head on 22 May 1965 during a south-west gale.

By the end of January some gannets have returned to their breeding stations; indeed some birds remain in attendance throughout mild winters. A curious fact, common to gannets, auks and shearwaters, is that large northward migrations are not apparent in spring—gannets always seem to be moving west. Hartley recorded only five northward movements off Land's End in four years of observation. Some of them were in the height of summer and doubtless represented birds returning to Grassholm after feeding flights. In 1945 Hartley noted that such movements were not uncommon in the late summer, but were always small and confined to the late morning, allowing the birds ample time to reach the Welsh colony which they invariably did near dawn. Larger northward movements have been noted just east of the Scillies; normally they must keep well out to sea at all times.

At Scilly most birds occur over the open sea around the islands, large numbers occurring among the islands only during storms. In September and October several hundred may occur off St Agnes and the Western Rocks in rough weather or when large shoals of fish come close inshore—about 750 on 20 October 1957. At other times of the year large flocks are exceptional, though parties of up to a dozen occur and up to fifty or so within a few hours can sometimes be seen out at sea to the south or west of St Agnes.

Gannets have been recovered in Cornwall mainly off the north coast or in Mount's Bay, but only two from the south coast. Most were found between July and September with a few winter records as late as March. They had been ringed at the following colonies—

Bass Rock, East Lothian, 3; Ailsa Craig, Ayrshire, 2; Grassholm, Pembs., 7 (others from here said to have been picked up at sea off the Wolf Rock); and Les Etacs, Alderney, 1.


# CORMORANT

*Phalacrocorax carbo*

The cormorant is widespread in Europe, breeding in Iceland, along much of the

# CORMORANT

ESTIMATED OCCUPIED NESTS – 1967

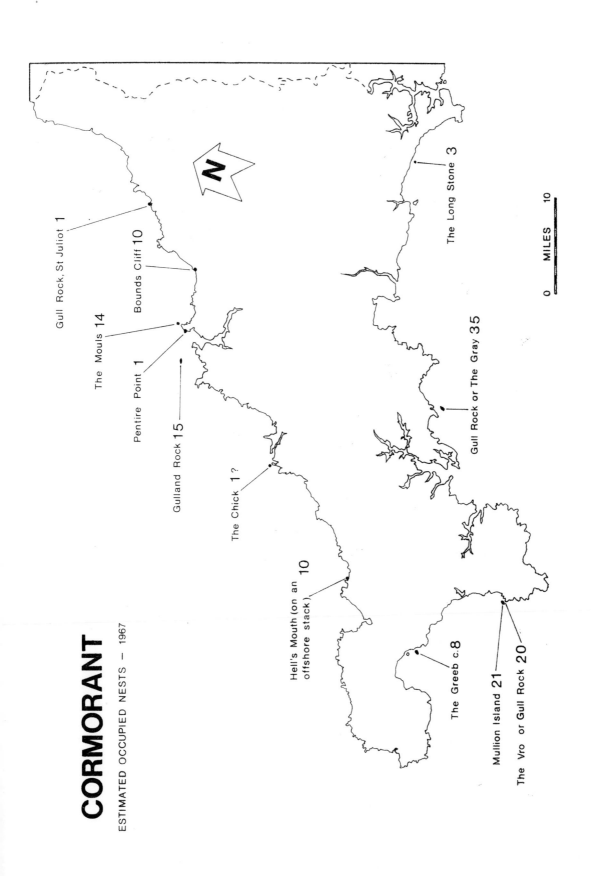

Gull Rock, St Juliot 1

Bounds Cliff 10

The Mouls 14

Pentire Point 1

Gulland Rock 15

The Long Stone 3

Gull Rock or The Gray 35

The Chick 1?

Hell's Mouth (on an offshore stack) 10

The Greeb c.8

Mullion Island 21

The Vro or Gull Rock 20

0    MILES    10

north and west coast of Scandinavia and in Britain except the south-east. In middle and southern Europe it is replaced by the southern or lesser cormorant *P. carbo sinensis* which has been recovered on the south coast of Britain from Kent to Dorset, but never identified in Cornwall.

The cormorant and shag are easily confused so it is natural that each name has been applied to both species in Devon and Cornwall. Shag or English derivative 'shagga' in particular was used in Cornwall. Moyle separated the cormorant and shag, but mistakenly thought the latter was represented by two distinct species in Cornwall—the black and the grey. The grey was described from a specimen shot in 1716 and clearly describes the young shag.

No truly Cornish name for either species has survived, but it was undoubtedly *morvran* (*mor-bran* sea-crow) which is still used in Welsh and Breton for the cormorant. A dialect name at Mousehole was 'spilgarn' which probably means 'carn-hoverer' from the habit both species have of drying their

Cormorant

outspread wings while perched on rocks. 'Trainygoat', also used at Mousehole, is a corruption of Cornish *tryn y gota* (lit. spread his coat) and clearly has the same origin of meaning as 'spilgarn'. At St Ives the cormorant was christened 'Jan Cockin(g)' perhaps after some local fisherman, but the origin is obscure.

In Cornwall the cormorant is greatly outnumbered as a breeding bird by the shag; the former holding about eighteen per cent of the total number of nests for the two species. More shags nest at Gull Rock, Veryan, than cormorants nest in the whole county.

Little is known of the past history of the cormorant colonies. Willughby and Ray (1662) found them nesting on Godrevy Island, but today they are confined to the mainland at Hell's Mouth where Harvey (BB, 1923–24) found about ten pairs—its present strength. Harvey also estimated 50 pairs at Gull Rock, Mullion—twice as many as at present. In 1931 a colony of about 35 pairs was said to exist between Boscastle and Crackington Haven, but nothing is known of it now. Up to eleven occupied nests were reported at Polzeath in the 1930's; this colony is known to have changed its position at least once and may now be represented by the few nesting at Pentire Point. Tree-nesting, a habit not uncommon on the Continent, is not known in Cornwall, but tree-roosting has been reported in recent years with up to 25 birds at Sheviock Wood bordering the River Lynher.

Cormorants avoid the open sea when feeding, remaining largely in estuarine waters, flying considerable distances to and from their breeding colonies. Birds from Gull Rock, Veryan, have been seen flying in from the direction of the Fal, five miles away and from the direction of the Fowey River, fifteen miles away. S. C. Madge[1] has recorded daily feeding flights up and down the Tamar well above Gunnislake—some perhaps reach Tamar Lake. On the Camel estuary R. J. Salmon has seen birds settling on the river beyond Egloshayle church and sometimes as far as Grogley Halt. Cormorants, unlike shags, will frequent inland stretches of water, especially reservoirs like Melancoose, Stithians, and Drift, where fishing is profitable.

There is evidence of a passage movement of cormorants and shags in the autumn. At

Godrevy Point, A. G. Parsons (1958) distinguished two movements. Soon after dawn there was an inshore movement of local birds, presumably to feed, while after about 8.00 a.m. twos and threes moved west low over the water, a long way to seaward of St Ives Island. These flights are presumably linked with the finding of cormorants and shags, ringed in other parts of Britain, on Cornish beaches in autumn and winter.

Nothing has been published on the wintering numbers of cormorants. Over 90 were seen in Falmouth Bay on 29 December 1943, but it is not known whether this total is abnormally large or not.

On the Scillies the cormorant may be seen fishing close inshore almost anywhere amongst the islands, but usually not more than two or three together except close to the breeding colonies. Cormorants regularly visit the freshwater pools. In June 1963, for instance, one went nearly every day to the Pool on St Agnes, catching an eel almost immediately and flying off as soon as it was swallowed.

No accurate census of nesting cormorants has ever been taken, though there is some evidence of a decline this century. Clark and Rodd (z, 1906) wrote of considerable numbers on the outer rocky islets. In 1903, for example, Inner Innisvouls was thickly populated, a large colony thrived on Melledgan, while 29 nests were on Rosevear. This statement suggests there were more nests on the first two islands than on Rosevear, making it probable that the population was around, or something over, 100 pairs. By 1945 Ryves and Quick (BB, 1946) believed about 60 pairs were breeding on two or three islands. In 1954, the estimate was 50 pairs—20 on Rosevear, 18 on Mincarlo and 12 on Melledgan and in 1963 there were about this number on the same three islands. In 1964 there were six nests on Guthers—the first time birds bred there for some years.

Clark and Rodd (z, 1906) noted the habit of this species to change its nesting station

annually or every few years. Thus in 1901 and 1903 the main colony was on Great (Inner) Innisvouls with no nests on either Little (Outer) Innisvouls or Menewethan; in the intervening years there were large colonies on the latter two islands but only three nests on Great Innisvouls. Subsequent changes have been recorded only infrequently. The main colony, or colonies, have been reported from the following islands and rocks in the following years—

| | | | |
|---|---|---|---|
| Castle Bryher | 1937 | Melledgan | 1902, 1911 |
| Great Crebawethan | 1949, 1951 | | 1914, 1962 |
| Great Innisvouls | 1901, 1903 | Menavawr | 1947 |
| Illiswilgig | 1949 | Menawethan | 1902 |
| Little Innisvouls | 1902 | Mincarlo | 1885, 1946 |
| | | | 1954, 1963 |
| | | | 1965 |
| | | Rosevear | 1903, 1954 |

King (MS) considered that Melledgan was the most frequently occupied island between about 1900 and 1928, and there has often been a colony here in recent years, although numbers fluctuate. Illiswilgig was apparently used for a number of years in the late 1940's, in 1951, and perhaps subsequently. Most of these islands have been occupied by smaller colonies in years other than those mentioned above, as have Rosevear, Hanjague, and Guthers. Single nests were found on Annet and Gorregan in 1947.

Nesting commences considerably earlier on Scilly than elsewhere in Britain. Incubation begins regularly in early March and most clutches are usually completed during this month or in early April, though a few not until May, or even early June. In some years the first eggs have been laid in the last two weeks of February. In 1914, for example, incubation must have commenced not later than 25 February and this was stated to have been by no means exceptional.

Only cormorants ringed in the British Isles have been recovered in Cornwall and the Scillies—most of them within twelve months of being ringed as nestlings. The longest surviving bird was ringed at St Margaret's Island, Pembs., 3 July 1961 and found dead on the Tamar on 11 January

1967. Most of the forty-three recoveries have been between September and February of birds ringed at—
The Lamb, East Lothian, 1; Mochrum, Wigtonshire, 4; Farne Islands, Northumberland, 1; Isle of Man, 2; Anglesey, 5; Saltee, Co. Wexford, 8; Pembrokeshire, 8; Lundy Island 4; and south Devon, 1.

Of birds ringed as nestlings at Scilly, mostly on Melledgan (none ringed on the Cornish mainland) nine have been recovered within the Scillies or Cornwall and only seven from other parts of Britain—
Devon, 4; Somerset, 1; Gower, Glamorgan, 1; and Suffolk, 1. There have been eleven recoveries from west France between September and February and two in July—
Finistère, 6; Côtes du Nord, 2; and Morbihan, 3. Three Spanish records are—

|  | Ringed as nestling | Recovered |
|---|---|---|
| Melledgan | 19.5.'14 | Pontevedra, Galicia 6.10.'14 |
| Melledgan | 8.6.'62 | Killed, Ria de Muros, Corunna 20.2.'64 |
| Melledgan | 22.6.'64 | Killed, Colunga, Oviedo, end of December '64 |

## SHAG                  *Phalacrocorax aristotelis*

Unlike the cormorant, the shag is confined to the north Atlantic, breeding on suitably rocky coasts from the Mediterranean to north Scandinavia and Iceland. In Britain only the south-east is largely unsuitable while in the north and west breeding numbers have generally increased, especially in the last twenty years.†

The shag has been condemned for eating too many fish of economic importance. In 1911 the Cornwall Sea Fisheries Committee offered a reward of one shilling for the head of every shag and cormorant killed within the Committee's jurisdiction, the reward becoming payable from 1st September that year. The scheme, dropped from July 1915 until September 1925 remained operative until the end of 1929 and accounted for a total of 10,959 heads. By this time many

† For local names see under cormorant.

people, fishermen included, doubted whether this slaughter was justifiable. Staff at the Marine Biological Laboratory at Plymouth therefore analysed the stomach contents of the two species from 1929 to 1933.

One hundred and eighty-eight shags and 27 cormorants which had been feeding around the Cornish coast, were shot and examined. The results shewed that the proportion of species of economic importance consumed by the shag was negligible—only five out of the 188 were found to have eaten flatfish. Even during stormy weather when forced to feed in estuaries, often in company with cormorants, shags seemed reluctant to eat flatfish. By contrast, the cormorants consumed nearly 50 per cent of marketable species. (G. A. Stevens, *Journal Marine Biological Assoc.*, 1933).

The shag has been exonerated of the crimes committed by the cormorant which, fortunately for the fishermen, is far less common, being outnumbered by about ten to one and possibly as much as fifty to one on the Scillies.

The shag is less of an estuarine feeder than the cormorant, being more at home off rocky coasts, relishing quite high seas in the most abysmal conditions. Breeding colonies are scattered along the steeper cliffs of the mainland—mainly in the north and west. Most nest on offshore islands—the largest single colony comprising about 150 pairs

Gulland Rock from Trevosa

being at Gull Rock, Veryan; only one pair bred on the mainland opposite in 1967. About 66 pairs on Mullion Island and 47 at nearby Gull Rock, give the west side of the Lizard peninsula the highest concentration in the county with about 200 breeding pairs between Gunwalloe and Cadgwith. More nest in the Land's End peninsula than indicated by the figures of the 1967 census, for unlike the cormorant, the species was badly affected here by the oil and detergent. Many of the traditionally occupied ledges between Morvah and St Ives remained empty while at The Brisons off Sennen, only about fifteen pairs nested although 250 non-breeding birds were disturbed on the day of the count. The figures on the map for the coast from St Ives to Botallack Head are for the possible normal population.

Too few figures have been published to recognise any definite trends in breeding numbers. A decrease seems certain in some areas, perhaps due to human disturbance, for at Bedruthan in St Eval, where five nests were counted in 1967, up to twenty occurred prior to 1947. It is also less common between Porthcothan and Park Head.

There is no proof of any change in status at Scilly. Shags are the commonest sea-birds nesting everywhere except on the inhabited and larger uninhabited islands, and most commonly on the exposed western rocks where on some islands virtually every suitable site is occupied. In 1962 and 1963, there were about 130 nests on Rosevear and 70 on Melledgan, mostly in cavities beneath high boulders, and also on Rosevear in the shelter of the old building and beneath the large sheets of iron left by the builders of the Bishop Rock lighthouse—a convenient and protective situation against the widespread depredations of the great black-backed gulls. The total breeding population for the islands is probably about a thousand pairs, several hundred more than on the Cornish mainland.

Nesting commences later than with the cormorant. Most eggs are not laid until late April or early May, no earlier than on the mainland. Indeed, breeding seems to have continued in Anglesey throughout the winter! The earliest date of egg laying in Cornwall is c. 16 February 1933 and 16 March 1914 at Scilly. While fledglings have been observed on nesting ledges in early September—one on 9 September 1963 at Kynance Cove, Mullion—most have fledged in July and many ledges are deserted in early August.

From the end of August there is evidence of a large westerly passage of shags off the Cornish coast. As with the cormorant, movements close inshore in the early morning are certainly local birds moving to feeding areas, but further out large numbers are recorded moving west, mostly before 8.00 a.m. while none are recorded moving in the opposite direction later in the day. Few figures have been published but off St Ives c. 110 were counted between 6.15 and 7.30 a.m. on 8 September 1959. Large gatherings are more frequently noticed at Scilly where flocks of several hundred may be seen throughout the year when conditions are favourable, especially late summer when the young have fledged but before some have disappeared from the islands for the winter. Then rafts of a thousand birds have been recorded—as on 26 August 1960— while gatherings half this size are not uncommon especially in September.

Little is known of wintering numbers in the county. Off the south-east coast large flocks assemble around Looe Island and to a lesser extent between Seaton and Looe, but elsewhere it is not normally seen in parties of more than ten (Madge[1]).

All the shags recovered in Cornwall and Scilly—most of them no more than a year old—were ringed at the following British breeding colonies—
Bardsey Island, 2; Ynys Gwalon Fawr, Caernarvonshire, 3; Skomer, 2; and Lundy Island, 57.

In Cornwall five ringed at Mullion have been recovered, but all others are from

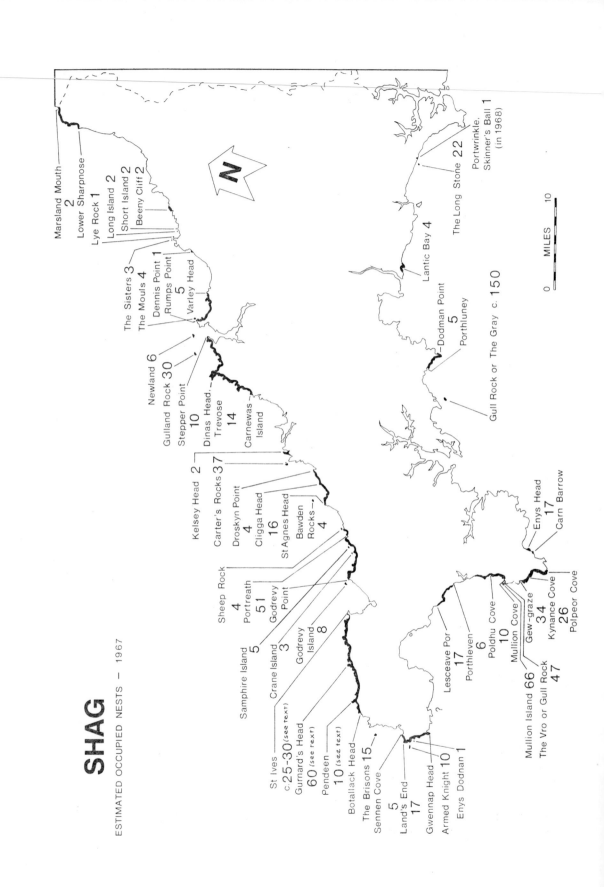

# SHAG

ESTIMATED OCCUPIED NESTS — 1967

Marsland Mouth 2
Lower Sharpnose
Lye Rock 1
Long Island 2
Short Island 2
Beeny Cliff 2

The Sisters 3
The Mouls 4
Dennis Point 1
Rumps Point
Varley Head 5

Newland 6
Gulland Rock 30
Stepper Point
Dinas Head.
Trevose 10
Carnewas Island 14

Kelsey Head 2
Carter's Rocks 37
Droskyn Point 4
Cligga Head 16
St Agnes Head
Bawden Rocks 4

Sheep Rock 4
Portreath 51
Godrevy Point
Godrevy Island 8

Samphire Island 5
Crane Island 3

St Ives c. 25–30 (see text)
Gurnard's Head 60 (see text)
Pendeen 10 (see text)
Botallack Head
The Brisons 15
Sennen Cove
Land's End 17
Gwennap Head
Armed Knight 10
Enys Dodnan 1

Lesceave Por ?
Porthleven 17
Poldhu Cove 6
Mullion Cove 10
Gew-graze 34
Kynance Cove 26
Polpeor Cove

Mullion Island 66
The Vro or Gull Rock 47

Enys Head 17
Carn Barrow

Lantic Bay 4
The Long Stone 22
Portwrinkle,
Skinner's Ball 1
(in 1968)

Dodman Point
Porthluney 5
Gull Rock or The Gray c. 150

N

0 ————— MILES ————— 10

Scilly. Excluding the large number of local recoveries, shags have been recovered in the following counties—

north Devon, 1; south Devon, 20; Gloucestershire, 1; Pembrokeshire, 1; and Caernarvonshire, 1.

One bird from Mullion was recovered in Finistère while fifty-three from Scilly were found abroad—mostly in western France between August and January—Finistère, 38; Côtes du Nord, 6; Manche, 1; Le Havre, 1; Loire Atlantique, 1; and Gironde, 1. Three have been recovered in the Channel Islands. Almost all the birds were one year old or less with a few up to three and a half. Quite exceptional was the recovery at Brest, Finistère on 6 November 1928 of a shag ringed somewhere at Scilly in June or July 1914.

The other foreign recoveries are—

|  | Ringed as nestling | Recovered |
|---|---|---|
| Rosevear | 29.6.'65 | Corunna Province, Spain, sometime late in 1965 |
| Annet | 26.6.'62 | found alive, Den Helder, Noord Holland 23.9.'62 |
| Annet | 26.6.'62 | found dead, Ijmuiden, Noord Holland 8.9.'62 |

# HERON                    *Ardea cinerea*

The common heron nests in a broad belt from western Europe to the Pacific coast, but is mostly absent from the Mediterranean and Arctic regions. In Britain it nests in almost every county.

In Cornish the heron was called *cherhit* which in late Cornish was probably more correctly written *kerghyth* (c.f. Welsh *crychydd*). The word survives in the place-name Polkerris (Polkeryes on Norden's map of 1584 and meaning heron pool) in Tywardreath. Hern, as recorded by Rodd (1880), is a dialect word common throughout England.

No heronry was reported in Cornwall until the nineteenth century. All are small, not one ever having exceeded about thirty pairs while all are now less than half this size. All heronries, whether extinct or still occupied are listed below. Much of the historical information is taken from E. M. Nicholson's 'Census of Heronries' (BB, 1928–29), A. G. Parson's census of 1948 (CBWPS) and J. F. Buxton's similar census of 1954 (BS, 1956).

BUDE AREA—Tamar Lake
One pair has bred here at least since 1961, usually rearing three young.

Bude Canal
For at least twenty years herons built in firs where the Tamar divides Whitstone and North Tamerton parishes. Six nests were successful in 1954, but lately there have been only two or three (Lott[1]). This is perhaps the new heronry discovered "in North Cornwall" in 1948.

LAUNCESTON AREA—
Werrington Park
Until oak trees outside the East Lodge of the estate were cut down about five years ago, some eight or ten pairs had nested annually since at least 1920, and probably before that. Until the recent county boundary changes this heronry was just in Devon (Commander Williams[1]).

ST GERMANS AREA—Sheviock Wood
A colony was established here about 1872 and contained three nests in 1873 and six or seven in 1877 (Z, 1877). It was probably an offshoot from the old-established colony at Warleigh six miles to the north-east on the Devon side of the Tamar. Deserted sometime after 1906 Sheviock Wood was reoccupied in 1921; in 1928 it contained about ten nests which remains its approximate size—nine nests in 1964, seven in 1966 and 1967.

Warren Point, Antony
An old-established site which was deserted in 1921 when the birds moved to Sheviock Wood. It was later reoccupied, holding four nests in 1948 and fourteen in 1954, only to be deserted again after tree-felling in 1960 in which year it held five or six nests.

St John's Lake
Two pairs have nested in pines on the north shore since 1965. Two pairs are said to have nested in Cornish elms on the south side about 1959 (Madge[1]).

LOOE AREA—Trenant Park, Duloe
A heronry has been here since at least 1820 and originally contained about eight nests in the old oak trees, but only two or three when Clegg wrote this account in 1872 (Z). Clark (VCH) wrote that it had contained up to thirty nests but only two or three in his day. However, it returned to its former strength and contained at least 28 nests in 1928. Further records are not available until 1953 when there were two pairs and three the

following year. Six pairs nested in 1966, five in 1967, but only one in 1968 due to tree-felling.

### FOWEY AREA—St Winnow

This is an old site and probably the one near Fowey mentioned by Rodd in 1864. In 1906 (VCH) two are mentioned on the Fowey River, but their exact location is not given. The St Winnow site contained eight nests in 1928, and fifteen (the most recorded) in 1946. During the 1950's it was gradually forsaken for a new site two miles downstream. Only one pair remained in 1959 although more have returned since— three pairs in 1967.

### Penpoll Creek

Birds from the St Winnow heronry first established themselves here about 1950. Thirteen nests were occupied in 1959, diminishing each year to six in 1962.

### PAR

One pair has nested in an alder tree in the marsh regularly since 1957. Two nested here in 1962 and 1966.

### FAL BASIN

The records from the River Fal, Helford River and adjoining creeks, are more fragmentary than most, but the large number of localities mentioned in the scattered reports probably refer to a smaller number of heronries which have changed their quarters from time to time—note the similar well documented change from the north to the south bank of the Camel River.

### Lamorran River

Rodd in 1864 mentioned a heronry here. This is probably the site in Borlase Wood, near Tolverne, marked on the six inch Ordnance Survey maps of 1906 and earlier. Seventeen, and possibly nineteen, nests were occupied in 1940, but only five nests were found in 1948 and four in 1969.

### Tregothnan

A heronry mentioned by Clark (VCH) on this estate was perhaps the one at Merther Pool adjoining the Tresillian River. It contained at least twelve nests in 1928 but has gradually diminished since—eight in 1954 and two in 1968.

### Kea Wood

Herons have nested here for at least twenty years, the maximum being about ten pairs, but were almost wiped out in the winter of 1962–63 (Craven[1]). About four pairs nested in 1969.

### Trelissick to Restronguet

Birds nested at Trelissick Wood prior to 1948 and presumably still do so. Other sites formerly occupied are at Pill Creek from 1937 to 1940 (five nests in 1940) and half a mile away at Camersands Wood two pairs nested in 1938. Herons are thought to have nested at Carclew

about 1890 (P, 1892) but this was never proved— no heronries are now known anywhere along Restronguet Creek.

### Porthcuel River

Sites were known here before 1948 at Trewince, North Wood, Quay Wood and Place. In 1966 a heronry was occupied at Porth Creek (the Trewince site) but the number of nests is not known.

### HELFORD RIVER

The fragmentation of Cornish heronries is very apparent along the Helford River. Between 1948 and 1953, A. G. Parsons found four sites simultaneously occupied within a short distance of each other—Bishop's Quay, in beech trees; Polwheveral, in beech trees; a 'splinter' from the above two sites a quarter of a mile away in Merthen Wood in scrub oak; and Bonallack, Constantine, in beech trees. The first record of a heronry at Helford was at Bosahan (presumably the one in St Anthony parish) before 1906 (VCH). There were three pairs at Bonallack prior to 1928. In Merthen Wood, near Groyne Point, there were also three nests in 1928 and about ten in 1948. Opposite Merthen at Tremayne were three nests in 1961 and two at Bishop's Quay in 1964. The heronry at Polwheveral, Constantine is known to have been occupied since the 1930's—twelve nests were recorded in 1947. At least until this date herons also nested at Polpenwith, Constantine.

Common heron

## MOUNT'S BAY—Marazion

Prior to 1948 two pairs nested in the pine trees below the Cheshire Homes, but for the next fifteen years moved half a mile up the valley to the long wood below Bowgheere Farm. This site has not been used since 1967, but may have been deserted earlier (Parsons[1]). In 1959 one pair nested in a low alder tree in the middle of Marazion Marsh, a site occupied ever since with a maximum of four nests in 1966.

### Penrose

An adult seen with three young birds on the Penrose estate, Helston in July 1959, are thought to have come from Helford. No herons are known to have nested on the banks of Loe Pool except for two pairs in 1927 or 1928 at Treginver Wood (Parsons[1]).

## CAMEL ESTUARY

A heronry was established at Prideaux Place before 1880. There are single records of nesting at St Cadoc, Padstow in 1928, one mile east of Wadebridge in 1927, and at Dinham the same year. However, the main colony was west of Dinham House at Trevelver which is thought to have been established about 1880 by birds which deserted Prideaux Place three miles away. Three nests were at Trevelver in 1920 rising to ten in 1928. The same number of nests, mostly in elms, was counted in 1941, but in 1943 the site was deserted, the colony having moved in that year, or in 1942, across the Camel estuary to the creek below Bodellick Farm, St Breock, sometimes called Pinskin Creek. Twelve nests were here in 1943, ten in 1948 eleven in 1958, fourteen in 1961, only 6 in 1962 and four after the disastrous winter of 1962–63 recovering by stages to fourteen in 1966.

Ryves wrote (1931) that a pair undoubtedly bred near St Mawgan in 1930 and 1931 "as the birds were up and down the valley during the season and about mid-July, in both years, four birds suddenly appeared—probably the parents and two young".

## BODMIN MOOR

Nests far from the estuaries are rare in Cornwall. A pair nested in fir trees at Jamaica Inn, Bolventor, in 1868. There was a heronry at Trebartha Hall, but as it was not mentioned by F. R. Rodd who owned the house, it may not have been founded until about 1920. Seven nests were occupied in that year and at least twelve in 1928 having altered its position two years previously. The colony was probably deserted in the 1930's. A recently discovered heronry is at Halvana Forest, a mile and a half east of Jamaica Inn, with eight nests in the tall conifers in 1965 and twelve in 1967. Since 1965 a few pairs have nested at Fernacre Plantation near Roughtor.

CLIFF NESTING — by solitary pairs occurs on a limited scale. From 1931 to 1933 a pair raised up to four young on the cliff at Dizzard Point, St Gennys. No breeding was proved subsequently although adult birds were about in 1935 and 1939. On the south coast in 1961 three young were hatched in a cliff nest at Polkerris, near Par. Between Polkerris and Gribbin, three pairs nested in 1966 and two in 1967.

From about the end of June onwards, the local population is augmented by birds from outside Cornwall. British birds are not thought to move far, but some breeding in the north clearly disperse to southern areas. However, only one British and two foreign ringed herons have been recovered in Cornwall (see below).

## ISLES OF SCILLY

Most herons in recent years have been reported on passage between August and October, the largest number being sixteen on "a small island" on 8 September 1959. The same year eleven flew over St Agnes on 5 October. Wintering birds leave in March and only a few are seen during spring and summer. Large numbers were seen sixty years ago or more—Clark and Rodd (z, 1906) wrote that twenty to thirty were not unusual on Stack Rock and at Guthers, while as many as sixty had been counted, but at what time of year is not recorded. Rodd (1880) mentioned that herons were "believed to breed on Stack Rock"—a flat-topped rock between St Martin's and Tresco and a favourite resort—but this was never proved.

| | Ringed as nestling | Recovered |
|---|---|---|
| Mepal, Cambs. | 9.5.'33 | found dead, St Breock, October '33 |
| Hillared, Vastergotland, Sweden | 10.6.'34 | Par, 12.11.'34 |
| Nodlandsvatnet, Rogaland, Norway | 10.6.'40 | found dead, St Teath, 12.1.'41 |

Over half the ringed birds in Britain come from Scandinavia.

# PURPLE HERON          *Ardea purpurea*

The purple heron is found in much the

same European localities as the little egret, but has become more common since about 1945. English records occur mainly between April and October in East Anglia.

| | |
|---|---|
| pre-1838 | Couch recorded that one alighted on a fisherman's boat about two to three leagues from the shore. |
| 1845 | One captured near Penzance (PZ). |
| 1846 | One killed in a sedgy grove at Killiow House, Kea on 9 April (Z). |
| 1850 | One shot at St Buryan (Z)—probably the specimen from Trewoofe Valley (WLE). |
| 1851 | A bird in a Plymouth poultry shop had been shot on the Tamar on 30 October (Z, 1859). |
| 1858 | One shot at Scilly (Z, 1906). |
| 1867 | A female obtained near the Lizard about 29 April (Z). |
| 1878 | An immature shot on St Mary's Moor on 30 August (Z). Two perfect adults had not been obtained in Cornwall in the last few years (Couch, 1878). |
| 1898 | One seen on Tresco was finally shot on St Mary's in April (Z, 1906). |

There are no more reports until—

| | |
|---|---|
| 1944 | One at Scilly on 25 April. |
| 1945 | Two, one adult, on Tresco on 17 April. |
| 1950 | An exhausted bird on St Martin's on 3 April. |
| 1958 | One on St Agnes from 22 to 24 April. |
| 1961 | Two at Porthellick Pool, St Mary's on 27 April, three from the 29th with one remaining until 23 May. |
| 1962 | An adult male at Porthellick Pool from 10 to 23 May. |
| 1965 | A male with a female or young male at Porthellick Pool on 3 May. |
| 1966 | A near adult at Porthellick Pool from 1 to 30 May (R) and an immature on Tresco from 14 to 18 May (R). S. C. Madge[1] (1968) saw one fly in from the sea at Downderry on 24 April and finally located the bird on the Erme estuary in south Devon where it remained for several days (R). |
| 1968 | One at Marazion Marsh on 5 June (R). |

## LITTLE EGRET     *Egretta garzetta*

The little egret breeds in isolated areas in southern Europe, becoming more widespread from the Balkans eastwards. It is now an annual visitor to southern counties.

A letter of Henry Mewburn of St Germans, dated 7 March 1826, says that a pair was taken in Cornwall within the previous eighteen months. Couch refers to them in his Cornish Fauna (1838) while Rowe (PI, 1862–63) noted that a pair, presumably referring to the same birds, had been taken on the Tamar.

No other records are known until 1943–44, when one remained on the Hayle estuary from November to 10 February. The next was reported at Trewornan Bridge on the Camel from 26 to 28 May 1949. Out of the nineteen years from 1949 to 1967, little egrets have been reported from the mainland or Scilly in twelve years. This is consistent with observations in other parts of Britain and seems to indicate an increase in birds and not bird-watchers.

Ordinarily only one little egret is seen in Cornwall in any one year; 1955 proved exceptional when five separate birds (possibly seven) were seen on various dates between 7 and 23 April at St Erth, Gwithian, Marazion Marsh, Penrose near Helston, Ruan Lanihorne, and on the Camel estuary. The only other locality where the little egret has been seen is at Gweek in 1957 and 1965.

Most Cornish records coincide with the spring migration in April and May. The earliest dates are 2 to 5 March 1952 when one was on the Camel estuary. The following

Purple heron

year one remained there from 19 May to
8 June. One migrating bird landed exhausted
on board the *Sara Stevenson* 30 miles S.W.
of the Lizard on 4 May 1961.

The autumn records are from Gweek on
10 to 18 September 1957 and Godrevy on
18 October 1959 with presumably the same
bird remaining at Hayle from 9 to 22
November. One was at Marazion Marsh
on 27 and 28 July 1963.

The only records from Scilly are—

1955 One at St Agnes from 13 May to 27 June.
[A bird shot since 1951 and in the Abbey
Collection may have been obtained in
April that year].
1962 One at St Agnes from 13 to 28 May.
1963 One at St Mary's from 3 to 30 April.
1966 One at Tresco from 6 to 9 May.

# GREAT EGRET
# (GREAT WHITE HERON)
*Egretta alba*

The great egret is a vagrant to Britain
from its nearest nesting areas in south-east
Europe.

1866 Bullmore reported one with two common herons at Pennance near Falmouth
on 4 February 1866. It remained for several
days but was so shy that no one could get
close enough to shoot it. Rodd (1880)
thought it was probably a spoonbill giving
no other reason than that the latter had
occurred in Cornwall. One reported at
Hedge Rock off St Martin's did prove to
be a spoonbill when shot on 26 December
1870.
1948 One at Loe Pool between 28 September
and 3 November also visited Porthleven,
and Gweek where it was photographed
on 4 October. This may be the bird seen
later in Sussex.
1951 One flushed with some common herons
at Godrevy Marsh on 29 May made off
across St Ives Bay.

# SQUACCO HERON
*Ardeola ralloides*

In Europe the squacco heron is largely
confined to southern Iberia, the Rhône and

Po valleys, and from the Balkans eastwards.
Formerly more widespread, it has not bred
in Holland since the last century. This,
perhaps, explains the lack of Cornish records
since 1915, although birds have since been
seen in Devon—as in 1958 and 1964.

c. One shot near Penzance—probably the
1834 specimen from Trereife, Madron—and
another seen a few days later at Hayle
(Couch, 1838 & z, 1843).
1842 One shot at Scilly in the autumn (z).
1843 One shot at Penzance about 12 April (z).
pre- Courtney refers to a bird, in Rodd's col-
1845 lection, from near Land's End—perhaps
the one Rodd (1880) lists from Sennen.
1849 A remarkable flight occurred in west
Cornwall about 15 May. One shot in a
tree at St Hilary, two shot near Land's
End, three (one report says five) shot at
Trevenwith in St Keverne, and the first
specimen was obtained at Scilly (z, & g,
8.5 & 22.5.'49).
1862 One shot about five miles from Camelford on 10 May, and another near Redruth at the end of April (z, & g, 9.5.'62).
pre- One or two known from the Tamar
1863 (pi).
1865 One captured at Caerhayes Castle on 14
May (z).
1867 Rodd examined one from the Land's End
on 7 May (z).
1871 One obtained near the Lizard in May (z).
pre- A near adult captured at Roskestal, St
1876 Levan (wle).
pre- From 1849 Clark and Rodd noted Scilly
1906 examples from Tresco, St Mary's, and
St Martin's.
1907 The specimen now in Truro Museum
was shot at Penwethers, Truro on 1 June.
1915 One shot on Tresco in April (ar).

# NIGHT HERON
*Nycticorax nycticorax*

The night heron is more widespread than
the little egret with the nearest colonies to
Britain on the Loire and, since 1946, in the
Netherlands. It is seen every year in eastern
England. Cornish records, mainly for April
and May, are—

pre- In the last three years a male had been
1838 obtained at Crowan, a female at or near
the Lizard, and a juvenile caught between
Penzance and Newlyn (ri).

1844    One shot in the fish pond at St John's near Torpoint (Yarrell).

1849    In a year when eight were shot in south Devon, one, perhaps two, was killed on Tresco on 15 May.

1850    One, probably female, killed at Penrose, Helston on 28 April (z) and a pair were shot at Gunwalloe in April (WLZ).

1855    One killed near the Lizard in October (Rodd, 1880).

1865    A female knocked down at Camerance Wood, St Just-in-Roseland (Bullmore, 1866).

1869    A pair shot at Hayle about 10 May (z) and another shot about this time at St Mawes (P).

1919    One at Tregorden Marsh, Egloshayle for about a week in May was perhaps the bird taken near Stratton on 10 May and presented to Truro Museum (RI).

1925    One at Scilly—presumably Tresco—in October (AR).

1944    One at Scilly on 6 May.

c.      One found shot at Menadarva, Camborne
1946    (Turk[1]).

1948    One at Manaccan from 11 September to
-'49    10 April.

1950    One at Carne Creek near Helford around 19 March, and another at Marazion Marsh on 23 May.

1955    An immature male was on St Mary's for about a month until shot on Tresco on 28 April.

1961    Two adults frequented Porthellick Pool, St Mary's from 29 April to 13 May. On 30 April they were joined by an immature which remained until 2 June.

1962    One on the Great Pool at Tresco during May.

1965    One on Tresco from 26 March to 1 April.

## BITTERN                 *Botaurus stellaris*

The bittern is a regular breeding bird in East Anglia and in recent years its range has extended to other eastern counties, but has little prospect of regaining its former status when breeding occurred as far west as Wales. There are no breeding records for Cornwall. Borlase (1758) counted it amongst the county's waterfowl without elaborating on its status. Polwhele (1816) and all later writers described it as rare.

Records since the last century shew it to be a winter visitor in varying numbers depending upon the severity of the season. 1838 saw an unusual number in Cornwall— "that five were taken to Penzance for stuffing" (G, 2 February 1838). More than usual appeared in 1867 when one or more were reported from Scilly and "a large number from the mainland" (z, 1868).

The crepuscular habits and secretive nature of the bittern may well give a false impression of its rarity. Many records have been for birds disturbed by wildfowlers or for birds which have flown into overhead wires and would otherwise have remained undetected. Few years now pass when at least one is not seen in Cornwall. Between 1945 and 1967 bitterns were not reported in 1955–1957 and 1964. While most have been seen in west Cornwall, they may be found in suitably marshy tracts throughout the county. In 1962 there were single birds at Tamar Lake; Marazion Marsh; and Smeaton Farm near Saltash. The bittern is solitary by nature, so that the occurrence of three near Camborne in 1964 is most unusual. British breeding birds are resident. Rather than migrate in severe weather they would prefer to starve in their Norfolk reed beds. Dutch birds are mostly sedentary, so that the emaciated specimens which turn up in Cornwall may have come from central or northern Europe. Apart from one seen at Dozmary Pool on 12 July 1960, all records are between early November and the end of March with most in January and early February.

At Scilly, Clark and Rodd (z, 1906) noted six or seven occurrences, but the only records since are—

1945    One at St Mary's on 25 January (AR).
1959    One on Tresco on 5 September.
1962    One found dead at St Agnes on 11 January.

## LITTLE BITTERN

*Ixobrychus minutus*

The little bittern is found over much of

Europe except in Scandinavia and Brittany. It has nested in East Anglia but can only be regarded as a rare visitor to south-east England with more sporadic records from elsewhere. Most have been seen in April and May.

1727 The 'Crab-catcher' taken alive near the sea at Gorran was probably this species. Kept at Mr Doucett's house for some months "neither he or many who saw it could tell what Bird it was, till this last Christmas 1733 . . . "(Tonkin). 'Crab-catcher' is probably derived from 'Clabitter' or 'claw-bittern', a local English name for the bittern. Tonkin describes the bird in great detail.

1832 One shot at St Mawgan-in-Pydar (G, 25.5.'32).

1838 A male killed on Newham Moors near Helston (WLZ).

1841 Another bird, a female, killed on Newham Moors (WLZ).

1866 A male obtained on Tresco on 10 June (Z).

1867 An exhausted female picked up at Coverack about 20 April (Z), and another killed in an orchard at St Hilary about 11 April (Z).

c. One obtained at Skewjack, Sennen (Z, 1868 1870).

1870 A female killed at Skewjack, Sennen in the last week of May (Z).

1901 A male captured in The Parade, Lostwithiel on 30 June (Z).

1910 A male caught by a dog near Land's End in April (BB) and one shot near New Mill, Gulval in November (Harvey, 1915).

1922 An exhausted female captured on the cliffs near Mousehole on 9 May (BB).

1952 One at Hayle Kimbro ponds, Ruan Major on 11 April.

1955 One on St Agnes Pool on 7 May.

1958 A dying juvenile picked up at Jacobstow in May.

1964 An adult on St Agnes and St Mary's on 11 and 18 April. A dying bird arrived at Falmouth on 3 May and another was seen alive on Sithney Common near Helston on 11 May.

1965 A male was found dying at a farm at Bedruthan Steps on 9 April.

# AMERICAN BITTERN
## *Botaurus lentiginosus*

The American bittern is a vagrant to Britain that is easily overlooked and misidentified. Rodd (1864) wrote that it was supposed to have been killed in Cornwall but no example was known to him. At least three shewn to Clark (RI, 1907) belonged to the European species. The following are assumed to be authentic—

1873 One shot at Tresamble, Gwennap on 4 November and sent to Gill the Falmouth taxidermist (RI, 1907).

1903 An emaciated bird caught on Bryher on 10 October lived for at least three years in the aviary on Tresco (Z, 1906).

1906 A male with a broken wing was killed near Porthcurno beach on 12 November after being chased down the valley (Z).

1927 One shot on Goss Moor on 28 November where another, thought to be the same species, was seen on 30 December (BB).

1953 One shot late in the year at Stratton (Treleaven[1]).

The specimen of little green heron now at Truro Museum

## (LITTLE) GREEN HERON
*Butorides virescens*

The only British record of this common North American species is the adult bird now displayed at the County Museum, Truro. It was shot by the gamekeeper at Penrice, who saw it at Hay Bottom, a swampy valley near Pentewan, on 27 October 1889 when trying for the proverbial "early woodcock". It was exhibited at the Linnaean Society in 1890 (z).

James Harting saw no reason to doubt the record, suggesting that this crepuscular bird came off shore at twilight and perched in a ship's rigging. Objections that it could not have survived the crossing were dismissed on the grounds that many birds have tremendous fasting powers in captivity. The green heron certainly seems an unlikely trans-Atlantic wanderer, but perhaps no more strange that the authenticated crossings of the American bittern.

## WHITE STORK            *Ciconia ciconia*

British records were far more common in the nineteenth century when the species bred in much of western Europe. Now the white stork is largely found east of a line from the Netherlands to the Balkans, and in parts of central Iberia.

1848   An adult killed at Mayon Pond, Sennen on 13 May (z).
1885   One seen at White Marsh, Lostwithiel in November (vch).
1952   One, perhaps an escape, was seen at Sea Mill on the Camel estuary in October.

## BLACK STORK            *Ciconia nigra*

The breeding range of the black stork has considerably attenuated in the last hundred years and is now restricted to part of Iberia and east of a line from northern Germany to the Balkans.

1831   The second British example was this bird shot on Beggar's Island in the River Lynher on 5 November (Couch, 1838 & vch).
1887   One obtained at Tresco in September (z, 1906).
1890   One shot on Scilly on 8 May (z).

## SPOONBILL            *Platalea leucorodia*

Until the mid-seventeenth century the spoonbill nested in East Anglia, but today the nearest long-established colonies are in the Netherlands and southern Spain.

It is a regular visitor to coastal areas of eastern and southern Britain and can scarcely be called a vagrant to Cornwall. Birds have been seen in the county in every month of the year, but usually in autumn with most in October. Some over-winter, and these, or New-Year arrivals, are generally gone by April. A few have remained until late June, while autumn arrivals have been seen in July—one on 19 July 1964 on the Tamar.

Records for the mainland early this century are lacking. One was seen on the Camel in January 1922 and another at Marazion Marsh in November 1927, but from 1935 when two wintered on the Camel from November onwards, spoonbills have been recorded annually apart from 1959, 1960 and 1966.

Although they will frequent freshwater sites, Marazion Marsh is the only one known to have been visited. Birds have been seen on all the major estuaries but most consistently on the Camel, and at Ruan Lanihorne. About half are of single occurrences, and half the remainder of pairs. Large parties are rare—eight (mostly immatures) at Ruan in November 1942 and January 1943, being the maximum. One to three sightings in any one year are usual, but in 1964 eight were reported, comprising five at Marazion Marsh on 29 March and single birds on the Tamar (19 July); Hayle (17–23

NORTH CLIFFS NEAR CAMBORNE—Reskajeage Cliffs, otherwise known as the North Cliffs, with their off-shore rocks, form a notable stretch of coast for nesting sea-birds. They are typical of the north coast cliffs formed of Devonian shales and thin sandy bands. This view is north-east from Hell's Mouth and shews the almost flat marine platform at about 230′ which ends in abrupt magnificence. In the distance, St Agnes Beacon rises like an island above the peneplain.

Over 1,000 pairs of kittiwakes now nest (1969) in Cornwall's largest sea-bird colony just west of St Agnes Head. The foreground cliffs offer ledges to 80–90 pairs of guillemots and 20–30 pairs of razorbills, but puffins are no longer found here. Large numbers of fulmars—which first occurred on these cliffs in the early 1940's—hundreds of gulls (mostly 'herring'), and about fifty pairs of shags, are amongst the resident population along with a few oystercatchers which nest in precarious positions well up the cliff face. [ *Photo:* D. B. BARTON ]

THE CAMEL ESTUARY—Typical of the winding rias, or drowned river valleys, of the south-west is the Camel. The Tamar-Lynher complex, the Fal with its many adjoining creeks, the Hayle estuary, and the Camel, are the most rewarding tidal waters in the county for bird-watchers. This aerial view, taken from above Stepper Point, looks up-river and shews Padstow in the middle distance.

The sands in the foreground, including the dangerous Doom Bar, provide an important feeding and resting ground for migrant terns. These lower reaches are also frequented by grebes and divers in winter.

Top left, on the further shore, is Pinskin Creek, site of one of Cornwall's larger heronries. The best place for watching waders is where the rivers Amble and Camel meet below Trewornan Bridge. The view from the observation hide recently constructed here, is sketched on page 17. Above Trewornan bridge is the Walmsley sanctuary, famous for its wintering flock of about 100 white-fronted geese.     [*Photo:* DEPT. OF AERIAL PHOTOGRAPHY, UNIVERSITY OF CAMBRIDGE]

September); and at Falmouth (11 December). The largest numbers seen this century were in the 1940's, when the spoonbill attempted to recolonize long-abandoned breeding areas on the Continent. In 1946 when they bred at the mouth of the Loire for the first time since before 1600, at least twelve birds were seen in Cornwall, with up to five at Ruan in December. About a dozen were also reported in 1948.

No record this century compares with that of 1843 when a flock of eleven flew over Hayle on 11 October and alighted on marshy ground at Gwithian where seven were killed at one shot from a single-barrelled gun (z & G, 20 November 1843). In the third week of the month nineteen were seen near Newquay and four of them killed (Couch, Supplement to 1838 *Fauna*). Courtney (1845), almost certainly referring to 1843, wrote that a flock was seen on the beach between Penzance and Marazion, and many were afterwards killed near Perranporth.

At Scilly, the spoonbill is an occasional visitor in autumn and winter. One was seen in April 1869 or 1870 at Tresco, and once in June—an adult male on the 7th in 1850. Clark and Rodd (z, 1906) record about a dozen, chiefly on Tresco, where a few remained for many weeks.

The only records this century are—

1909. At least one in October at Tresco (AR). Spoonbills were seen in four of the six years 1940–45—mainly on Tresco and include one flock of thirteen on 2 October 1940. Since two were reported on 15 November 1945, the only record has been of seven at St Agnes on 24 November 1966 as well as an immature bird on St Mary's from 23rd to 27th of the same month.

British records are likely to become increasingly sporadic as the number of European birds decline. More were seen in this country in the first quarter of the present century than at any other time, 1920 being the exceptional year.

| | |
|---|---|
| pre-1829 | One shot at Hayle was presented to Truro Museum (RI). In 1838 Couch wrote that several were known from Cornwall. |
| pre-1845 | Courtney records one shot at Paul near Penzance. |
| 1854 | One shot on Tresco on 19 September (z). |
| 1866 | One shot at Scilly on 8 October (z). |
| 1883 | One seen on Tresco in November (z). |
| 1900 | One obtained at Hayle in November, and another near Saltash in October (RI, 1902. z, 1907 reverses the months). |
| 1902 | Two at Tresco on 11 October—one shot at Penzance Gate, the other flew off over Pentle Rock (z, 1906). |
| 1906 | A male shot near Sennen Cove on 25 October (z). |
| 1908 | One shot near Land's End in November (BB). |
| 1909 | One shot at Paul on 25 October (Harvey, 1915). |
| 1920 | Ten very tame birds were seen at Marazion Marsh on 19 September; two were still there on 1 October. Two, probably from this party, were at Land's End on 30 September (BB). |

## GLOSSY IBIS    *Plegadis falcinellus*

With breeding birds restricted to the Carmargue, the Po valley, and the Balkans,

Glossy ibis

1932   One on Scilly in the autumn (Parslow[1]).

1940   Seven remained on Tresco for about two weeks from 18 October.

1964   A very tame bird which arrived near
-'65   Wadebridge on 31 December, spent many weeks on a very muddy farmyard pond near Egloshayle church and was last seen lower down the Camel at Dinham on 16 April. Probably the same bird was earlier seen in Devon.

## FLAMINGO            *Phoenicopteridae* sp.

A flamingo of indeterminable species was seen at Penzance sometime in 1912, and later shot on Scilly. It was regarded as an escape (Harvey, 1915).

During the autumn of 1964, a scattering of flamingos occurred in many coastal counties from Northumberland to Cornwall. Close examination shewed them to belong to the South American race *P. chilensis* which is regularly imported into Britain and parts of the Continent (BB).

## MALLARD              *Anas platyrhynchos*

The mallard is one of the most widespread of breeding ducks in the Old and New Worlds, and in Britain it nests in all counties. In Cornwall the species is first mentioned by Carew (1602) who gives no indication of its status. At present it is the most common resident duck, but comparatively few breeding records have been published. The following information, partly derived from unpublished sources, may well be far from complete.

North-east Cornwall. Three or four pairs regularly nest at Tamar Lake and at least four pairs on the Bude Canal. Many of the latter birds shew signs of albinism due to crossing with farmyard ducks. On the cliff at Efford, just south of Bude, one or two pairs nest under gorse bushes, making the long trek to the Bude Canal with the ducklings. In the Launceston area at least one

pair nests on the river below Netherbridge, but little is known of the bird's status in this part of the county (Lott[1] & Treleaven[1]).

Bodmin Moor. The only recent record is of a female flushed from a nest with ten eggs at Halvana Plantation, Altarnun, on 3 June 1947. Col. Almond (1959) wrote that a few mallards and teal are seen in St Breward parish at migration time but none are known to breed. Clark (VCH) wrote that they bred on the Moor at the turn of the present century, while according to Hitchens and Drew (*History of Cornwall*, 1824), "in the vicinity of Dozmary Pool scarcely a season elapses in which wild ducks do not hatch their infant broods".

Camel estuary. Ryves and Quick (BB, 1946) wrote that numbers had decreased in the Wadebridge area. Numbers at the present time are not known—some may nest undetected in the Walmsley Sanctuary. In 1965 at least two pairs were thought to have nested between Wadebridge and Rock. Hand-reared birds introduced by wildfowlers have obscured the picture still further.

Melancoose reservoir. In 1965, six females nested, and another three may have done so. The early nesters were said to be more successful being less disturbed by man.

West Penwith. Clark (VCH) wrote that at the turn of the century mallards nested on freshwater pools in the area—presumably thinking of Skewjack in Sennen and similar sites—but the only locality yielding modern records is Marazion Marsh where one or more pairs nest annually. Breeding was first recorded here by Borlase (1758)—the first county record. Birds have nested in the wet fields behind the Hayle estuary, as in 1933, but apparently do not do so now.

Loe Pool, Helston. Up to three pairs have reared young here, as in 1951, and nesting is presumably annual.

Hayle Kimbro Pool. Two females were known to have nested in 1965, and one in 1968 was seen with five or six young.

Tresillian. A pair annually nests on

Kiggon Pond, hatching eleven young in 1966, and usually at Tresemple Pool as in 1969. On the Tregothnan estate (Jarvis[1]) mallards nest in the woodland over a wide area usually within easy reach of ditches and small streams which eventually lead them to salt water.

Ruan Lanihorne. A pair was seen with three young below Sett Bridge in May 1965. They may have nested within the boundary of the Tregothnan estate.

Clark (RI, 1902) wrote that in the last few years birds had nested at Bishop's Wood, Truro; on the edge of Baldhu Moors; near Old Kea; near Constantine; and in 1898 at Pendarves, Camborne. No recent records come from these localities. The only published site from west Cornwall not given above, refers to a female which reared eight ducklings at Gunwalloe Marsh in 1939.

The only breeding records from the Par area are of a nest with ten eggs found in a disused quarry close to St Blazey railway sidings in 1955 and two on the edge of the sea cliff at Little Hell in 1967.

South-east Cornwall (Madge[1]). East Looe River. Ten females were known to have bred in 1966 on an artificial lake two and a half miles from Looe. Lynher. One female nested, and six may have done so in 1965. River Tiddy, St Germans. One female nested but as many as fifteen may have done so in 1965. Crafthole reservoir. One female reared eleven ducklings in 1966.

Isles of Scilly. Nests sparingly with records going back to the mid-nineteenth century. In 1903 nests were found on Tresco; at Porthellick, St Mary's; among the bracken on Samson; St Helens; and Tean (z, 1906). At present about twenty-five breed annually on Tresco, St Mary's, Samson, and probably the other small islands mentioned above (Hunt[1]).

Since British breeding mallards are thought to be largely sedentary, it can only be assumed that the increased winter population is built up mainly of Continental birds. Winter numbers do not shew—as do wigeon, for example—a steady rise and fall with a peak about January. A second peak, sometimes giving the highest total of the year, usually occurs about September or October and clearly indicates a movement of passage birds. Most estuaries and stretches of suitable freshwater annually support a winter population. Some birds are also found on the sea in sheltered bays—a more common feature than published records would indicate. They are not uncommon most years off Perranuthnoe, sometimes accompanied by shovelers (Parsons[1])—others have in recent years been seen in Veryan

*St Clement on the Tresillian River - the riverside walk from here to Tresillian is renowned among local ornithologists*

Bay. In 1943 mallards were described as frequent in the shelter of the north side of the Rumps Point, St Minver, where that year a maximum of 300 was seen on 24 December and 200 on 24 January. In 1932, fifty to a hundred were said to be usual there, but there are no recent records. Birds from Melancoose reservoir frequently commute between the reservoir and The Chick off Kelsey Head, where they spend the day resting on the island or on the open sea.

Wintering numbers, taken mainly from the Wildfowl Census figures are—

Mallard

| Loc. | Cnt. Period | Av. Nos. | Max. Nos. | Date |
|---|---|---|---|---|
| Tamar Lake | 1954–5 to 1966–7 | 30 | 95 | October 1966 |
| Camel and Walmsley Sanctuary | 1959–60 to 1965–66 | 75 | 185 | Walmsley January 1962 |
| Gannel | — | few | 20 | recorded (w) |
| Melancoose reservoir | 1961–2 to 1966–7 | 60 | 110 | January 1961 |
| Hayle | — | usually absent | 10 | November 1965 |
| Drift reservoir | — | 2–4 usual | 26 | November 1965 |
| Marazion Marsh | — | not always seen— usually less than 40 | 100 | November 1965 most unusual |
| Loe Pool | 1959–60 to 1966–67 | 180 | | with allowance made for the abnormal total of 800 plus in the cold spell in January 1963 |
| Stithians reservoir | — | — | | 33 in Nov. 1965 c. 100 17 January 1966 |
| Restronguet Creek | 1962–3 to 1965–6 | 25 | 38 | November 1963 |
| Tresillian River | 1962–3 to 1965–6 | 65 | 163 | December 1966 |
| Ruan Lanihorne | not reg'rly counted | 60 to 100 thought average | 210 | October 1961 |
| Par Beach | a few times | — | 11 | December 1961 |
| Looe | only rec'tly counted | — | 76 | October 1965 |
| Fowey | not normally counted | Average thought to be 30 (w) | | |
| St John's Lake | only recently counted | — | 250 | January 1966 |
| Lynher | 1959–60 to 1965–66 | — | 70 | November 1965 |
| Tamar estuary | 1954–5 to 1966–7 | 90 | 170 | September 1954 |

(mallards are said to prefer the Devon side of the river (w) )

In winter, increased numbers occur at Scilly, especially on the pools at Tresco, but there is little information on numbers.

Fifteen mallards, none of them nestlings, ringed in Britain have been recovered in Cornwall; ten were ringed at Slimbridge, Gloucestershire, and single birds at Coln St Dennis, Gloucestershire; Peakirk, Northamptonshire; Ludham, Norfolk; Abberton, Essex; and West Wycombe, Buckinghamshire. Recoveries of foreign ringed birds are—

| Ringed | | | Recovered |
|---|---|---|---|
| Selbjerg Vejle, Jutland, Denmark, | nestling | 21.7.'63 | shot near Mullion January '64 |
| De Koog, Texel, Holland | full grown | 18.8.'53 | shot Boyton 12.1.'56 |
| Hallum, Friesland, Holland, | full grown | 25.11.'53 | near Camborne 30.1.'54 |

## TEAL                    *Anas crecca*

The diminutive teal is one of the most widespread wildfowl in the northern hemisphere, and most plentiful in northerly latitudes. In Britain it is widespread but local in the south.

Borlase (1758) recorded teal as winter visitors. F. R. Rodd (MS) wrote that "a few still breed with us", but only Clark (VCH) supplied any details. Birds regularly nested on Bodmin Moor, small numbers on Goss Moor, and sometimes further west "for young teal are not infrequently reported in the summer months" in the Truro-Falmouth district. The number of records since 1931 is less than half a dozen, while in the past twenty years the only record refers to suspected breeding at Tamar Lake in 1953.

There are unconfirmed reports that teal nested on Porkellis Moor, Wendron until the early 1950's (Parsons[1]).

Teal winter on both freshwaters and estuaries. The number seen on a given estuary may fluctuate enormously from month to month because the birds wander about estuary complexes, as in the Tamar-Lynher-St John's Lake area. At Lambe Creek near Truro the teal always remain in a restricted area and the annual build-up and decline is easily recorded. 150 to 200 are normal here in January.

The average figures given below are calculated by taking the average of the annual maxima on Wildfowl Counts irrespective of the month in which the maxima occurred.

| Locality | Average | Greatest Number |
|---|---|---|
| Tamar Lake | 60 | 100, December 1963 |
| Tamar estuary | 100 | 500, December 1953 |
| Camel estuary and Walmsley Sanctuary | 200 | 450, December 1962— up to 1,000 said to have been counted at high tide when birds take to the freshwater pools on the Sanctuary. |
| Hayle estuary | 300 | c. 650, December 1962 & 1963 |
| Loe Pool | 120 | c. 400, January 1963 |
| Lynher | 140 | 260, March 1965 |

Areas for which fewer figures are available—

| | | |
|---|---|---|
| St John's Lake | — | 250, 15 January 1966 |
| Par Beach | — | over 100, 10 December 1967 |
| Ruan Lanihorne | — | 80, 23 December 1966 (regular counting would certainly shew greater numbers here) |
| Restronguet Creek | Not always present | 200, January 1963 |
| Stithians reservoir | — | 107, 3 January 1967 |
| Melancoose reservoir | 20–30 | over 60, 27 February 1964 |
| Drift reservoir | 20–30 | 45, January 1966 |
| Marazion Marsh | Well below 50 | 100, November 1965 |

First birds arrive about mid-September. Early dates are 26 July 1963 at Marazion, and 29 July 1967 at Walmsley. A great increase normally occurs in November. While most teal depart in March, a few are often seen well into April. On Scilly there is evidence of regular passage in April and September. Extreme dates are 29 August 1959 on St Agnes, and 15 April 1958 on St Agnes. Fifty-three teal ringed in Britain and thirty-four ringed on the Continent have been recovered in Cornwall; all records are for autumn or winter. Recoveries from ringing stations are—

Abbeton, Essex, 33; Orielton, Pembs., 12; Slimbridge, Glos., 4; Peakirk, Northants., 1; Deeping St James, Deeping St Nicholas, and Sutton Bridge, Lincs., 1 each.

Foreign recoveries are from Holland, 18; Denmark, 8; Flanders, 5; and one from each of Sweden, Finland, and France (mouth of the Rhône). A full grown teal ringed at Fanø, Denmark on 15 October 1907 and shot at Tregothnan, Truro on 17 January 1908 is the earliest bird recovery in Cornwall.

## GREEN-WINGED TEAL
*Anas crecca carolinensis*

This American bird resembles the European teal so closely that most ornithologists now regard it as a subspecies. Only the male birds are distinguishable. In Britain, one or more examples has been recorded annually since 1958.

| | |
|---|---|
| 1962 | One at Marazion Marsh from 4 February to 22 April (R). |
| 1963 | Another at the same place on 15 May (R). |
| 1968 | One on the Lynher on 10 February stayed until at least 28 March (R). |

## GARGANEY
*Anas querquedula*

Garganey breed across Europe outside most of the Mediterranean region and the far north. In Britain, on the edge of its breeding range, nesting is largely confined to the south-east.

In Cornwall the garganey is almost exclusively a passage migrant. Clark (VCH) said it was not uncommon in the Truro-Falmouth region, where it is rarely seen now, the only recent records being two at Tresillian on 24 March 1960 and one on 28 October 1967. Clark's statement that it was not infrequent in the Penzance-Lizard area still holds good—in fact it is certainly an annual visitor there. It is also a regular visitor to east Cornwall where previously it was overlooked.

At Scilly the only records known to Clark and Rodd (z, 1906) were one killed on Tresco, 29 March 1881; five shot in March 1883, and one at Porthellick, St Mary's at Christmas 1900. Two were present on Tresco on 20 January 1945 (AR). Since 1957 they have been seen almost annually, mainly from March to May, but also in September. In 1959 they were especially numerous between 17 March and 31 May when a maximum of twelve were at Porthellick Pool and five on St Agnes. In the autumn up to ten appeared on Tresco between 11 and 17 September. That year a pair nested unsuccessfully on Tresco where the species is said to have bred once before.

On the mainland, spring passage normally starts sometime between 10 and 20 March and dies off between 20 April and the first few days of May. There is no well defined peak movement, but maximum numbers are more often seen at the end of March or early April. The earliest dates are one on the sea—itself unusual—off Par on 27 February 1965, and one at Marazion Marsh on 26 February 1943.

In 1959, a female with several young, thought to be garganey, were flushed from reeds on the Amble marshes on 30 June. At Marazion Marsh in 1961, a pair was seen on several dates in June and July, while in 1964 a pair apparently attempted to nest there. The first fully authenticated breeding records for Cornwall are in 1968 and 1969 —the locality remains a secret.

A light autumn passage has been noted every year since 1958, mostly between mid-August and mid-September. Late dates include one at Loe Pool on 19 October 1949, and the bird at Tresillian already mentioned, while the maximum number was twelve at Marazion Marsh on 15 August 1945.

The garganey visits freshwater pools favouring those, like Marazion Marsh and Tamar Lake, which possess a rich fringe of reeds and grasses. A good indication of the sites visited and the maximum numbers likely to be encountered, may be obtained from a résumé of the unusually large spring migration of 1959.

| Locality | Dates in 1959 | Max. No. seen and Date |
|---|---|---|
| Marazion Marsh | 19 March–8 May | 20, 3 April |
| Loe Pool | 3 April | 1 |
| Clowance Pool | 17–19 March | 1 |
| Tory Pond, Stithians | 25–30 March | 1 |
| Copper Bottoms, Praze | 20 March–24 April | 6, 20 March |
| Walmsley Sanctuary and Amble Marshes | 28 March–1 May (breeding suspected) later in year) | 9, 27 April |
| Par Beach pool | 13 March–23 April | 12, 18 March |
| Tamar Lake | 31 March–6 May | 6, 24 April |
| Isles of Scilly— | | |
| Porthellick Pool | 17 March–11 April | 12 |
| St Agnes | 19 March–22 April | 5, 15 April |
| | 15–19 May | 1 |
| Tresco | 31 March–2 April | 7 |

Other localities visited by garganey since 1960 include—Gwithian Pool (ten on 10 April 1960), Gunwalloe, Cargoll in Newlyn East, Tehidy Pond, Melancoose reservoir, and St John's Lake.

## GADWALL                    *Anas strepera*

The breeding distribution of this species in Europe is irregular. In Britain it breeds mainly in the south-east, but has spread, partly due to introduced birds.

In Cornwall there is a marked dichotomy in its status between the mainland and the Isles of Scilly. Formerly it was rare at Scilly —the only record known to Clark (z, 1906) being a bird shot on Tresco on 1 January 1900—but since 1934 birds have bred on Tresco. The gamekeeper (Wardle[1]) said that the resident population stems from a drake which was shot in the wing, pinioned, and later released on the Pool. This bird subsequently paired with a wild female resulting in a gradual build-up to the present population of about twelve pairs. Winter numbers, between 40 and 60 (65 on 14 October 1967), are mainly birds of the year.

Since many are shot, their numbers do not increase beyond their present strength. The gadwall rarely wander from Tresco, even outside the breeding season, while the only nest on another island was found on Tean about 1944 (Ryves & Quick, BB, 1946).

On the mainland the gadwall has become more common in the past twenty years, and is an annual visitor in small numbers. The species favours freshwater localities but has been seen almost every year on the Hayle estuary, with a maximum of six on 20 January 1965, when some wintered there from 11 November to 15 March. Most records are of one or two birds. Up to four have been reported from Tamar Lake as in February 1962, and three at Melancoose reservoir as in November 1964 and 1965. The most regularly visited stretch of water is Loe Pool, where five were usual in the late 1940's and early 1950's, but where records now seem more sporadic. Since 1950 there have been occasional records from Tamar Lake, Amble Marshes on the Camel estuary, Clowance pond or Crowan reservoir, and single occurrences from the Lynher, Par Beach pool, the Gannel, Drift reservoir, Gunwalloe marsh, and Tresemple pond near Tresillian.

There is no sign of breeding on the mainland, although pairs have been seen at Marazion marsh in May and early June in 1964 and 1965.

Most birds are reported between late November and late February; early dates including 4 and 14 September 1959 at Tamar Lake and the Camel estuary respectively, and 15 October 1962 at Tamar Lake. A late record is of two at Gunwalloe marsh on 10 April 1960.

## WIGEON                  *Anas penelope*

In Europe the wigeon breeds mainly in Scandinavia, the Russian taiga, and Iceland. In this country it is well established only in Scotland. Birds have nested as far south as Kent, but never in the south-west.

Wigeon are common winter visitors to Cornwall recorded by Carew (1602) and Borlase (1758). The latter (MS) wrote that the wigeon was known locally as the 'Whistling Wigeon' to distinguish it from the 'Tamar Wigeon' (pochard) and 'Pyed Wigeon' (goldeneye).

First birds often arrive in early September, but there are a few August records—the 7th on the Tamar in 1959, 26th at Hayle in 1967, and 29th on the Lynher 1965. While most leave the county in March, a few commonly remain into April—the 25th at Hayle in 1965. On the Camel estuary, six passage migrants were seen as late as 23 May 1967, and an eclipse male was seen at Crowdy Marsh, Camelford on 8 June 1952.

Wigeon are certainly the commonest wintering ducks in Cornwall. At least 8,000 were estimated in January 1965, over 70 per cent of them in the Tamar area.

| Locality | Seasons | Av. Max. Nos. | Greatest Nos.[1] |
|---|---|---|---|
| St John's Lake | six (non-consecutive) | 2,175 | 5,000 January 1966 |
| Lynher | 1959–60—65–66 | 1,000 | 1,200 December 1960 |
| Tamar estuary | 1954–55—66–67 | 555 | 2,000 December 1957 |
| Tamar Lake | 1954–55—66–67 | 40 | 123 February 1961 |
| Camel estuary and Walmsley Sanctuary | 1959–60—65–66 | 360[2] | 1,600 January 1963 |
| Hayle estuary | 1959–60—65–66 | 470 | 750 January 1965 |
| Loe Pool | 1959–60—65–66 | 180[2] | 1,000 January 1963 |

AVERAGE WINTERING NUMBERS OF WIGEON ON THE HAYLE ESTUARY: 1959–60 to 65–66

| Sept. | Oct. | Nov. | Dec. | Jan. | Feb. | March |
|---|---|---|---|---|---|---|
| 16 | 84 | 232 | 402 | 397 | 318 | 38 |

Although not the main wintering area, the Hayle estuary provides more accurate figures than localities like the Tamar where the picture is complicated by considerable movement between estuaries. The figures are taken from the average monthly totals of the Wildfowl Census which produce a rather conservative result. Thus, the average maximum number for January during the same period taken from the C.B.W.P.S. reports, totals 604.

[1] Figures mostly from the CBWPS reports.
[2] Excluding the abnormally high figures in the winter of 1962–63.

There are few figures from Ruan Lani-horne, but an average winter maximum of 200 to 250 is estimated. Birds are rarely seen on the Gannel—90 were there on 28 December 1961. The maximum at Tresillian is 150 on 28 December 1964—only a dozen or so are normally seen here at irregular intervals. Wigeon are irregular visitors to Melancoose reservoir, where 28 were seen in January 1962, and Crowan reservoir where 350 were present in January 1964.

On Scilly, most authors described the wigeon as "not uncommon", F. R. Rodd, for example, noting 150 at Tresco Pool on Christmas Day 1864. Nowadays small flocks visit the pools on St Mary's and St Agnes with larger numbers on Tresco (Quick, 1964), but few figures have been published. Many occurred in the hard weather of January 1963 when up to 30 were present on St Agnes. The latest dates are of single birds on Tresco on 13 May 1964 and 18 May 1967.

Wigeon

Five ringed wigeon have been recovered in Cornwall in winter. All were ringed on migration at Abberton, Colchester (1); Orielton Decoy, Pembs. (1); and three in Holland. Most British wintering birds, however, are known to be of Russian origin.

## PINTAIL                                    *Anas acuta*

The pintail breeds in many areas in northern Europe, Asia, and North America. Numbers have increased in Britain but there is no Cornish breeding record. A pair was said to have raised seven young at Skewjack Pond, Sennen in 1938, but although the record is published in *The Handbook*, the find circumstances were so unsatisfactory that local ornithologists who have read the correspondence involved feel the record should be deleated. Only occasional summer records are known—for example, a bird seen at Marazion Marsh on 6 June 1961.

Until the early years of the present century, pintails were described as not uncommon in hard winters in the west of the county and, according to Clark (VCH) on Bodmin Moor. In 1853 one of the most devastating shots made with a double-barrelled shoulder gun dispatched 37 pintails out of a large flock on the Helford River. They were sold in Falmouth with their tails cut off to make them appear "more duck-like" (Bullmore, 1866). In 1915, Harvey described the pintail in west Cornwall as a regular visitor, its numbers depending on the severity of the winter. A decline is then apparent for Ryves (1948) found the species to be rare until 1942, after which numbers increased with at least 55 on the Camel estuary in January 1945. There is also a change in distribution; from being more common in the west, the pintail now favours the eastern parts of the county. There are, for example, no recent records from Helford River. The main wintering areas are the Camel estuary (including the Walmsley sanctuary) and the River Lynher. The average winter maximum at Ince in the winters 1961–62 to 1965–66, is 70, with a maximum around 80, and the average for the Camel in the same period is 66 with 100 on 11 January 1964. A few birds are regularly reported from Hayle, Marazion Marsh, and Loe Pool, and were unusually numerous in the hard weather early in 1963 when there were seventeen at Hayle on 7 February and twelve at Loe Pool on 12 January. Records are sporadic elsewhere, but include reports from Restronguet, Ruan Lanihorne, Par beach, Crowan reservoir, Stithians reservoir, Dozmary Pool, and Tamar Lake. Few are ever reported at the inland localities—the most being nine at Crowan reservoir in January 1963.

First birds arrive from about 20 October whilst most leave at the end of February or early March. Figures from the Camel or Lynher do not shew a passage movement, but isolated records from Tamar Lake, Marazion Marsh and elsewhere shew movements in August and September and in April.

The pintail is an uncommon and by no means annual visitor to Scilly in ones or twos in mid-winter, to Porthellick Pool, or St Agnes. Unusual was a drake at Tresco on 2 June 1965, and five on Tresco and St Agnes on 4 and 27 October 1966.

## SHOVELER                  *Anas clypeata*

The shoveler breeds throughout Europe except in the Mediterranean region and the far north. It has greatly increased in Britain where it is now widespread, although still local, and has nested at Scilly. The first record is for a clutch of ten eggs on 17 May 1958, perhaps on Tresco where two pairs have since nested but probably not regularly (Hunt[1]). There are no mainland records, although Harvey (1915) thought it may have nested at Marazion Marsh where a few birds have summered in recent years.

The shoveler is principally a winter visitor arriving from mid-September and leaving in March. Rodd (1880) and Clark (VCH) considered it the most abundant duck in west Cornwall in some winters, a flock of over 100 was seen on the Land's End marshes in late January 1894. Today flocks of fifty have been recorded at Loe Pool with a maximum of 108 in January 1964.

The average January maximum here from 1960 to 1966 is 24. Birds appear to move between Loe Pool and Marazion where up to 20 are seen almost annually on the Marsh and 56 on 10 December 1962. At Tamar Lake it is an irregular visitor in parties of up to half a dozen and is similarly fitful in the Tamar-Lynher area. Forty-three on the Tamar in March 1956 were certainly migrants. Shovelers frequently appear elsewhere and since 1960 up to 36 have been counted at Ruan Lanihorne on 28 December 1961, nineteen at Melancoose reservoir on 22 December 1963, seventeen on 20 January 1963 at Hayle where only one or two are usual, over twenty at the Walmsley Sanctuary in December 1946, and seven early in 1962 at Crowan reservoir where shovelers are rare. Parties have sometimes been reported from sheltered bays, for example in Mount's Bay near Perranuthnoe.

On the Scillies most reports are of small winter parties on Tresco. More occur in hard weather but few figures have been published. A maximum of twenty was on Tresco from 20 to 27 January 1965, and parties of about a dozen occur fairly regularly in September and October. Migrants have been reported on St Agnes, but no more than four birds on any single occasion.

| *Ringed* | *Recovered* |
|---|---|
| De Koog, Texel, Holland adult male, 28.12.'61 | shot, Ruan Pool, Lizard, 1.1.'63 |
| Naardermeer, Noord Holland full grown, 11.10.'62 | shot, Bodmin, 23.12.'62 |

## RED-CRESTED POCHARD
*Netta rufina*

The red-crested pochard nests in scattered areas in Europe as far north as Denmark, but more commonly near the Mediterranean. A few annually reach Britain, but it is impossible to distinguish wild birds from escapes.

1845   One shot at Swanpool near Falmouth in February (Bullmore, 1866).
1927(?) One at Scilly on 21 November (AR).
1952   A female at Tamar Lake on 13 January.

1953    Another female at the same place on 8 January.
1961    A male on Helston Park Lake and Loe
-'62    Pool from 29 December to 17 March.
1963    Three females at Tamar Lake on 8 September.

scaup

## SCAUP                    *Aythya marila*

The scaup breeds in the northern taiga and tundra and has done so occasionally in northern Scotland since 1899.

In Cornwall it is a regular passage migrant and winter visitor—exceptionally are more than a dozen recorded in a season between late November and the end of February. There are scattered records of migrants in September and October, the earliest being two at Loe Pool on 29 August 1960. Some March records, as nine off Feock in mid-March 1961, also suggest a passage movement. There are no recent records for April, but several in May and June as in 1965 when there were two at Hayle from 17 May to 3 June and one until 6 June.

The scaup is essentially a sea-duck, but regularly frequents freshwaters near the sea —notably Marazion Marsh and Loe Pool, with other recent records from the Drift, Melancoose, Stithians and Argal reservoirs, as well as Swanpool. Unusual was one on Clowance pond at Crowan from 17 to 25 February 1959. From estuaries and sheltered bays there are records at Hayle (most often), the Camel, Mount's Bay (Penzance area),

the Fal, and the Lynher-St John's Lake area. During the cold spell of January and February 1963, only single birds were reported from west Cornwall except for a maximum of three off Penzance. In east Cornwall, by contrast, they were more numerous with thirteen at St John's Lake on 9 February and fifteen off Torpoint (perhaps the same flock) on the 19th, while seven remained on the Lynher until 10 March. Large numbers were reported from west Cornwall in the 1953–54 season—five at Loe Pool in October, ten at Argal reservoir on 23 February, six at Hayle on 13 February, and three in Prussia Cove on 7 March.

At Scilly, the scaup is an irregular visitor in ones or twos. Rather more, probably migrants, have been seen in October than at other times, mainly on freshwater pools as Porthellick on St Mary's, Tresco Great Pool, and St Agnes Pool. Unusual was a male on Tresco on 24 June 1964 (Parslow[1]). Birds rarely remain for more than a day, but a drake on Tresco stayed from 29 August to 5 September 1962.

A nestling ringed at Husavik, Iceland on 22 July 1928 was recovered at Trewern, Madron, in mid-February 1929. Most British recoveries are of Icelandic birds.

## TUFTED DUCK            *Aythya fuligula*

The tufted duck is increasing as a breeding bird in much of northern Europe, including Iceland. In Britain the increase has been marked where birds have exploited new reservoirs. In Cornwall a pair has summered at Stithians reservoir since 1966 while others have remained almost annually on the Argal reservoirs since the last war, but without any sign of nesting. The only breeding records are for Tamar Lake in 1961 when a pair with three juveniles were seen on 7 July, and for "a Cornish reservoir" (perhaps Tamar Lake) in 1937. A pair with six young just able to fly were seen on the Tamar at Cargreen on 21 July 1966 (Musson[1]). Fully winged adults were recently introduced to ponds at Trago Mills near Liskeard but they did not nest in 1968. Unpinioned young formerly kept at Trebartha Hall, North Hill, used to leave in the autumn and return the following spring to breed (VCH).

The tufted duck is increasing as a winter visitor. In 1838 Couch described it as scarce and Clark (VCH) found it to be irregular in small flocks in south and west Cornwall, while Ryves (1948) described it as "not regular" and occurring mainly in severe weather. Today it is certainly a regular visitor to areas of freshwater.

One hundred to 150 are regular winter maxima at Loe Pool and the Argal reservoirs, with up to 300 at the former in January 1963. Up to 100 have been counted at Drift reservoir as late in 1965, and up to 40 at Stithians reservoir on 13 January 1967. At Tamar Lake, the only important locality in east Cornwall, about 50 is a regular maximum with as many as 120 in December 1956. In the hard weather of January and February 1963 many occurred where few or none are normal—Clowance Pond, 154; Crowan reservoirs, 119; Swanpool near Falmouth, 60; nearly 30 on the sea at Poldhu and also about Penzance harbour; and up to 45 at the Hayle estuary. In the south-east, by contrast, only five were counted on the Tamar and sixteen at St John's Lake in the same period.

A few birds reported in July-August and April-May are passage migrants. Wintering birds arrive from mid-September—when about six are commonly present at Tamar Lake—and early October when first arrivals appear at Loe Pool. Numbers increase considerably by mid-November. Birds leave during March, few remaining until the end of the month. At Loe Pool there were 46 on 13 March 1966, but only one on the same date in 1964.

At Scilly, tufted ducks are irregular visitors to freshwater pools in parties of six or less, mostly from December to May although there are records for every month.

Maximum numbers are six to ten on Porthellick Pool and St Agnes Great Pool in December 1961 and January 1963.

| *Ringed* | *Recovered* |
|---|---|
| Nakskov, Denmark | shot at the Lizard, |
| adult male, 14.5.'62 | c. 15.1.'63 |

## POCHARD *Aythya ferina*

The pochard breeds throughout much of Europe except Scandinavia, most of France and the Mediterranean region. In Britain there has been a marked increase although it is still local.

In Cornwall the pochard is a winter visitor. Couch (1838) described it as rare but most later writers recognised it as a regular visitor in small flocks. Numbers have certainly increased greatly in recent years, no doubt as a result of the building of new reservoirs.

Tamar Lake and Loe Pool are traditional haunts. Wildfowl Census figures for Loe Pool in January give the average as 93 birds from 1959 to 1965. Maximum numbers, not coinciding with those taken on the census days, have consistently been over 100 in recent years, with 250 on 29 December 1961. The maximum counted at Tamar Lake is about 100 in January 1957. Below

*Tufted duck - shoveler in background*

are given the average numbers of pochards at Tamar Lake from 1954-55 to 1966-67.

| Sept. | Oct. | Nov. | Dec. | Jan. | Feb. | March |
|---|---|---|---|---|---|---|
| 2 | 12 | 28 | 38 | 27 | 14 | 6 |

Stithians reservoir has become an important area with about 240 on 14 January 1966 and over 200 in January and December 1967. Figures from the Drift and Argal reservoirs are few, but in 1965 the maxima were 110 and about 200 respectively. Pochards are not regular visitors to Marazion Marsh, but 50 were counted on 30 December 1961. Less than 50 are regularly reported from Melancoose and Crowan reservoirs. Clowance Pond normally holds only a few but 122 were counted on 10 February 1962. In east Cornwall, apart from Tamar Lake, pochards are seen regularly only at Dozmary Pool where a few dozen are usual, the maximum being 68 on 25 January 1962.

Few are recorded before mid-September —earliest date is 25 August 1963 at Marazion Marsh. Most pochards have departed by mid-March—latest date is 7 April 1960 at Dozmary Pool.

Small numbers of pochards visit Scilly, especially St Agnes where the maximum was about 70 in November 1963. On Porthellick Pool, St Mary's, 30 were counted on 4 January 1966—double the normal maximum. The latest departure date is 31 March 1947 when several were present on Tresco.

The only ringed birds recovered are single adults ringed at Slimbridge, Gloucestershire, and Abbotsbury, Dorset, and shot near Penryn in winter.

## FERRUGINOUS DUCK (WHITE-EYED POCHARD)
### Aythya nyroca

The number of ferruginous ducks breeding in Europe has decreased considerably this century and is now found in the west only in isolated areas. It is an annual vagrant to eastern Britain but extremely rare elsewhere. Some birds may well be escapes.

| | |
|---|---|
| pre-1857 | One purchased at Mrs. Dunning's game shop in Falmouth was presumably shot somewhere locally (P). |
| 1905 | An exhausted bird was killed on a beach near Mylor on 11 March (Z, 1907). |
| 1943 | A male shot on Tresco on 15 January (AR). |
| 1952 | A male at Tamar Lake on 3 January. |
| 1954 | One (female?) at Prideaux ponds, Luxulyan on 9 and 16 February. |
| 1955 | A male at Loe Pool on 16 March. |
| 1957 | An immature at Tamar Lake on 17 April. |

## BUFFLEHEAD          *Bucephala albeola*

The bufflehead breeds in arctic North America and winters as far south as the Gulf of Mexico. Only about six have been reported in Britain, the fourth example being a female shot on Tresco Great Pool on 7 January 1920 (BB) and now in the Abbey Collection.

## GOLDENEYE          *Bucephala clangula*

The goldeneye has a circumpolar distribution and nests widely in the forests south of the tundra in northern Europe. In 1931 and 1932 it bred in Cheshire. Birds wintering in this country come mostly from Scandinavia.

A regular winter visitor to Cornwall in small numbers, the status of the goldeneye has probably not altered since the last century. Maximum numbers seem to occur in mid-winter and not at migration time as frequently occurs elsewhere. Usually it is found in ones or twos, but eight have been counted on Loe Pool—one of its most frequented haunts. Larger groups include twelve on the Fal on 30 January 1965, eleven at Hayle on 20 January 1963, and nine at Stithians reservoir on 6 February 1967. All the larger estuaries are visited, but records are rare or absent from the Fowey estuary, the upper reaches of the Truro-Fal complex, Helford River, and the Gannel. Most large freshwaters have been visited as well as Trenance lake at Newquay (1965), Helston Park lake (1961), and Treloweth pond at St Erth (1963). While shunning the open sea, goldeneyes have been reported from sheltered areas like St Ives Bay and Mount's Bay. Three females were seen off the Lizard on 10 February 1967.

Goldeneyes are usually seen between late October and late March, extreme dates being 30 September 1960 at Clowance pond, and 21 April 1951 at Loe Pool. A male remained at Carnsew Pool, Hayle from December 1960 to 18 August 1961.

Goldeneye

On the Scillies, one or two are reported in most years from either Porthellick Pool or St Agnes Pool. Four at Porthellick on 7 March 1965 is the largest group yet seen. Few remain for more than a day or two.

Exceptional were the numbers in 1937–38. A flock of at least 22 was in Mount's Bay between mid-December and February, while another twenty off Sennen Cove reached 50 on 10 March; fifteen remained on 1 April. Most are recorded between mid-November and the end of February. Extreme dates are 19 October 1952 at St Ives, and 24 April 1958 at Hayle. The majority of records come from St Ives Bay, Hayle estuary, Mount's Bay, and Loe Pool, but others occur at south coast localities such as Par Bay and Carrick Roads.

Being a sea-duck, inland records are rare —they include one at Tamar Lake on 19 November 1938 (BB, 1944), and two in January and one in April 1944 at the same place, and a female at Trenance lake, Newquay in autumn 1948.

The only published records from the Scillies are for 1960–61 (two, one as early as 12 October 1960 on St Mary's), 1964–65 (two), and 1967 (at least three). The only other records are of single birds obtained in November 1911 and on 31 October 1950 (AR). In the last century four immatures were obtained—two shot on different occasions on Tresco and St Mary's before 1852, one on Tresco in 1854, and another in November 1864 (Z, 1906).

## LONG-TAILED DUCK
### *Clangula hyemalis*

The long-tailed duck nests chiefly in the tundra throughout the northern hemisphere, and once nested on Orkney in 1911. Birds winter at sea, usually in the arctic, but occur almost annually in Cornwall. Since 1952 more have been reported than previously, but its status is probably the same as in the last century.

Most records are of single birds. Three were in Mount's Bay on 27 January 1962, and at least six at Harlyn Bay in late November 1957—at least fourteen individuals were seen in Cornwall that winter.

Long-tailed duck

## VELVET SCOTER
### *Melanitta fusca*

The velvet scoter nests in Scandinavia and northern Russia, and may have done so in Shetland. Birds winter along the Atlantic

sea-board. James (1808) first noted this uncommon visitor to Cornwall. It was unknown on Scilly until 1911 when one was
seen on 23 March (Parslow[1]). The only
other records from the islands are for two
on 28 November 1957, one on 8 November
1959, and two on 19 December 1962.

On the mainland there are few records
until 1952, but the largest known flock
consisted of about twenty seen along with
150 common scoters off The Rumps, Polzeath between February and April 1940.
Since 1952, velvet scoters have been reported nearly every year, with up to
eighteen individuals in November and
December 1957. Most are seen in St Ives
Bay and Mount's Bay—especially off Loe
Bar and between Marazion and Newlyn—
with only a scatter of reports from elsewhere,
and usually between early November and
late January. Extreme dates are for nine
migrating birds at St Ives on 16 October
1960, and three off Looe on 19 April 1954.

## SURF SCOTER
### *Melanitta perspicillata*

The surf scoter is an American visitor to
Britain mostly seen off Orkney and Shetland. Some have taken to wintering on the
Solway, but there are no recent records
from Cornwall.

1845  After violent winter gales a decaying
      specimen was picked up in the cove by
      the powder magazine at Pendennis
      Castle. Cocks very graphically described
      the remains as giving off a powerful
      *noli-me-tangere-effluvia* (P, 1857).

1865  A dying adult was picked up close to
      Carn Thomas, St Mary's on 22 Septem-
      ber (z & pz, 1888–89).

1867  An immature male shot off Skirt Point,
      Tresco was sent to Penzance on 28
      October (z).

1906  An adult male and two velvet scoters
      were shot at Helford on 16 December (z).

## COMMON SCOTER
### *Melanitta nigra*

The common scoter breeds in Iceland,

Scandinavia, north Russia, and in small but
increasing numbers in Scotland and Northern Ireland. In Cornwall it is a common
passage migrant and winter visitor whose
status has not changed since the last century.
Although always more rare on Scilly, in
recent years one or two small parties have
been reported almost annually, particularly
in October—the most being about 24 in
Crow Sound in November 1957.

The common scoter is essentially a sea-
duck. It has been recorded after bad weather
at Tamar Lake (five on 16 November 1953),
and at Marazion Marsh on several occasions
but is rare even in harbours. The scoters like
feeding on sandy floors in 30 to 40 feet of
water which doubtless accounts for the bulk
of records from Mount's Bay and St Ives
Bay, where these depths exist up to two
miles out. Similar conditions occur in St
Austell Bay and immediately east of Pentire
Point.

Scoters have been seen in every month of
the year, although very rarely in May or
June as ten in Carrick Roads on 20 May
1961. Twenty or more off Penzance on
30 June 1959 perhaps saw an early start to
the autumn migration which usually commences about mid-July. Movement continues well into November and even
December, but becomes confused with
wintering birds. During the peak migration
in September and early October, from one
to 50 or more have been counted passing St
Ives Island in a day with as many as 230 on
8 October 1961 and a record 500 in a four
hour watch in November 1959 (w). Such
movements have been noted along all the
Cornish coastline but only commonly in
the west.

Wintering numbers are difficult to assess.
In recent years between 25 and 50 have been
reported annually from St Ives or Mount's
Bay in mid-winter with a recorded maximum of 70 in Mount's Bay on 25 January
1964. Flocks of 50 have also been reported
from Pentire Point, Widemouth Bay and
Whitsand Bay; 150 off Pentire between

February and April 1940 is the largest flock ever reported in the county. Spring passage is from about early March to late April. Although the evidence is scanty, the bulk of wintering flocks consists of females. Thus, there was only one male out of 55 birds at Pentire Point on 8 February 1964.

## COMMON EIDER
### *Somateria mollissima*

The common eider breeds on the Atlantic coast of North America, Greenland, Iceland, and Europe. In Britain it nests in increasing numbers as far south as Lancashire. This increase, with a corresponding rise in Holland, surely accounts for the greater numbers now reported off the Cornish coast. In the nineteenth century Rodd (1880) thought it almost as rare as the surf scoter and up to 1900 there are only eight published records, the earliest being for one shot at Looe on Christmas Eve 1839 (RI).

Between 1931 and 1951 eiders were reported in only seven years, all single birds except for thirteen on the Camel in February 1934. Since 1952 records are annual and birds have been seen in every month of the year. Most are wintering birds from early November to late February. There may be a passage movement in November but evidence is inconclusive. A few eider seen as late as April and May could be non-breeding birds remaining in south-western waters. Since 1957 some individuals have been watched throughout the summer in St Ives Bay and (once) off Penzance.

Winter records come mostly from St Ives Bay, Mount's Bay—especially in the Newlyn-Marazion area, the mouth of the Camel estuary, and from Daymer Bay to Constantine Bay. There are other records from Newquay, Par Bay, and Looe. More than usual were seen in the winter of 1962-63. The extreme dates and maxima are—

St Ives Bay, 22 October (two) to 30 May (nine) —16 on 17 January.
Mounts Bay, one throughout the summer of 1962. 19 December (two) to 3 May—up to fifteen in January and February.
Par Bay, up to four between 26 November and 3 May.
Camel estuary, two between 15 December and 2 January.

A few others were reported from St John's Lake, off the Lizard, Newquay, and Portreath. The only other large parties are eleven in Constantine Bay and St Ives Bay on 27 December 1965.

Miss Quick (1964) described the eider as an occasional visitor to Scilly but the only records ever published are—

A pair shot sometime in the 1870's (z, 1906).
1882   The male of a pair shot on 5 April (PZ).
1891   Three birds present for six weeks were shot in Tean Sound on 18 December (z, 1906).
1923   An immature female shot off Tresco a few days before Christmas (BB).
1929   Two females and a male seen on 16 March (BB).
1961   One off the Eastern Isles on 31 December.

## RED-BREASTED MERGANSER      *Mergus serrator*

A regular winter visitor to Cornwall, the red-breasted merganser is the commonest of the three species of saw-bills. It is circumpolar in temperate latitudes, but does extend further north than the goosander. In Britain it is well distributed in Scotland and Ireland and in the 1950's colonized northern Eng-

Eider ducks

land and North Wales. Continental birds attempt to ride out the winter on ice-free waters within their breeding range so that British wintering numbers depend largely on the severity of the weather.

Mergansers may be found in any sheltered bays and estuary mouths around the entire coast—Carrick Roads is a favourite locality, while many records come from the Tamar and adjoining waters, and the Camel estuary.

Mergansers may be seen from early November onwards, but there are a number of October records including the 9th at Marazion Marsh in 1950, and one flying past St Ives Island on the 5th in 1963. Unusual was a 'brown-head'—adult males are comparatively scarce—at Helford River from 30 August to 18 September 1958. Most are recorded from early December to early March, but a few are seen in early April almost annually. Later dates include three at St John's Lake on 20 April 1966, and one at Hayle on 29 April 1957. The only May record refers to a male at Hayle from 20th to 25th in 1967. One was seen on the Camel on 6 June 1948 about which time a female was also reported at Bude.

Red-breasted merganser

Most records are of single birds. Parties of four or five are not rare, and the large flocks listed below might prove more common with consistent watching. Notable numbers in Carrick Roads are 24 (ten males) off Turnaware Point on 31 December 1966, 21 in December-January 1938, nineteen on 6 March 1949, fifteen on 5 March 1960, up to

fifteen in January 1961 and at least fourteen (six males) on 26 December 1965. Outside the Fal, a party of nineteen flew past Looe on 6 January 1966 and eleven flew past Whitsand Bay on the 22nd of the same month. Many of these records suggest a spring passage movement. Curiously, no more than usual were seen in the hard weather of January 1963—the record year is 1966 when over 100 individuals were reported.

On the Scillies, the merganser, like the goosander, is but rarely reported. Since 1947 the only sightings have been—1947, 2 April (one); 1962, late December (two); 1963, January (one); 1965, in January (possibly two), and one in November 1967. This is in contrast to the late nineteenth century when Smart (PZ, 1885) wrote that it was "exceedingly common in winter" although it was not recorded by Rodd (1880). Clark and Rodd (1906) also described it as fairly common in winter.

## GOOSANDER        *Mergus merganser*

The goosander, largest of the saw-bills, breeds in boreal and temperate regions around the northern hemisphere. It has been a widespread though scarce nester in Scotland since 1871 and after 1940 extended its range south to include Northumberland and Cumberland.

Winter records in Cornwall have increased considerably in recent years. Since 1955, at least one to four sightings have been published annually. Almost all comprise single birds—the largest flock being eleven on the Camel on 12 December 1959. In 1962–63, over 70 individuals were reported around the coast and at inland sites, between 30 December and the end of January, the maximum number being eight at Loe Pool, where two remained until 28 February. Records after mid-February are rare. The latest dates include a male at Tamar Lake on 6 April 1963, a female at Hayle on 3 April

ST AGNES, ISLES OF SCILLY—St Agnes is the most south-westerly of the inhabited islands and covers only 312 acres. This view, from the lighthouse at the centre of the island, looks north-west to the pool and shews the Bird Observatory, at Lower Town farmhouse, in the middle.

The Observatory, opened in 1957, is manned by volunteers who normally maintain a continuous watch from late March to November. Their main work involves the daily census of migrants; full details are sent to the British Trust for Ornithology and are published in *Bird Migration*.

Several thousand birds are ringed annually, continuing the pioneering studies in this rewarding field by H. W. Robinson and N. H. Joy as early as 1911, and A. W. Boyd in the mid-1920's. Not only are the rarities ringed, for which the islands are second to none, but also—and more important—nesting species such as shags, cormorants, auks, and terns. Regular visits have been made to Annet, half a mile away, to ring storm petrels and Manx shearwaters.    [*Photo:* J. L. F. PARSLOW]

THE HAYLE ESTUARY—For many bird-watchers, Cornwall's most popular stretch of tidal mud and sand is certainly the Hayle estuary. This view down river at low tide is taken from the road near the Old Quay House seen in the sketch on page 111. The causeway carrying the main A30 road flanks the estuary out of view on the right, while the embankment of the St Erth–St Ives railway line may be seen skirting the left bank. These vantage points make Hayle one of the most easily watched estuaries in the south-west. It is particularly noted for its migrant waders and wintering wildfowl.

Below and to the right of Hayle power station is the dark bank which forms the boundary to Carnsew Pool—a tidal reservoir of nearly 37 acres. Here in winter may be seen, often at close quarters, great northern divers, slavonian and black-necked grebes, mergansers, and such species as scoter, goldeneye, and long-tailed duck.

[*Photo:* D. B. BARTON]

1949, a male at Stithians reservoir on 11 April 1967, and a female at Carnsew Pool, Hayle from 27 to 29 May 1967. Rarely are the first goosanders seen before 15 to 20 December. Most unusual were five immatures at Loe Pool on 24 November 1956. The majority of goosanders are 'brown-heads'—females or immature males.

Many records come from the Camel estuary, but all estuaries, even so far upstream as Tresillian and the more important stretches of freshwater from Tamar Lake to Loe Pool, have been visited in recent years. Even diminutive Clowance Pond, and Swanpool at Falmouth, formed suitable refuges in January 1963.

On the Scillies goosanders are very rare. A maximum of four off St Mary's on 4 January and one in Tresco Channel on 18 December 1963, plus an immature male killed on Tresco on 22 December 1934 (AR), are the only published records this century.

SMEW                  *Mergus albellus*

This strikingly handsome saw-bill from the forest belt between northern Scandinavia and eastern Asia is a hardy species which moves far south in winter only in severe weather. It was first mentioned as an occasional visitor to Cornwall by James (1808).

Johnes (in Bray's *Tamar and Tavy*, 1836) gave 'white nun' as a local name for the male and 'weasel-headed coot' for the brown-heads (females and young males) which he had seen shot far inland on the Tamar. The latter name is connected with 'vare wigeon' used in north Devon (Montagu, 1802) from the resemblance of the head to that of a vare or weasel.

There are few early published records—for example, only two from Scilly, one shot in December 1869 and two shot out of three in January 1891, but Clark and Rodd (1906) stated that others were known. On the mainland Ryves (1948) knew of only three

occurrences after 1931, but its status has probably changed little since the nineteenth century and from 1947 to 1967 birds were seen in every year except 1952, 1958, 1961, and 1965.

Most are seen in January and February with a few in late December. The earliest arrivals are one at Crowan reservoir on 16

*Smew*

November 1963 and another at Stithians reservoir on 21 November 1967. The latest dates are for a female off Compass Point, Bude on 24 April 1951, and a male on the Camel estuary on 13 April 1956. Since 1947 only 20 per cent have been identified as adult males. Nearly a third of the records comprise single birds—exceptional were fifteen (six of them males) on the Camel in early February 1952, and twelve (one male) on the Tamar on 3 March 1956. In the hard winter of 1963, four at Marazion Marsh on 1 January was the largest party, but at least 25 individuals were seen throughout the county—the most in any one winter.

Favoured localities are the lower reaches of the Camel and Tamar estuaries; Marazion on the marsh or off-shore; and Loe Pool, but records have been received from most of the reservoirs and from an unlikely place as Tory Pond, Stithians in 1963.

The only recent records from Scilly are—

1954  One at St Agnes on 9 March.
1957  One on Tresco on 28 November.
1959  One in Tresco channel on 11 December.

## SHELDUCK                    *Tadorna tadorna*

In Europe the shelduck breeds mainly in coastal areas of western Scandinavia, the Baltic, and southwards to Burgundy. In Britain it nests in most maritime counties, and has generally increased.

In Cornwall the shelduck was formerly called the 'burranet', a local variation of the more widely used name of burrow-duck, a reference to its habit of nesting in old rabbit burrows. Carew (1602) gives the following delightful account—"The Burranet hath like breeding [i.e. like the puffin] and, after her young ones are hatched shee leadeth them sometimes over-land, the space of a mile or better, into the haven, where such as have leasure to take their pastime, chace them one by one with a boate, and stones, to often diving, untill, through weariness, they are taken up at the boates side by hand, carried home, and kept tame with the Ducks . . ." This was possibly for eating as Carew lists them amongst the birds which are edible although "these content not the stomacke, all with a like savorinesse". Clearly the shelduck bred in Cornwall in the sixteenth century, but it was not recorded doing so again for some three hundred years. Borlase (1758) wrote that the "shell-drake is rare, but in the hard winter of 1739, I had one brought to me exactly answering the description of Ray's Willoughby". Throughout the nineteenth century it increased but was still commonly seen only in hard weather, as in 1875 (z, 1877) and 1891 (Clark, 1902). A few pairs nested in Devon but apparently did so in Cornwall for the first time about the turn of the present century, for Clark in 1906 (VCH) wrote that it "nests regularly and in increasing numbers at the mouth of the

Camel, its only breeding station in the county". By 1925 nesting had spread to the Tamar where Dewhurst (BB, 1930–31) counted seven pairs on two tidal creeks. About the same time it nested on Scilly in a semi-protected state (Wallis, BB, 1923–24)—the eggs were dug out of the burrows and placed under hens to protect them from the great black-backed gulls, but the practice is not recorded since then.

A marked spread in Cornwall occurred in the 1930's and early 1940's. Birds nested near St Clement on the Tresillian river in 1931 and 1932, at Tremayne Creek near Helford in 1933, while two pairs regularly did so by 1936 at Helford. Young were first seen on the Hayle estuary in 1943. Ryves (1948) said that birds had bred at Fowey, but this was not confirmed until 1958 or 1959. Breeding numbers at the present time are imperfectly known partly due to the difficulty of finding nests. Moreover, juveniles from different broods are herded together and shepherded by 'nurse' birds, and while the members of one family may be identifiable by their larger sizes, it is not possible to sort them all out as large parties may contain youngsters of every conceivable size.

Tamar: A few pairs breed in the Cargreen-Salters Mill area. A pair with ducklings were seen on Kingsmill Lake in August 1966.

Lynher: Four pairs known to have nested in 1965, two in 1966, and at least five in 1967.

St John's Lake: Two pairs (possibly five) nested in 1966.

Wilcove, near Torpoint: A pair at Thanckes Lake in 1966 probably bred at Wilcove.

Fowey River: Nesting occurred in 1959, possibly in 1958, but there are no subsequent records until 1967 when three pairs with 25 juveniles were seen at St Winnow.

Ruan Lanihorne and Tresillian: Over 50 young were counted at Ruan in 1965 and a brood annually frequents the Tresillian River. These birds are mostly reared in the peace and quiet of the Tregothnan estate which stretches between the two rivers. Here the bird is a common nester in banks and in the open woodland, often in rabbit holes. About ten years ago five young were hatched at Treveor, some three miles from the river, and it took them five to six days to reach Lamorran Pond (Jarvis[1]). Shelducks also nest on the south bank of the Ruan river at Ardevora Creek (Rundle[1]).

On the south coast a few pairs nest in rabbit burrows amongst the gorse in the soft, sandy cliff-tops of Gerrans Bay. In May 1968, P. Marriott saw a duck enter a hole near Pebyah Rock, Pendower. Two pairs nest annually at Kiberick Cove, near Portloe. Although young reared in Gerrans Bay are seen on the sea there, it appears that the birds are eventually walked across the Roseland peninsula to Ardevora—well over two miles by the most direct route—for young have been seen walking along the road at Treworthal and Trelugga near Philleigh in the early morning (Rundle[1]).

Red River: Young have been seen taken down the valley below Roseworthy towards Gwithian, and some twelve or more years ago young were seen on a farm at Nanterrow. These birds are thought to have nested in burrows about 'Engine House Wood' (Parsons[1]) but there is no evidence of recent nesting in the area.

Hayle Estuary: Two broods have been reared in recent years, as in 1966, in the railway embankment of the main Penzance line, but none were reared in 1967.

Marazion Marsh: Birds first bred here in 1961 or 1962. The only other record is for 1965.

Helford River: A few pairs presumably still breed in the locality but there are no records since 1949 when three families nested near Bishop's Quay.

Camel estuary: At least one pair nested in 1966, and ten may have done so. Breeding probably takes place in the Walmsley sanctuary where entry is not permitted. In the 1930's, a pair nested for several seasons at the Rumps "in a thorny place". In the late 1940's, R. B. Treleaven[1] remembers birds breeding in a rabbit burrow near Rock, and about this time birds probably nested at Daymer Bay. However, the area is now too disturbed to be attractive to the birds.

Scilly: About twelve pairs now breed on the islands since the first record on Samson in 1958. About 1963 they spread to the Eastern Islands (Hunt[1]).

Shelducks leave Cornwall in or about July, for the duration of their flightless moulting period. Most local ornithologists have assumed that our birds make for Bridgwater Bay, Britain's only moulting station. However, few of the 5,000 or so

Bridgwater birds seen in July remain there (BB, 1963) for, after a short period, most fly off to Knechtsand near Bremerhaven, Germany.

Shelducks return to Cornwall slowly during the autumn. Not many are seen before mid-November, although it has been claimed that a few birds never leave the county. Shelducks are absent, or extremely rare, at freshwater sites like Loe Pool and the reservoirs. Even at Marazion, few are seen on the marsh in the winter months for these birds are almost exclusively estuarine. Occasionally in very hard weather, as in January and February 1963, they appear in sheltered bays. In that year there were twenty in Widemouth Bay, and up to 31 in Mount's Bay.

The numbers wintering on the various Cornish estuaries may be summarised as follows—

| Locality | Count Years | Average Annual Max. | Highest Total |
|---|---|---|---|
| Camel and Walmsley Sanctuary | 1959–60 to 1965–66 | 100 | c. 250, December 1965 |
| Tamar | 1954–55 to 1966–67 | 100 | 217, February 1965 |
| Lynher | 1959–60 to 1965–66 | 120 | 350, February 1965 |
| St John's Lake | 1964–1966 | 170 | 205, February 1966 |
| Tresillian | 1962–63 to 1965–66 | 160 | 300+, February 1963 |
| Restronguet | 1962–63 to 1965–66 | 40 | 84, March 1965 |
| Hayle | 1959–60 to 1965–66 | 30 | 42, February 1965 |

| Ringed | Recovered |
|---|---|
| Topsham, Devon 10.8.'56 | found dead near Saltash 27.12.'56 |
| Near Sutton Bridge, Lincolnshire 27.8.'66 | found dead, Calenick Creek, Truro 26.11.'66 |

None ringed abroad have been recovered in Cornwall, but birds from the German moulting areas have been found in Devon.

# RUDDY SHELDUCK
*Tadorna ferruginea*

In Britain the ruddy shelduck is a vagrant from the Black Sea area and Asia Minor. A remarkable invasion took place in 1892 with flocks of twenty reported in some places. In Cornwall, however, only one occurred on the Helford River (VCH), whilst the only other mainland record, possibly of an escaped bird, refers to one on the Camel estuary on 15 November 1942 (BB). On Scilly, one was obtained sometime between 1906 and 1923 according to Clark (letter, 9 September 1923).

## GREY LAG GOOSE     *Anser anser*

The grey lag, ancestor of the farmyard goose, has an uneven European distribution much reduced by persecution although artificially maintained in places. Both wild and semi-feral birds nest in Scotland. Grey lags winter directly south of their breeding grounds but few now reach Cornwall.

In the eighteenth century it was more common for Walter Moyle wrote that "they are very common in Cornwall in hard winters. In that of 1709–10 I had five brought me in one morning, killed at one shot in Mellingy Moors under Lambriggan [Perranzabuloe], which were fat and very good meat". Couch (1838) briefly noted it as a winter visitor, but only six occurrences were reported on the mainland from 1848 to 1901. On Scilly one was seen in November 1863, one on Tresco in October 1870, while two killed on Tresco in October 1885 are the last recorded there (Z, 1906).

During this century most grey lag geese have been seen at the Walmsley Sanctuary, the largest gaggle being fifteen in the winter of 1923–24. Later it appeared that birds

might become regular visitors with the white-fronted geese. In 1939, six which arrived on 14 November had increased to thirteen at the end of the year and remained with the white-fronts until 9 April. Birds were also at the Sanctuary in 1941–42 (two) and 1942–43 (six), but since then only single birds have been seen in 1954, 1956, 1960, and 1962. Stragglers seen elsewhere include birds at Hayle in 1954, two at Dozmary Pool in December–January 1961–62, two on the Lynher in November 1963, one at Loe Pool from 6 November 1965 to 15 January 1966, and one at Stithians reservoir from 26 May to 4 July 1966.

## WHITE-FRONTED GOOSE
*Anser albifrons*

White-fronts breed in the U.S.S.R. and North America, mainly north of the Arctic Circle, leaving a large area around the north Atlantic only partly filled by the Greenland race (see below). They winter as far south as the Mediterranean on marshlands and wet meadows.

In the nineteenth century the white-front was an irregular winter visitor, not uncommon in severe winters such as 1829–30 when Couch (1838) recorded large flocks, and 1877 when many were killed on the Cornish moors (Z, 1878). Published records however, note birds in only nine years up to the blizzard winter of early 1891. Between 1919 and 1932, Wilcocks recorded about twenty on the Camel, but never more than five at once.

The white-front is now the most common wild goose in Cornwall, annually visiting the wet meadows of the Walmsley Sanctuary between Trewornan Bridge and Chapel Amble. The white-fronts' story of success began with a party of 24 seen between 16 and 21 December 1935. In the years that followed both the numbers of birds and the length of their stay increased. They first remained into the new year in

*Greylag goose (western form)*

1939-40, departing on 9 April—later than at the present time, and first reached treble figures in 1945-46 when about 200 were present on 4 February. By contrast only twenty remained at the Sanctuary in 1948-49 and only nine at the beginning of 1950. Numbers still fluctuate—increasing with the severity of the weather—but since 1960 at least 100 seem to comprise the normal 'resident' flock: 120 is considered the optimum maximum number which the Sanctuary could adequately maintain for any length of time (w). The maximum number occurs in February or early March, suggesting the addition of passage migrants to the 'resident' party a few weeks before their final departure.

Birds arrive at Walmsley any time between early October (the 5th in 1960) and early December (the 13th in 1962) most returning in mid-December. Departure invariably occurs within a day or two of 15 to 18 March, but is often preceded by some birds leaving from 1 to 15 March (Parsons[1]). From 9 January 1967 for about a month one to three melanistic birds remained at the Sanctuary. They were completely dark except for the tip of the tail and an indistinct white patch close to the bill.

Outside the Sanctuary and the sand-banks on the Camel estuary which the flocks visit, white-fronts are uncommon. In the early 1950's the Landulph section of the Tamar was regularly visited, but some factor, human disturbance possibly, discouraged them. Areas like Tamar Lake and Bude Marsh have supported white-fronts for varying periods on several occasions. The cold weather of January and February 1963 brought unprecedented numbers to many areas of Cornwall where they had been previously unrecorded. The Walmsley Sanctuary remained their principal quarters and here at least 2,000 were present on 20 February. Throughout January and February about 500 were seen around Week St Mary, and 200 at Widemouth in January roosted on the Bay at night. Up to 250 were reported from the Tamar. In the St Columb area flocks varied from a dozen to over 200 mainly near Trevose Head but also inland at St Merryn, St Columb, and near the A39 road to Wadebridge. Fewer were seen in west Cornwall, with a maximum of 106 at Hayle on 10 January, and up to 80 in a field on Camborne North Cliffs.

The white-front remains a rare visitor to Scilly, the only recent reports being in 1951 (three), 1962 (one), 1963 (one), 1964 when

White-fronted geese

six were seen at St Agnes, and 1967 (two).

The Greenland race of the white-fronted goose, *Anser albifrons flavirostris*, winters exclusively in Britain—mainly in Ireland—but few have been recorded in Cornwall. At the Walmsley Sanctuary five were seen on 2 February 1964, and a party of seven in 1947 was probably of this form. One was identified at Tresco, 26–29 February 1965.

Two birds ringed at Slimbridge, Glos., in March and five ringed in Holland in December or January have been recovered in Cornwall, but there are no recoveries in the county of birds ringed at their breeding grounds.

## BEAN GOOSE          *Anser arvensis*

There are a number of geographically distinct forms, all breeding in the high arctic. Excluding the pink-footed goose, here dealt with separately, the typical form wintering in Britain is the forest or taiga form *Anser arvensis arvensis*.

In Cornwall the bean goose was formerly more plentiful and according to Rodd (z, 1864) was the commonest goose, comprising 90 per cent of the flocks which arrived, "sometimes in considerable numbers", after hard frosts in the north. They were abundant in the winter of 1890–91 with flocks seen throughout the county, including Scilly (VCH) where only one has occurred since—in November 1905 (z). In 1915 Harvey wrote that the brent was the most common species of goose in west Cornwall, and since then the only published reports of bean geese are—

1931   One at the Walmsley Sanctuary for two weeks from 3 November.
1941   One shot on a farm near the Gannel estuary.
1942   A bird almost certainly of this species was seen at the Walmsley Sanctuary on 26 January.
1951   A bird identified by its almost completely black bill as the tundra or Russian bean goose *Anser arvensis rossicus*, was seen at the Walmsley Sanctuary in early February. Some ornithologists maintain that

identification based on the bill colour is not reliable, and that *all* belong to the form *A. arvensis arvensis*.

## PINK-FOOTED (BEAN) GOOSE
### *Anser arvensis brachyrhynchus*

The pink-footed goose breeds in Greenland, Iceland, Spitsbergen, and perhaps Franz Joseph Land. Birds from the first two localities winter mainly in north and east Britain.

Although the most numerous of Britain's wintering geese (*c.* 60,000), few ever reach south-west England. They were unknown in Cornwall until Clark wrote in a letter that one had been seen at Scilly between 1906 and 1923. The only other records are—

1947   One with about 100 white-fronted geese at the Walmsley Sanctuary on 24 February, was last seen on 14 March.
1951   One at Gwennap Head near Land's End on 24 October.
1954   Twenty flew down the valley at Mawgan Porth on 16 September.
1962   A party flying over St Agnes on 5 October were identified by their call notes.
1963   One at Tamar Lake from 20 December to mid-January.
1965   Up to three present at the Walmsley Sanctuary from the end of 1964, remained until 8 March. One was seen on the River Lynher on 7 November.

## BRENT GOOSE (DARK-BREASTED)
### *Branta bernicla bernicla*

Brent geese breed on the arctic coasts and islets around the world, but not in western

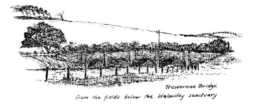

*Trevornan Bridge*
*from the fields below the Walmsley sanctuary*

Europe or Iceland. The dark-breasted form breeds in Arctic Russia and Siberia. In Britain most birds winter around the Wash or in Essex.

In Cornwall it was first recorded by Moyle in 1715–16. He obtained three that winter and wrote "we have them frequently in Cornwall soon after Harvest; I have shot many of them upon Lambriggan [Perranzabuloe] and found them to be very good Meat". How many were to be seen in Cornwall in the nineteenth century was never accurately recorded. Bullmore (1866) wrote that he frequently saw half a dozen locally shot birds at Webber's poultry shop in Falmouth. "Considerable flocks" occurred in hard winters, as in 1890–91, January 1895, and January 1902. At such times, fishermen from the Scillies reported "sea-geese"— probably 'brents'—well out at sea (z, 1906). Near the mainland, Mount's Bay was a favourite locality and much havoc was wrought by sportsmen using 'puntguns' amongst the birds which liked to stay between a half and one mile out in the Bay (Rodd, 1880, & vch). Harvey (1915) wrote that it was the commonest goose seen nearly every year between Marazion and Newlyn. The largest gaggle later recorded here was nineteen on 11 December 1932.

In many parts of Europe an epidemic, which started in 1931 and became general by 1934, destroyed 90 per cent of eelgrass (*zostera marina*), a staple food of the brent goose, and there seems to have been little change in the abundance of the plant since then. The extent to which Cornish eelgrass was damaged is not known, but it is not thought to have been less badly affected than in other areas.

Between 1931 and 1965, single birds or gaggles were reported from the Hayle estuary and St Ives Bay on 20 occasions; the Camel estuary and Constantine Bay, fourteen; Mount's Bay and Loe Pool, ten; St Austell Bay to Gerrans Bay, eight; Tamar estuary and Tamar Lake, six (probably it is more common in the Tamar-St John's Lake

area than records suggest); Helford and Maenporth, three; Ruan Lanihorn, two; the Gannel, two; and on three occasions elsewhere. In Mount's Bay they have been reported in only six years, including four before 1940. The largest gaggle is 30 at St John's Lake in February 1937.

Numbers fluctuate greatly from year to year and there is no regular wintering flock. None has been reported in six winters since 1940–41, and only one sighting in another seven winters. A maximum of at least 90 individuals was seen in the hard winter of 1962–63.

In recent years most reports are from November to the end of February, but migrants have been reported as early as 13 September in 1954 when twenty flew into Mount's Bay at Marazion. Few remain into March although in 1933, twelve were at Lelant until 28 April, while one was shot at Marazion in May 1897 (vch).

On the Scillies it was not uncommon according to Rodd (1880) but only one is known to have been obtained there—shot on 1 October 1860 (z, 1906). The only reports this century are five at Tresco on 18 February 1942 (ar): 50 at Tresco on 24 September 1953 and one at Tresco in March 1960.

An adult ringed at Jorssand Island, Jutland, Denmark on 11 October 1961, was shot at Helford River on 26 December 1961.

## BRENT GOOSE (LIGHT-BREASTED)
*Branta bernicla hrota*

This form of the brent goose breeds in eastern Canada and Greenland. Most birds wintering in Ireland are of Greenland stock, and those seen in Cornwall are assumed to come from the same area.

The first recorded in Cornwall was one on the Camel estuary on 10 December 1953. Since then, twelve were seen at Hayle from 17 to 20 September 1960; three on the

Camel on 5 April 1961; one shot at Pen-
dower on 30 December 1961; three in St
Ives Bay on 26 October 1962; and ten on
St Agnes on 8 October 1964.

## BARNACLE GOOSE

*Branta leucopsis*

The barnacle goose has an extremely
limited breeding range in southern Norway,
eastern Greenland, Spitzbergen, and Novaya
Zemlya. In Britain, Greenland birds winter
off the Scottish islands and Ireland, while
those from Spitzbergen frequent the Solway.
Where Cornish birds come from is uncertain.

The barnacle goose is less common in
Cornwall than formerly. Carew mentions
it in his survey (1602), although this need
not indicate any contemporary abundance
for the species attracted attention because
of its supposedly remarkable life-history.
Moyle (Tonkin MS) described a specimen
obtained in 1716 but gave no indication of
the species' status. In the nineteenth century,
it was described as not uncommon in hard
weather, as in 1895 when a large flock was
seen at Helford (Clark, 1902).

At Scilly it has always been rare. First
noted in 1876, there were two gaggles
(12 birds shot) in September 1880 (PZ), three
on Tresco in January 1884, fifteen in
January 1895 (Z, 1906) followed by a complete blank until five were reported on
St Agnes on 28 October 1960, one on
Wingletang Down, St Agnes on 26 December
1961 and four on St Agnes on 17 October
1967.

Records this century from the mainland
are few. Dr. Harvey (CBWPS, 1931) said it
was unknown to him in the Land's End
peninsula where, in the nineteenth century,
it had been reported on the marshes and in
Mount's Bay.

pre-    One November day, three on the Camel
1914    (Ryves, 1948).
1938    Seven, probably of this species, at Loe
        Pool on 4 September.

1943    One on the Camel on 7 November.
1949    One at Tamar Lake on 27 October and
        seven sitting on Polzeath Cliffs on 10
        March.
1952    30 flying up the Tamar on 17 September.
1955    One on a pool near Land's End from 13 to
        15 November.
1959    One at Loe Pool between 1 November
-'60    and 5 January.
1962    One at Marazion on 23 and 24 February
        and three flying west past St Ives Island
        on 28 October.
1965    One at Treweege Farm, Stithians on 3
        December.
1968    One at the Hayle estuary from 29 to 30
        October.

## CANADA GOOSE

*Branta canadensis*

Introduced into Britain from North
America sometime before 1678, the Canada
goose has since become naturalized and has
spread to many areas including Devon. Ten
artificially-reared birds were released at
Shobrooke Park in 1949, had multiplied to
160 by 1963 and spread to other waters in
the county. In 1923 it was found domesticated on Tresco, but its subsequent history
here is not known. In Cornwall it remains
an occasional visitor.

1819    One obtained by Henry Mewburn of St
        Germans was figured by Bewick in sub-
        sequent editions of his *British Birds*.
1849    One purchased by Cocks at 'Mr. Chard's
        game-shop' in Falmouth (Bullmore,
        1866).
pre-
1863    One obtained at Scilly (Z, 1906).
1871    One shot near Falmouth in January
        (Rodd, 1880).
1948    Several at Tresco in March and April
        (Parslow[1]).
1954    Two at Par beach on 8 February, and one
        on the 9th which may have been the same
        bird as seen at the Walmsley Sanctury on
        the 10th.
1957    Four, known to be escapes, seen on Hel-
        ford River.
1959    Three to four at Tresco in April and five
        on 17 September.
1962    One on St Mary's on 7 to 8 January.

1963   An unprecedented number were brought into the county by the cold weather at the beginning of the year. Maximum numbers were—

Lynher, eighteen reduced by shooting and last seen 27 February; Walmsley Sanctuary, nineteen on 19 January, 60 on 1 February, and 40 remaining on 20 February; Gwithian Pool, eleven on 16 January; St Ives Bay, seven in flight on 20 January; Clifton, Tamar, ten on 2 March with three remaining until 7 May; Hayle, three on 25 January; Marazion Marsh, two on 1 March; Crowan reservoir, one on 26 January; Lizard Head, one out at sea on 20 January. Scilly, none seen in the cold weather, but the following November one was watched in flight.

also kept at Bicton by Lady Rolle, and also near Crediton (D & M, 1892).

1841   Three recently shot at Skewjack, Sennen were said to be the first obtained in Cornwall (G, 31.12.'41).

1848   One shot near Gunwalloe in November (G, 24.11.'48).

1849   One was shot in the autumn by the Helford River ferryman (P, 1851) and another shot at Loe Pool (WLZ).

1851   One purchased in Plymouth market on 22 December had been shot near Launceston (N).

1870   Two birds mistaken for spur-winged geese, flew in from the sea and were shot at Seaton near St Germans on 1 October (Z).

1878   A male and female were sent from Cornwall to a Plymouth taxidermist on 13 and 14 December (Z).

## EGYPTIAN GOOSE
### *Alopochen aegyptiacus*

The Egyptian goose, not officially on the British-Irish check-list of birds, is a species introduced from Africa and Palestine which has become semi-feral in a few areas—notably Norfolk. Claims that specimens seen in Cornwall in the last century were genuinely wild, cannot be taken seriously. Courtney (1845) recorded that Augustus Smith had introduced birds to Tresco and exhibited them on the mainland. On 11 May 1854 Smith wrote—"the Egyptian Geese I was afraid to disturb this year, wishing for a brood of young ones; in this, however, I have been disappointed, as the eggs have turned out addled" (*Letters of Augustus Smith*, 1873). In Devon birds were

## SPUR-WINGED GOOSE
### *Plectropterus gambensis*

The spur-winged goose is a native of tropical Africa and like the Egyptian goose is not on the official British-Irish list.

The first example obtained in Britain, and the only one from Cornwall, was seen for about a week in the neighbourhood of St Germans. It was eventually shot in a wheatfield at Sconnor by John Brickford whose wife, unable to stuff it, cut the wings off to use as dusters and threw away the skin. About three weeks later it was recovered, with its head torn off, by Henry Mewburn of St Germans who sent it to Thomas Bewick at the Newcastle Museum. The

View across the Fal to Ardevora near Ruan Lanihorne – one of the finest spots for watching waders in southern Cornwall

latter figured it in his *British Birds* (1826 edition). The specimen was excellently restored and it remained at Newcastle for many years but had apparently disappeared by 1870 (z).

## MUTE SWAN                    *Cygnus olor*

The mute swan is increasing as a breeding bird in Europe but still occurs mainly around the Baltic, in Holland and the British Isles. It is indigenous, at least to East Anglia, but numbers have been augmented by introduced birds. Domesticated and regarded as a Royal bird since the twelfth century, it became especially popular in Elizabethan times when over 900 swan-marks were registered. The species now lives mainly in a semi-feral state.

The history of the mute swan in Cornwall is veiled in obscurity. No one registered a swan mark. Several families sported swans on their heraldic achievements, but this only indicates the popularity of the charge, probably for artistic reasons alone.

Camden (*Britannia*, 1610) wrote that swans abounded on the Scillies without stating whether wild or mute. Both Carew (1602) and Borlase (1758) are unusually reticent on the subject of swans which were certainly kept by the seventeenth century Cornish gentry for Thomas Tonkin (MS begun in 1700) refers to two swanneries. The best known of these, near Falmouth "behind Arwennick . . . is a large pool . . . It is commonly called the Swan Pool, for that Sir Peter Killigrew, to whom it belongs, kept abundance of swans here". Of the Manor of Elerky in Veryan, Tonkin wrote that "In Domesday Book it is called Elerchi which signifies the swans' house or swan-nery; for Elerk in Cornish is a swan and there are the remains of a large pool under the house which seems to have been designed to that end." The word *elerch* is found in Old Cornish (Cottonian Vocabulary, *c.* late 12th century) and is the plural of the presumed form *alarch* which is not

known in written form. *Elerch* may well have referred to both wild and mute swans, for Moyle (Tonkin MS) called the wild swan an Elk or Hooper, the former name clearly being a corruption of the Cornish.

A swanpool is marked on the six-inch O.S. map at Trebartha Hall in North Hill, but the ornithologist F. R. Rodd who lived there never mentioned any swans. Indeed, the nineteenth century is as little informative as earlier periods. James (1808) wrote that they occurred "sometimes in very hard winters" while Rodd (1880) knew only of domesticated birds and gives a single occurrence at Swanpool in 1856, of "partially wild birds" attempting to nest in the county (see also Cocks, P, 1857). It can only be inferred that in nineteenth century Cornwall some landowners kept swans, but that the breeding of semi-feral birds was rare, and that few visited the county in winter. This is precisely the picture drawn for Devon by D'Urban & Mathew (1892).

Swans were kept at Trengwainton where in Victorian days the area around the three ponds west of the house was laid out for pony cart drives. The swans, introduced and kept on the top pond, disappeared during the second World War when the pond became very grown in (Bolitho[1]). A pair was always kept at Clowance, Crowan, until 1918; birds were also kept at Tre-vethoe, Lelant (St Aubyn[1]). At Boconnoc, near Liskeard, two cobs were kept before the first World War to eat weed on the lake (Fortescue[1]).

Recent breeding records are as follows—

Tamar Lake:   Normally two or three pairs and once four pairs each with four cygnets. None bred in 1967 (Lott[1]).

Bude Canal:   One pair in most years (Lott[1]).

Bodmin Moor:   Two young reared at Temple Tor pond in 1967—the first record from Bodmin Moor.

Helford River:   The same pair have bred at Port Navas for at least the past fourteen years. The nest is usually swamped at high tide and has to be built up artificially. In 1967 three hatched but only one survived.

Camel Estuary: About five pairs usually nest at Wadebridge, but in 1967, as they interfered with domestic geese, the Council removed their artificial islands so that only one pair bred in the area (Weeks[1]).

Lamorran: A pair nests on the pond in most years, but the cygnets are usually killed by people shooting from the roadside (Jarvis[1]).

Truro area: A pair nested almost annually at Tresemple Pool, but now nests nearer Tresillian. At Truro a pair hatched three young at Boscawen Park in 1967.

South-east Cornwall: Single pairs nest annually at Millbrook Lake (three young, 1967); St John's Lake (six young, 1967); River Lynher (deserted in 1967 as in former years); at Haye Creek off the Tamar high tides washed a nest away in 1967; and at a freshwater pool adjoining the East Looe river.

Stithians reservoir: In 1966 a pair nested and produced six cygnets, but in 1967 the birds deserted.

Swanpool, Falmouth: A pair, unsuccessful in 1966, hatched four young in 1967. Three were hatched at Maenporth Marsh in 1967.

Scilly: One or two pairs nest annually on Great Pool, Tresco (Hunt[1]).

While the mute swan is largely sedentary, dispersal movements within the British Isles are large enough to considerably augment the native population in winter. Varying numbers may be found on all the coastal waters of the county.

Tamar Lake—up to about fifteen are usual. Tamar estuary and environs—the only large flock is at St John's Lake where 40 regularly winter and 59 were counted on 11 November 1967. The East Looe river normally holds about 30, but numbers on the Lynher are negligible (Madge[1]). For the following localities, numbers are given for the hard winter of 1962–63 which tend to be above average. Tresillian river, sixteen; Restronguet, twenty; Hayle, twelve; and Loe Pool, four. Some 60 or more commonly winter on the Camel, but in 1967 no more than eighteen were seen on 30 September. Figures for the Scillies are absent except for nineteen reported on 8 October 1963.

## WHOOPER SWAN
### Cygnus cygnus

The whooper swan breeds south of the tundra in northern Russia, parts of Scandinavia, and Iceland, while a few may still breed in the Scottish Highlands. The British wintering population, which derives largely from Iceland, is concentrated in northern Britain, especially in central and eastern Scotland.

The wild swan was first recorded in Cornwall by Moyle (Tonkin MS) who wrote that it was "called also an Elk, or Hooper, plentiful in Cornwall in hard winters". Moyle shot and 'cased' an example in January 1715–16. Over a dozen references are scattered throughout the nineteenth century literature after one (described as a Whistling Swan) was shot at St Clement near Truro, and presented to the Museum in 1829–30 (RI), but many clearly went unrecorded. The "big years" were the hard winter of 1870–71 with up to seventeen birds reported at Scilly (Rodd, 1880) and 1890–91 when several flocks were observed west of Truro, and up to twelve were seen on Tresco at Christmas (VCH).

During the present century birds were reported on only seven occasions between 1924 and 1950. This does not give a true indication of its status for increased observations since then have shewn the whooper swan to be a regular visitor between late November and the end of

Mute swans

January. 1958 was the only year in which none was reported. On the Scillies visits are more sporadic—with records in only seven years from 1950 to 1967.

Early arrivals include one on the Camel estuary on 26 September 1948. In 1967 two were seen on Bryher, Scilly on 10 October, and two (different birds) on St Agnes from 21 October to 5 November. Three at Tamar Lake on 28 October 1951 remained until 10 March, and an immature at Scilly until 9th April 1954 was exceptionally late.

East Cornwall has provided most records. Between 1950 and 1967, the number of occurrences has been—
Tamar Lake, seven; Camel estuary and Walmsley Sanctuary, five; Gwithian Pool and Hayle estuary, three each; Dozmary Pool and River Tamar, two each. There are single records from a clay-pit on Temple Moor; a pool at Retallick near Winnard's Perch; Mawgan Porth; Lynher and Helford rivers, Loe Pool; Crowan reservoir; Clowance Pool, and Stithians reservoir. Marazion Marsh had not produced a published record since one out of a group of three was shot on 23 February 1871 (G, 25.2.'71) until 24 to 25 October 1966 when two adults were seen—probably the extent of water is normally too small for them; mute swans are rare on the marsh for the same reason.

There is no regular wintering population. Some birds, for example the flock of nineteen on the Tamar on 9 November 1952, are clearly migrants. Some stop for a short time while others winter as did two on Tamar Lake from 17 October 1952 to 22 February. The party of nineteen mentioned above, and twenty at St Agnes in February 1956, are the largest herds reported. The total number recorded in the hard winter of 1962–63 was fourteen individuals, double the average since the winter of 1951–52.

# BEWICK'S SWAN

*Cygnus bewickii*

The Bewick's swan breeds in the Finnish and Russian tundra mainly further north than the whooper. The main wintering area in Britain is in the south-east with a smaller nucleus in Ireland.

The species was first distinguished from the whooper by Wingate in 1829. Cocks (P, 1857) stated that two from a party of six were shot off Falmouth in January 1830. Although published records number less than half a dozen up to 1907, its status is probably the same as today's. D'Urban and Mathew (1892) wrote that in south-west England as a whole, Bewick's swan was more common than the whooper. Certainly the terrible frosts of 1861–62 brought many to Cornwall if a newspaper report can be relied upon—". . . an old bird and an immature specimen have been sent to Mr. Vingoe of Penzance for preservation. A flock of 25 to 30 were seen passing over Penzance a day or two since, and from their small sizes it is supposed they were all of this species" (G, 18.1.'61). During the blizzard winter of 1890–91, un-numbered herds were reported as well as twelve on Tresco, some of which remained until 23 March (Z, 1906). In 1907 at least sixteen were seen on the north coast in January—three at Newquay, eleven at Hayle, and others at Bude and Mousehole. From then until 1950 there are only three reports including 25 at Scilly during the big British influx of 1938–39 (BB).

Since 1951 the species has been seen in most winters, sometimes in greater numbers than the whooper. Early in 1963 there were at least 37—and possibly 66—individuals in the county compared with fourteen whoopers. Most are reported from late November until the end of February in parties of up to five or six. The largest herd in recent years comprised nineteen birds on Temple Tor Pool on 1 January 1967—this included the dozen on Dozmary Pool the previous month which had built up from five which arrived on or before 13 November. Early arrivals include two at Dozmary on 28 October 1961 which remained until 15

December, and four at Drift reservoir on 3 November 1967. One bird at Trewornan on the Camel estuary on 19 February 1960 remained until 11 April. Other late birds, probably migrants, include six at Hayle Kimbro Pool near the Lizard on 18 March 1962, and four at Dozmary Pool from 16 to 25 April 1956.

The Bewick's swan frequents more waters in Cornwall than the whooper, with records from most of the main estuaries and reservoirs and several sightings from such small waters as Gwithian Pool, Clowance Pond, and once even at Tehidy Pond.

The only recent records from Scilly are—

1956   Three at St Agnes and St Mary's from 30 March to 1 April.
1962   One at Tresco on 24 November.
1963   Two at St Agnes from 14 to 20 January.

The only previous records are for 1890 and 1938–39 (given above) and for the winter of 1895–96 when nine were on Tresco for five weeks (z, 1906).

## COMMON CRANE   *Grus grus*

The crane is another of the many species whose breeding range has greatly contracted within historic times. Now it is largely confined to northern Europe from Scandinavia and the Baltic eastwards. Birds from this area winter in north Africa, but until about 1800 small numbers did so in Britain. Indeed, until about 1600 it bred in East Anglia.

Early records must be viewed with care since the name 'crane' was locally applied to both the heron and shag. Camden (*Britannia*, 1610) certainly meant shag in his description of the Isles of Scilly. Carew (1602) counted the crane amongst the "Citizens of the ayre", and here one is on safer ground as he also mentions the shag and heron by name. Borlase (1758), while noting the etymological confusion, does not count it amongst the county's avifauna. While Couch in 1838 said that "one or two specimens have been recognised as Cornish",

only one can be traced prior to that date.

1826   One frequented the banks of the Tamar 'for some time' in the autumn. It was eventually shot near Buckland Monachorum in Devon. (PI, 1830).
1845   One shot at Hendra Bridge, Menheniot on 17 March (P, 1846).
1881   One shot at the Long Pool, Tresco on 13 April (z, 1906).
1939   From about 23 to 25 April, a very wary bird frequented the Walmsley Sanctuary.
1949   A very large heron-like bird, thought to be of this species, was seen flying high over Penrose, Helston, on 4 September.
1961   At Trelonk on the River Fal, four were seen on 15 November; two were still there on the 23rd (R).
1963   On 6 November, seven (three immature) were seen at Trevehor, St Buryan. This record formed part of an unprecedented invasion of Britain resulting from unusual weather conditions. Probably over 500 birds were involved, making landfalls on all southcoast counties as far east as Essex (BB, 1964).

## WATER RAIL   *Rallus aquaticus*

The water rail is found in many parts of Europe from the Mediterranean to southern Scandinavia. Very little information exists concerning its status in Cornwall. It seems to be less common now, as over most of Britain where land-drainage has destroyed many habitats. James (1808) described the water rail as very common in Cornwall, and all writers to the end of the century refer to it as "not uncommon". Only Clark provided details of its distribution (VCH); at the turn of the century it had become scarcer but still bred at Bude, sparingly on the Goss Moors, at Bishop's Wood near Truro, and until recently near St Erth.

There are few recent breeding records, but the species is certainly overlooked. In 1968 birds reared young at Chapel Amble in St Kew, at Ventongimps in Perranzabuloe, and at Marazion Marsh. Others were reported in mid-Cornwall during the breeding season at Holywell, Summercourt, Newlyn East and Perranporth (per Musson[1]).

Young have been seen at Tresemple and Kiggon ponds near Tresillian, and once (about 1960) near Devoran (Allsop[1]). Birds holding territory—but never any young—have been seen at Lelant by the stream close to the rubbish dump. There are summer records from Par but none from south-east Cornwall. None are thought to nest on Bodmin Moor and the only bird reported from St Breward parish was a dead migrant which had evidently flown into overhead wires (Almond[1]). On the Scillies a few pairs nest about the Great Pool, Tresco (Hunt[1]).

Water rails are much more in evidence as migrants and winter visitors. Few dates have been published, but the autumn passage is certainly under way in September. Arrival dates are 5 August 1967 at Holywell in Crantock, 10 August 1966 at Porthgwarra, and 18 August 1966 at Tresemple pool near Tresillian.

At St Agnes far more were recorded in autumn 1959, probably due to the low water level of the Pool exposing more mud and reeds. One was seen on 13 May and daily from 21 August to 3 October with up to four at a time before 13 September and on 24 September. One or two were recorded on 8 days between 11 October and 11 November. In 1967, fifty were recorded at the Great Pool on 18 October.

On present information, or rather lack of it, winter numbers can only be described as 'not uncommon', for many are seen in cold spells close to farms and gardens. A few are not unusual in the winter months in gardens backing on to the Kenwyn river within a mile of the centre of Truro.

There is no evidence of a marked spring passage, but single birds have been found dead from late March to late April on St Agnes, and Annet and (29 March 1960) one on the catwalk of Bishop Rock lighthouse. Wintering birds leave Scilly in March, for in 1965, at least twelve were at the Tresco pools in late January, but no more than three by late March. On the mainland birds were last reported in 1967 in April at Swanpool

on the 14th, at Porthcothan on the 15th, and at Porthgwarra and Marazion Marsh on the 16th.

Many British wintering birds are from northern Europe and there is one recovery in Cornwall—a bird ringed as a juvenile on 2 September 1961 at Rantum in the North Frisian Islands, was killed by a dog near Wadebridge on 5 January 1962.

## SPOTTED CRAKE
*Porzana porzana*

Although widely distributed throughout much of Europe except in northern Scandinavia and Russia, the range and status of the spotted crake is not known with any accuracy, for it is an elusive bird, and like many rails, come across more by luck than by diligent watching and waiting. In Britain it remains a scarce annual nester in a handful of English counties, the trickle of published information pointing to Somerset as one of its strongholds.

In Cornwall, the spotted crake appears to be far less common than a century ago. Records go back to the beginning of the nineteenth century, for James wrote (1808) that he had shot two himself. N. Hare (PZ, 1848) possessed a bird killed near Dozmary Pool in 1846, and Rodd (1880) said that sportsmen after snipe in the marshes and wet moorland often found these birds which proved to be not uncommon in some years. F. R. Rodd shot two couples within four hours at Dozmary and the Cheesewring sometime in autumn 1868 (z) and at Crowdy Marsh shot three on 30 September 1860. Bullmore (1866) also said they were not uncommon in the Falmouth area. Clark in 1906 (VCH) regarded it as a regular autumn and winter visitor to the snipe marshes throughout Cornwall except in the Lizard, about Penzance, and the north coast, where it was a casual visitor. The only breeding records published by Clark are at Crowdy Marsh in 1860 and 1862, and near

Dozmary Pool in 1874. Harvey (1915) described this crake as a winter visitor "probably often overlooked", but no more is heard of the species until 1947.

On the Scillies the first spotted crake was shot in the autumn of 1849, and only two others are known to have been shot—in 1860 at Tresco Abbey gardens, and on 8 October 1880. There are no certain breeding records, but in 1903 at the end of May, a bird was flushed on two successive days from a likely nesting site on the Higher Moors of St Mary's (z, 1906).

Recent records are so few that all can be given below. The dates suggest that the spotted crake is now an uncommon passage migrant, chiefly in the autumn, and perhaps a winter resident.

1947  One observed at close quarters on 6 August in a marshy stream at Venn Farm, Launcells, just over one mile from the Devon border (R. J. Beswetherick[1]).

1949  One flushed on 5 February near Loe Bar, Helston (Parsons[1]).

1950  One picked up dead under telegraph wires near St Breward on 13 September.

1951  One picked up dead under telegraph wires at Marazion station on 17 September. Another picked up two days later in a back garden was eventually released on the Bude canal.

1953  One at Marazion Marsh on 1 October.

1956  One picked up dead on St Mary's, on 19 April.

1957  One trapped and ringed on Tresco on 19 April, and another found dead near Mullion on 6 November.

1959  One briefly seen at St Agnes Pool on 20 October.

1962  Another flushed from St Agnes Pool on 13 October.

1966  Four individuals sighted—at Porthgwarra on 10 September, at Porth near Newquay on 4 October, and at Scilly on St Mary's on 19 September and St Agnes from 25 to 29 September.

1967  One seen at close range at the edge of the Abbey Pool, Tresco on 2 October, and another at the Great Pool on 18 and 19 October. At St Agnes, single birds were identified from 2 to 9 September and on 16 October.

## BAILLON'S CRAKE
*Porzana pusilla*

Little is known of the precise distribution of this species which is reported from widely scattered areas of Europe, mainly in the south. Because of its secretive nature few are reported, and the only Cornish records belong to the period when Baillon's crake occasionally nested in East Anglia—it last did so in 1889.

pre-1850  An adult obtained within the basin of Penzance pier (z).

pre-1858  An adult shot in Zennor parish (Rodd, 1880).

1858  A mature male was captured on 8 July in a narrow ravine leading down to the sea near Land's End (z).

1877  An immature shot at Marazion Marsh on 12 October (z).

## LITTLE CRAKE          *Porzana parva*

Like Baillon's crake, the little crake is such a retiring species that its distribution remains obscure. It is found in some marshy areas of western Europe but is more common further east. Chance alone seems

Stithians reservoir · completed in 1965 it covers over 600 acres and is the largest in Cornwall

to determine when it visits this country.

early    One killed by Pechell at Scilly (z, 1906).
1850's
1878    An adult female captured by a cat at St
         Dominick about 19 March (z).
1892    One obtained by G. Harrison on 25
         October, but no locality given (VCH).
1966    One seen at St Agnes observatory on 25
         September was not accepted (R).

## CORNCRAKE                          *Crex crex*

The corncrake is a summer visitor to
much of Europe. The species has decreased
greatly in the last hundred years because of
its preference for nesting in hay fields and
similar habitats where eggs and young stand
little chance of surviving the inimical blade
of a mechanical cutter. In Britain, west
Scotland and Ireland remain the stronghold
of this once familiar ventriloquist.

Tonkin in 1715 described the 'Daker Hen'
as "a common bird with us"; Polwhele
(1812) said it was "never absent", while an
anonymous script of about 1860 (CRO, X.
256/7) refers to it in the Tregony area as still
"very numerous". In 1857, sixteen were
shot with a single gun on the Lower Moors
of St Mary's, on 19 September and every
tuft of grass in swamp and morass was
described as "safe in holding two", but this
was exceptional even for that date (z, 1857
& 1906). Rodd (1880), while noting that
it was not uncommon in grass fields and
clover seed, wrote that the nests were
frequently cut by mowers and in 1906,
Clark (VCH) wrote that it had become less
common although breeding annually on the
mainland and the Scillies. By 1915, A. W. H.
Harvey described it as "sparingly distributed" in the Penzance-Land's End area
although still a regular summer visitor. In
1931, G. H. Harvey in Penzance, and Ryves
in St Mawgan-in-Pydar, had noted sum-
mers when they failed to hear its un-
mistakable call in their own district. If
published records of birds heard in late May

and June may be taken as reasonable
evidence for at least attempted breeding,
then one or two pairs nested in most years
down to 1951 when two families were
reared in Breage parish. Later published
records are more scattered—

1953    Possibly attempted to breed at Mylor.
1959    Nested unsuccessfully near Boscoppa, St
         Austell.
1960    Again seen at Boscoppa on 27 May.
1965    Heard calling in a hay field near Nans-
         tallon, Bodmin, on 19 and 26 June, but
         after the field was cut on 10 July, not a
         bird was heard.
1967    A nest, with four young, was destroyed
         near Bodmin on 13 June. Two young
         apparently escaped with a parent.

Breeding birds may not be so rare as
published records suggest for a Newlyn
East farmer told the author that he had
heard, and usually saw, corncrakes throughout every summer in fields near the church
—1968 was the first year they had escaped
his notice. A. H. Glanville, however, found
three males holding territory in this area in
1968.

On the Scillies the corncrakes bred fairly
regularly until 1947 (Quick, 1964). The
only subsequent records are—

1960    A pair reported 'at Scilly' (Parslow[1]).
1966    A mother, with six young, was watched
         moving through a hay field on 1 June.
1967    Birds nested in Parting Carn field, St
         Mary's—there were possibly two nests.

Corncrakes are now best known as
passage migrants. In spring most arrive
from late April until mid-May; early dates
include 13 March and 18 April 1957 at St
Agnes, and 10 April 1955 at Mawgan
Porth. From the increased number of birds
heard calling in August, the autumn passage
would seem to start in the latter half of that
month. The main exodus, however, is in
September to early October. Late October
records are not unusual—as on St Agnes,
from 23 to 25 October 1966. The
latest dates are for a bird found dead near
Camborne on 1 November 1952, one at
Scilly on 4 November 1959, and one at

Nanstallon near Bodmin on 23 November 1967. Couch reported one shot in Cornwall on 24 December (pre-1838) after frost and snow, and knew of another obliged to remain there through injury. Clark (VCH) wrote that a few had wintered in the county, but there are no recent records other than those of an injured bird which spent the winter of 1943-44 in a shrubbery at Burniere, near Wadebridge, and one found injured near Redruth on 12 January 1967.

## MOORHEN *Gallinula chloropus*

The moorhen breeds throughout Europe as far north as southern Scandinavia. It is common in Britain and may have increased its numbers, but information is scanty. Little has been published on its status in Cornwall.

James (1808) described the moorhen as "rather scarce" while the other nineteenth century authors called it common or rather common. While one may regard James' statement with some scepticism, moorhens did become more plentiful on the Isles of Scilly when reeds were planted by the Tresco Abbey ponds in the early 1850's. Previously moorhens had been noticed on autumn migration and one specimen had been killed in April or May 1841. With the planting of reeds they soon became common and bred regularly at Tresco, and occasionally at St Mary's before 1860. In 1903 they were breeding freely round the Abbey Pools and in some numbers at St Mary's while two nests were found on Tean (z, 1906). The present breeding population on Tresco is about twenty pairs (Hunt[1]). A pair nested on St Agnes in 1950 and one or two have done so annually since.

Information from the mainland is scanty. It is certainly widely distributed and common on ponds and slow moving rivers except on Bodmin Moor where they must be thin on the ground but known to occur up to 900 feet (Musson[1]). Since 1955—and probably long before—two pairs nested on an area of marsh and small pools near Stannon Clay Works until recent operations made the area unsuitable (Almond[1]). A few birds have been seen at Dozmary Pool at migration time, but the lack of cover makes it unsuitable for nesting. Birds have bred at Temple Tor Pools.

Few figures have been published which give an idea of the increase in the winter population. A survey on Tresco in 1965 shewed that 50 to 70 were present from 23 to 27 January and only about 35 from 26 to 29 March; 56 were present from 17 to 20 September. A maximum of 150 plus was counted at the Abbey Pool on 22 October 1964. The few mainland figures published include 138 at Marazion Marsh on 6 January 1967, and over 100 in a field (presumably near the Argal reservoirs) on 5 January 1946, 70 at Newlyn East on 15 October 1967, and 80 at Caerhayes Castle on 2 December 1967.

The origin of wintering birds is obscure—most British and south European birds are assumed to be resident, but none ringed has been recovered in the county. As British birds are disinclined to migrate, they suffer severely in bad weather. The arctic conditions early in 1963 resulted in losses of about 75 per cent in St Breward parish on Bodmin Moor (Almond[1]). On lower ground, only a slight decrease was noted by R. J. Salmon, in the Lanivet area.

The only recoveries refer to three moorhens ringed on St Agnes, Scilly, in autumn and found dead on Tresco (2) and St Mary's.

## COOT *Fulica atra*

The coot is a widespread breeding bird throughout much of Europe and is extending its range into northern Scandinavia and Russia.

It is probably more common in Britain than formerly and is certainly more plentiful in Cornwall as a nesting species. Coots

G

are first mentioned in the county by Carew (1602) who counted them amongst the fowl that could be eaten—a fact also mentioned by Rodd (1880), who added that they afforded good sport to wildfowlers. The first writer to give any idea of the bird's status was James (1808) who said it was scarce, but whether he was referring to breeding birds, or to wintering numbers, is not possible to say. Certainly they were not scarce by the end of the century. Coots were formerly scarce and irregular winter visitors to the Scillies, but according to Clark and Rodd (z, 1906) in autumn 1859 they arrived in such numbers that as many as 100 were seen on the Abbey Pool, Tresco, at one time. The following spring two or three pairs nested, although Smart (PZ, 1885) and Smith (z, 1885) wrote that they did not breed on Tresco at that date— Smart adding that only "a chance bird or two, possibly slightly disabled, stays through the summer". A few pairs were breeding at the beginning of the present century, and nowadays some twenty pairs breed in the islands, mostly on Tresco, with a few on St Agnes since 1951, and at Porthellick Pool on St Mary's (Hunt[1]).

On the mainland, Clark in 1906 (VCH) wrote that the coot was a widely diffused resident that bred sparingly on Bodmin Moor, Goss Moor, Marazion Marsh, and very occasionally about Looe and in the Truro-Falmouth area. Coots regularly nested at Carclew ponds (P, 1892). Of these localities, only at Marazion Marsh is nesting still regularly reported. Harvey (1915), presumably referring to Marazion Marsh, called it an uncommon nester and years later (CBWPS, 1944) recorded that he had seen a nest at the marsh in May 1911 which had broken loose and floated about with a bird sitting on it. In 1945, coots were said to be breeding annually near Callington, but there are no more recent records anywhere in south-east Cornwall. This, and the 1911 record, were the only ones published by Ryves (1948). While some nesting must have gone unrecorded, there has certainly been an increase in breeding birds since new nesting sites have been created at such reservoirs as Melancoose and Stithians. Recent breeding numbers are—

Tamar Lake: Usually two pairs have nested since 1952—no previous records—with four or five in 1966.

Par beach pool: At least four pairs in 1966.

Caerhayes Castle: One or two pairs have bred, probably annually, since at least 1947.

Melancoose reservoir: One pair in 1963, and almost certainly annually since.

Tregothnan: Young have been seen on this estate where Merther Pool is the most likely breeding site (Jarvis[1]).

Stithians reservoir: At least nine pairs bred in 1966 and at least seven in 1967.

Loe Pool: A pair has been recorded here in most years since 1949.

Marazion Marsh: At least one pair nests annually, as in 1967.

Clowance Pond: A pair first bred successfully at this small pond in 1967, and again in 1968.

Crowan reservoir: A pair bred successfully in 1967, but not in 1968.

At Temple Tor pools on Bodmin Moor young have been seen recently, but birds have probably nested here for many years. A juvenile and two adults were seen on Goss Moor in August 1959, but there are no subsequent records.

Coot

Although large flocks of wintering coots are found on freshwater with surface feeding ducks—especially tufted ducks—their numbers have not been so well recorded as those of the wildfowl. The following figures refer to winter numbers obtained in various years since 1960 and are only approximate—

| Locality | Average Nos. | Maximum |
|---|---|---|
| Loe Pool | 290 | 500, mid-December 1964 |
| Helston Park Lake | probably less than 25 | 140, in stormy weather on 23 December 1945 |
| Marazion Marsh | 280 | 500, 3 March 1963 |
| Stithians reservoir | — | 400, 24 January 1966 |
| Drift reservoir | c. 250–300 | 300, December 1965—January 1966, and on 25 December 1967 |
| Melancoose reservoir | usually less than 50 | 200, 6 January 1962 |
| Par Beach pool | — | 230, 7 December 1966 |
| Tamar Lake | probably 100 to 200 | — |
| Argal reservoirs | — | c. 260, on the two reservoirs on 3 December 1967 |
| Heamoor reservoir, Penzance | 10–20 | 50, 22 February 1963 |

Few arrival and departure dates have been published, but careful watching at Drift reservoir since the winter of 1965–66, shews that a small number (usually less than 50) arrive during October, and that the main influx takes place in November. Peak numbers are maintained from mid-December to late January with a slow decline following in February and the main exodus in March; no more than about 50 are left by early April (Griffiths[1]). There is little evidence of passage movements, but one is detectable at Scilly in March and April (Parslow[1]). Fifty to 100 regularly winter on Tresco.

Except in cold weather, few coots are seen on estuaries or sheltered bays, and even then they are rare on the Camel or the Walmsley Sanctuary where less than half a dozen are usual. About 30 wintered at St John's Lake in the severe weather of 1947. In similar conditions in 1963, 110 were seen at Hayle on 5 January; 130 at Looe on 2 February; and about 100 on the Camel in January. The largest flock at Hayle is 120 in late December 1933, when many more than usual occurred in west Cornwall—between 300 and 350 were around the Hogus rocks in Mount's Bay and a small number remained near the Albert Pier, Penzance, until early February 1934. In recent years, the largest flock in Mount's Bay totalled 220 off Marazion on 27 December 1962, but it is thought they were driven there only because of a shoot at Marazion Marsh.

A full grown coot ringed at Ratzeburg, Schleswig-Holstein on 26 December 1953 was found dead on Tresco on 22 January 1957.

## PURPLE GALLINULE
### Porphyrula martinica

The only European recovery of this gaudy resident of the southern U.S.A. is an immature found in a very weak condition in the High Street of St Mary's, Scilly, on 7 November 1958. It died two days later and was sent to the British Museum for identification. Dr. Nesbet (quoted in Bannerman) wrote that the purple gallinule is one of a group of species which migrates directly across the width of the Gulf of Mexico, where its migration is occasionally interrupted by cyclonic storms. For this reason it is tempting to relate the Scilly record with a storm in the Gulf of Mexico a few days earlier, crossing the Georgia coast on the nights of 1–2 November, turning north-east to blow out in the Atlantic on the 4th and 5th. The gallinule, caught up in this storm, would then in mid-Atlantic, pick up a moderate south-westerly airstream without difficulty and be newly arrived at St Mary's on 7 November.

## OYSTERCATCHER
### Haematopus ostralegus

The oystercatcher is a common breeding bird along much of the European coast. In Britain it is more common in the north where it also nests along moorland rivers.

After decreasing in the last century, the population is generally increasing, although in Cornwall, by contrast, a decrease since the 1930's followed an increase from the late nineteenth century. Writers like Polwhele (1816) and Couch (1838) called it scarce or uncommon, the latter knowing it only as a winter visitor (*Imperial Magazine*, 1822). Rodd (1864) gave only Scilly as a breeding locality, but Clark (1902, & VCH) wrote that in the past thirty years the species had gradually extended from Scilly to Bude and Looe, nesting in small scattered colonies as at Perranporth. West Penwith, however, was never colonized.

On the north Cornish coast in the 1930's and early 1940's, Ryves and others noted breeding at Godrevy cliffs and along much of the Newquay-Padstow coast including records from the Huer's hut and Kelsey Head at Newquay, Bedruthan, Trevone, and Cataclews Point. Between Watergate Bay and Treyarnon, F. R. Smith[1] found nesting pairs at the following sites in the 1950's—on the eastern side of Stem Cove, Beacon Cove near Beryl's Point, Mawgan Porth near Beryl's Point and Trenance Point, and between High Cove and Bedruthan Steps. In most years a pair bred between Bedruthan and Park Head, while on the latter headland a pair always nested at the north-western corner with sometimes a second pair on the eastern side, and one pair on the west side of Porthmeor. Nests were usually placed in the top half of the cliff and were rarely accessible without ropes, the favourite sites being at the base of a bed of sea-pinks and close to a near vertical drop. Nests were very difficult to locate so it is not surprising that no accurate estimate of the population exists. Cursory observations by Smith since 1960 suggest that the resident population in this area remains about the same—probably no more than ten pairs in the seven miles between Watergate and Treyarnon, but it would be unwise to regard this as representative of the whole of the north coast. Dare's estimate of 40 to 80 breeding pairs between Godrevy and the Devon border is probably too high (*Fishery Investigations*, Series II Vol. xxv No. 5). The 1967 *Torrey Canyon* Census shewed breeding birds to be confined to only two other mainland areas. A few still breed between Hell's Mouth and Ralph's Cupboard, Portreath. R. Khan[1] has found pairs in the past ten years between Hell's Mouth and Fishing Cove, at Deadman's Cove and at Nancekuke, but believes no more than about four pairs nest here annually, although others may be undetected on off-shore stacks. One pair near Hell's Mouth nested each year on an earthy ledge about one hundred feet up—the young of the first clutch always fell over the cliff but at a second attempt single birds were sometimes successful.

North of the Camel estuary birds have nested in the Tintagel area in the 1930's and 1940's as at Willapark and Dizzard Point, but now are confined to the coast from the Devon border to Crackington Haven. Here they usually nest at the base of the cliff among the stones and pebbles or occasionally on the top of the high ridges formed by the near vertical strata. Breeding numbers are not accurately known, but are said to be higher north of Bude. South of the town there are perhaps no more than a dozen pairs. R. B. Treleaven[1] has found nests at Penkenna Point, the small point north of it, and at Upton where one pair nests unsuccessfully every year near the coastguard station.

In the Lizard area G. H. Harvey knew of nests between Halzaphron and Gunwalloe (CBWPS, 1932), but the only recent record from Mount's Bay is of a pair at Beny's Cove near Prah Sands in 1949 (Khan[1]). On the south coast a few pairs probably nest annually but the only records are single pairs at Lantivet Bay (1952), St. Austell Bay (1961), Dodman Point (1968), and Lansallos (1968) (Stevens[1] & Musson[1]).

Flocks of several hundred occur on migration on estuaries like the Camel and

Fal in spring and autumn but few figures have been published. Four hundred at St John's Lake on 5 March 1966 seemed an especially large gathering for Cornwall. Wintering parties not uncommonly feed away from the shore, especially in hard weather, on fields, grass-lands and coastal golf-links—77 were counted on 1 December 1967 on St Mawgan Airfield.

On the Scillies the oystercatcher is one of the most abundant and conspicuous of shore birds. It was described as a common nesting species in the last century and its status probably remains unchanged—the present population is estimated to be 100 to 150 pairs (Parslow[1]), at least a few nesting on every island. About sixteen to twenty pairs nest on Annet although there is usually a flock of about 60 non-breeding birds present. On St Agnes and Gugh there were nine breeding birds in 1950 while in 1962 and 1963 the total for the two islands was ten and nine pairs respectively. Nests are usually spaced out around the shores of the larger islands but on some smaller ones like Guthers and Green Island off Samson, four or five nests have been found within a few yards of each other in the midst of a ternary. The normal clutch size is three, but as many as five eggs were found in nests on Samson (May 1948) and Tean (May 1961).

Outside the breeding season flocks of up to 200 were recorded by Clark and Rodd (1906) while King (1924) once saw a flock of this size on St Martin's. Today such numbers are common, especially on the sand flats off Samson but also on islands such as St Agnes where the maximum count from August to November has exceeded 200. In spring a peak of 100 to 130 is normal in April and up to 80 non-breeding birds have been seen in June.

Birds ringed as young at Fetlar, Shetland; Inverness; Isle of Man (2); Anglesey; and Skokholm, have been recovered on Cornish estuaries. Locally ringed birds—two on Tresco and one near Newquay—were found close to the ringing area. Foreign recoveries are—

| *Ringed as Nestlings* | *Recovered* |
| --- | --- |
| Storhofdi, Vestmann Islands Iceland 18.6.'59 | found dead near Truro May or June 1961 |
| Bokholmen, Utvaer, Norway 27.6.'48 | found dead Padstow 3.7.'50 |

## LAPWING                    *Vanellus vanellus*

The lapwing breeds throughout much of Europe and has extended its range northwards. It is still widespread in Britain, but has largely decreased in the south as a result of intensified farming techniques.

A dialect name for the lapwing in Devon and Cornwall is 'horniwink'—an allusion to its projecting crest. Up to this century lap-

*View across Carminowe Creek - the southern extension of Loe Pool*

wings bred on most of the Cornish moors. There are records from Trevear in Sennen and Tregavara Moor, Madron (Rodd, 1864), Trekieve and Carkeek in St Cleer (N. Hare, PZ, 1849), Trewartha and Black Moor marsh "and considerable numbers in a lonely marsh west of Bodmin Moor" (F. R. Rodd MS). Clark (VCH) recorded occasional nesting at Lady Downs near Penzance and Carnon Downs near Truro, small numbers in the Tamar Valley, and more widely on Goss and Bodmin moors. Harvey (1915) knew of nests in the neighbourhood of Castle-an-Dinas, Ludgvan, but G. H. Harvey (1931) knew of none in Penwith apart from two at Marazion Marsh in 1926. Ryves (1948) wrote that lapwings bred in small colonies in many localities, though sparsely in the west, and in 1933 he found a colony containing ten pairs on three to four acres of rough ground which generally held five to eight nests.

There are few recently published breeding records. In the west it is certainly rare. None now nest at Carnon Downs, while the spread of caravans around Perranporth has ousted it from the dunes where a pair bred as recently as 1962. Breeding is annual near the Lizard—several pairs nesting on Predannack Downs. Three nests were found here in 1966 and there may have been two more. In West Penwith nesting is probably sporadic rather than regular; one pair raised four young at Trewey Down, Zennor in 1963. In east Cornwall the species still nests widely on Bodmin Moor, as in St Breward parish, but its exact status is far from clear. Nesting has also occurred near Bude (1947) and Tamar Lake (1953), Stokeclimsland (1947) and in a neighbouring parish a few years before, at Luxulyan in a marshy field (1948), and at Par Beach (1944). After 1940 a few nested regularly on the Amble marshes, at least until 1952 when four nests were found, and may still do so. Nesting is certainly more widespread than records suggest in areas like St Breock Down and Goss Moor. Three pairs at least

probably bred at Tregoss Moor in 1967 (Julyan[1]).

Breeding takes place normally in April and May although Ryves recorded one nest with two young and a chipping egg as late as 2 July and a full clutch as early as 22 March. Lapwings begin to flock in June with parties of a score or more occurring on the downs early in the month. Thus, 22 at St Eval on 10 June 1965 increased to over 60 the next day, and 170 on St Breock Down on 22 June 1966 had increased to over 250 the next day. At Stithians reservoir 27 on 13 June 1966 numbered over 300 by early September.

How soon passage birds and migrants from other parts of Britain and the Continent augment the local flocks is uncertain, although probably by mid-July. Large flocks will keep to the uplands as well as the estuaries in mid-winter, but leave the high ground when the weather deteriorates. Immense flocks arrive in severe weather, especially ahead of snow belts. 2,000 were counted flying west over Saltash in four hours on 28 December 1964. On New Year's Eve 1961, large numbers congregated around the Lizard, including the village green. Throughout the morning and afternoon birds flew off towards Brittany—the snow arrived later in the evening. With warmer weather flocks soon return as Col. Almond described at St Breward in 1958. Between 20 and 24 January many flocks flew south-west and west over the parish, but a sudden thaw on the night of the 24–25th reversed the situation and by dawn flocks of up to 200 were passing eastwards, mainly in the morning, but continuing on the 26th. It is impossible to give an accurate account of the numbers present on estuaries in winter, but among the largest flocks estimated are 3,000 on the Lynher on 24 February 1966, 6,000 in a ten acre field near Trewornan Bridge on 27 January 1962, and about 4,000 on the Camel estuary on 19 December 1967. At Hayle over a thousand were counted on various dates in January

1964, and over 1,500 at Ruan Lanihorne on 24 October 1967.

The return to the breeding grounds takes place in March and only isolated non-breeding birds linger on the estuaries into May.

The lapwing has never been known to nest on Scilly.

Two or three commonly appear in September and irregularly as early as June to August, but rarely remain for more than a few days. The main autumn passage occurs between late October and November. Numbers are not generally large—the largest wing recorded on St Agnes between 1957 and 1964 comprising 74 on 24 October 1958. Larger numbers sometimes appear on the open fields about St Mary's airport. Only in hard weather does the lapwing become conspicuous when flocks of a thousand or more are seen resting in the fields or flying southwards. At such times new arrivals are frequently very emaciated and early in 1963 scores were picked up dead or dying, while others quickly became extremely tame and so hungry that they even resorted to feeding on chicken food. On 13 February 1900 a flock estimated to be three miles long passed over the islands from the north-west and the next day the islands were full of lapwings, many of which died (z, 1906).

Spring migration is usually smaller than that in autumn and follows the departure of the winter visitors. Small flocks appear in March and April and a few birds may be seen in May. Only following hard weather has the passage in March comprised wings of a hundred or so birds.

Fourteen lapwings recovered in Cornwall had been ringed as nestlings in the following counties—

Glenorchard, Sterling, 3; Yorkshire, 2; Cheshire, 3; and one from each of Perthshire, Cumberland, Norfolk, Buckinghamshire; Oxfordshire, and Berkshire.

Foreign recoveries are—

| Ringed as Nestlings | Recovered |
| --- | --- |
| NORWAY | |
| Bryne, Jaeren 26.5.'41 | shot, Tresco c. 12.2.'45 |
| Klepp, Rogaland 20.5.'46 | found dead near Newquay 1.2.'54 |
| Line, Rogaland 15.5.'50 | found dead, Hayle 7.2.'54 |
| SWEDEN | |
| nr. Malmo 9.5.'48 | Kilkhampton 3.1.'51 |
| Kristianstad 11.5.'55 | found long dead, Polzeath 3.8.'56 |
| DENMARK | |
| Vandet, Jutland 8.7.'27 | Gwithian 21.12.'27 |
| Gjol, Jutland 20.6.'42 | Bude January 1947. |
| Hojer, Jutland 17.5.'52 | found dead, Falmouth 7.2.'54 |
| Korsor, Sjaelland 12.5.'52 | found dead, Jacobstow 6.2.'56 |
| HOLLAND | |
| Aarle Rixtel, Noord Brabant 25.5.'59 | Lizard 5.1.'60 |
| Petten, Noord Holland 27.5.'59 | Carn Brea 15.1.'60 |
| BELGIUM | |
| Le Zoute, West Flanders 1.6.'51 | Davidstow 19.11.'55 |
| CZECHOSLOVAKIA | |
| Cecelice 4.5.'61 | found dead, Falmouth 29.1.'63 |

Lapwing

# RINGED PLOVER
## Charadrius hiaticula

The ringed plover nests on much of the European coast. In Britain it is widespread but more rare than formerly, especially in the south. In Cornwall (but not Scilly) it is virtually extinct as a breeding species, for the shingle beach is its favourite habitat and as tourism has increased so nest records have diminished. During the 19th century it was generally distributed along the sea-shore (Rodd, 1880) and still fairly common early this century when Clark (VCH) made special mention of the beaches about Looe, and "here and there from Prussia Cove to Newlyn and less commonly further west". Harvey (1915) found it at suitable places in West Penwith, but the last nesting known to G. H. Harvey was on Eastern Green, Penzance in 1922 when three eggs were found on 3 August. A pair apparently nested at Sennen in 1924, another pair at Hayle in the late 1920's and at Gwithian about 1931. Small numbers still nested in the St Mawgan-in-Pydar area in the early 1930's, while in 1948 Ryves recalled a time past when he was able to find three nests within half-an-hour. Between 1922 and 1938, the Constantine Bay—Trevose area was watched fairly regularly by Mrs. Weeks[1] who always found a nest by the stream on Constantine beach, another near Parson's Heet, and a third further along Booby Bay. By 1948 it was scarce here.

Since the 1940's the only nesting records published are—1943, a nest at Point, Devoran; 1946, a pair with one young at Godrevy on 19 May; 1949, a pair with a chick at Loe Bar, Helston in early July; 1952, three very young birds at Loe Bar on 19 May—an early hatch; 1959, J. Sheldon (1968[1]) found a nest at Loe Bar, Helston, with four young birds which were photographed by his daughter; 1964, one pair at Booby Bay, St Merryn.

F. R. Smith[1] wrote that between 1950 and 1960 when searching for breeding oyster-catchers along the coast between Watergate Bay and Treyarnon, he never found any ringed plovers' nests, but on different occasions saw birds displaying at Mawgan Porth, at Constantine, and once at Rock on the north side of the Camel estuary. Probably these birds would have nested if the area were undisturbed. S. C. Madge[1] who has made extensive searches from the Tamar to Looe, has found no evidence here, while Loe Bar, Helston, clearly a former strong-hold, seems too disturbed for future nesting to be successful.

The ringed plover is not known to have nested inland in Cornwall; indeed, inland records are comparatively rare at any time, consisting of a few birds on autumn migration at reservoirs like Drift, Crowan and Stithians. Many migrants, especially early birds in July and August, probably belong to the arctic form *Charadrius hiaticula tundrae* which winters south of the Sahara, but its presence has not been confirmed by the recovery of ringed birds. The largest flights arrive in late August and in September, when parties of over a hundred are not uncommon. Thus, in 1966 some 200 were seen at Hayle on 7 August, while at the end of the month similar sized flocks passed through Hayle on the 26th, and the Camel estuary and the Ruan River on the 28th. In late August, 200 were also present at St John's Lake.

Montagu (1813) was the first to shew that the 'dulwilly' remained in Cornwall and Devon, even in the most severe winters, seeking shelter in the creeks and inlets. Wintering flocks are smaller than those seen on migration. Few figures have been published but on the Camel estuary in 1964 over 300 were present in early September, but only 50 or more by early November.

On the Scillies the ringed plover is still a common breeding bird, its status being apparently unchanged from a century ago. No figures were published but North (1850) wrote that eggs could be found without difficulty in the loose shingle above high tide. Birds still nest commonly on all the inhabited islands as well as on many larger uninhabited ones like Annet, Samson, and Tean. Since 1950 the population has certainly remained stable on St Agnes and Gugh, for an estimated twelve to fourteen breeding pairs in 1950 (Parslow[1]) remained the same in 1961-63. Birds nest on sandy beaches above high water mark, less frequently on banks of shingle or small shells, and often amongst short heather and grass, sometimes some distance inland. Clutches, as on the mainland, are normally of four, but in June 1963 nests of five eggs were found on St Agnes and St Mary's.

The main passage is in October when the usual population on St Agnes is from 80 to 100 birds, but sometimes higher—160 on 11 October 1958. In winter, parties of 50 to 100 are present on St Agnes, but reached a peak of 200 at the start of the extremely cold conditions in late December 1963. There is some evidence of a small return passage in spring—the highest total being 65 on 29 March 1957.

| Ringed | Recovered |
|---|---|
| Foulness Island, Essex, nestling 5.7.'59 | found dead, Sennen Cove 23.1.'63. |
| Bradwell-on-Sea, Essex, juvenile 12.10.'58 | found dead, Portreath 24.1.'63 |
| St Agnes, first winter 5.9.'60 | Laredo, Santander, Spain 3.10.'60 |

## LITTLE RINGED PLOVER
### Charadrius dubius

The little ringed plover is well distributed in Europe and since 1938 has nested in Britain where it is extending its range. While still extremely rare in Cornwall, increased records can be expected—indeed, future nesting may not be impossible at deserted china-clay pits as its spread elsewhere has been due largely to the utilization of artificial sites such as gravel pits.

1844 Cocks examined a specimen shot in the
-'49 Falmouth area between these dates (MS).
1851 One said to have been shot on Scilly in September (Morris, *A History of British Birds*, 1851–57).
1863 An immature shot at the Abbey Pool, Tresco on 27 October (z).
1956 One at Pentewan beach on 12 April.
1965 Two at Par beach pool on 1 April and another at Hayle on 11 May.
1966 One at Hayle on 17 April.
1968 Single birds were at Gwithian Pool from about 30 March to 2 April and Marazion Marsh on 6 July.

## KENTISH PLOVER
### Charadrius alexandrinus

Although found on much of the temper-

ate and Mediterranean coasts of Europe, the Kentish plover is an uncommon visitor to Britain and no longer nests in the county from which it gets its English name. Cornish records have increased in the past twenty years—probably because of the greater number of bird-watchers.

1852 A male killed at Long Rock near Penzance on 17 April (z).
1858 A female killed at the same place, also on 17 April (z).
1871 One shot near Penzance about 24 August (z).
1881 One seen at the Abbey Pool, Tresco in September (z, 1906).
1926 Fifteen said to have been seen on Lelant Beach on 31 August. This incredible record cannot be accepted because of insufficient evidence. A record of four at Daymer Bay on 21 September 1945 was backed by evidence "scarcely sufficient" to establish it satisfactorily (BB).
1946 One on the Camel estuary on 4 September.
1948 Four seen with ringed plovers at Trewornan on the Camel estuary on 18 September. This record seems more satisfactory than that of 1945.
1950 One on the Hayle estuary on 23 August.
1951 One near the breakwater at Bude on 31 May.
1956 Two at Penryn mudflats on 28 August.
1960 Two at Mawgan Porth on 31 August.
1965 Single birds were reported at Par beach from 20 to 25 August, on St Mary's on 10 October, and on St Agnes from 29 March to 10 April.

## KILLDEER (PLOVER)
### Charadrius vociferus

The killdeer is a North American species occupying the eccological niche filled by the lapwing in Europe.

1885 A female, "fat and hearty", which frequented the Long Pool on Tresco for several days, was shot on 14 or 15 January (z).
1957 A bird seen on St Agnes on 12 December after a severe gale, may have been the same one shot at Trenoweth Wood, St Columb Major on 26 December.

1959　A bird in full breeding dress was watched at close quarters at Tamar Lake on 27 July.

1963 -'64　At least two were on St Martin's from 19 November to 16 January.

# GREY PLOVER
*Pluvialis squatarola*

The grey plover is one of Europe's most renowned migrants. From its summer haunts in extreme northern Siberia it winters as far south as the Cape of Good Hope. Non-breeding birds also summer in this country so that the species has been recorded in Cornwall in every month of the year.

The main southward movements takes place from mid-September, early records including birds at Hayle on 25 July 1965, at Porthcothan in St Minver on 10 August 1963, and on the Lynher on 14 August 1965. Since the majority winter south of our shores the greatest numbers might be expected on passage—indeed, both Rodd (1880) and Clark (VCH) described it as a spring and autumn visitor with a few winter records, mainly of immature birds, although 'many' were reported at St Buryan in the winter of 1887–88. Sixteen constituted the largest wintering flock on the Camel known to Ryves (1931), but now equally large flocks may occur from December to February as on migration. A hundred or more are frequently seen on the Camel estuary in mid-winter. At St John's Lake there were up to 150 in December 1963 and 120 on 24 December 1965, while on the Tamar over 200 were reported near Cargreen on 23 January 1966.

In spring birds depart from about early March, all normally vacating the estuaries by early May. Later dates include 27 May 1956 at Hayle, the same date at Par in 1959, 28 May 1966 at Marazion Marsh, and 4 June 1958 at Hayle.

Outside the breeding season the grey plover is very much a coastal bird. Inland records are rare, although in recent years birds have been seen foraging up to several miles inland about Trevose—as were 27 on the headland on 21 February 1963. Only rarely are they reported further inland—for example, two at Crowan reservoir on 18 September and 6 October 1959, and one at Stithians reservoir on 18 September 1967. The only record known to Col. Almond[1] from St Breward parish is of one bird associating with lapwings on the moor on 16 November 1957.

Clark and Rodd (z, 1906) wrote that it was not uncommon at Scilly in autumn and winter, sometimes singly, and sometimes in parties of three or four but was rarely seen anywhere except on beaches—especially on Samson. Recent records from St Agnes shew it to be an annual migrant, mostly single birds from mid-September to mid-October—nine on 14 September 1959 are the most seen together. Up to five are recorded in winter on St Agnes, though possibly numbers are higher on other islands like Samson where there are extensive sand-flats. The species is less regular on spring passage—since 1957 it has been reported on only three occasions. The latest spring record is 5 May 1958 and 1962 on St Agnes, and the earliest in autumn is 7 August 1945 on Tresco.

# GOLDEN PLOVER
*Pluvialis apricaria*

Two forms of this plover are recognisable in full breeding plumage; the southern *Pluvialis apricaria apricaria* which nests in Britain and about the southern Baltic, and the northern *Pluvialis apricaria altifrons* found in Iceland, Scandinavia, parts of northern Russia and occasionally in northern Britain.

Nesting in Britain is now largely confined to Scotland and the north of England, but since 1950 a few pairs have bred on Dartmoor after an hiatus of nearly a century. Dr. Moore (PI, 1830) recorded that a brood of six was obtained on the banks of the Tamar in 1827, the nearest that breeding birds have apparently been to Cornwall.

The golden plover is one of the commonest waders in Cornwall in winter. Rather strangely, neither Carew (1602) nor Borlase (1758) mentioned the species' abundance, but James (1808) wrote that it occurred in amazing flocks. The earliest arrival dates are of one near St Neot on 28 July 1967, a flock of 30 on the Camel estuary on 20 August 1967, fifteen which flew over the Lizard on 26 August 1966 (*The Lizard*, 1967) and a few at Porthgwarra on the 27th the same year. Most begin to arrive in the latter half of September. Col. Almond (1959) wrote that at St Breward golden plovers usually arrived between 22 September and 11 October but that in 1958 a few had arrived by the end of the third week in August. Congregations of 1,000 have been reported in recent years by mid-October, and 2,000 or more by the end of the year. Over a thousand regularly occur on the Tamar estuary, the Camel and Walmsley sanctuary, Restronguet Creek, Hayle, and at inland localities like Crowdy Marsh near Camelford, and Rosenannon Downs in St Wenn. Large flocks are probably much more widespread at inland localities than records suggest.

Maximum numbers reported on the Amble Marshes are 5,000 on 4 February 1967 and 3,000 on 19 November 1967. On the Tamar 3,000 were estimated in one congregation on 1 March 1964, and 2,500 on 21 October 1967. Most golden plovers depart during March. Thus, in 1961 birds were last seen in St Breward on the 30th, but in 1963 were still about the moors until 22 April where few are generally seen after the second week of April. Small numbers, probably of passage migrants, are not uncommon on the estuaries until late April while a few stragglers occur in May. Most unusual is the report by Ryves in 1943 of a flock of 100—150 flying north over St Mawgan-in-Pydar on 5 June and a further flock of 25–30 on the 12th—the only June records from Cornwall.

Golden plovers are much affected by weather conditions so are seen on the higher moors in mild weather. In the severe conditions of January 1963 they seemed to leave the county altogether—a note in the Lanarth Gamebook states that not one was seen between 8 January and 1 March. The plovers massed on the Lizard at the beginning of January—199 were shot there on the 4th—a most remarkable total. The season's bag reached 331 compared with the usual twenty to thirty.

From early April golden plovers are not uncommon in near or full breeding plumage allowing separation of the two races. As far back as 1808, James of St Keverne referred to the northern *P. apricaria altifrons* when he wrote of "a variety with black and white bellies and breasts". 550 at Dinham on the Camel estuary in 1967 and 200 at Allet, near

The old quay at the head of the Hayle estuary from which may be obtained the finest view of this notable locality

Truro on 22 April 1960 are the largest recorded gatherings. These may have been birds of passage, but a single individual in almost complete breeding plumage as early as 31 January 1965, indicates that some winter in the county. The recovery in Britain of ringed birds suggests that our northern form is largely derived from Iceland.

On the Scillies the golden plover has been described by all authors as a common winter visitor occurring in especially large flocks in severe weather. It seems most plentiful in the larger, more open fields as at St Mary's airport, but occurs regularly on the heather 'downs' on most of the larger islands, as well as on the shores.

The first autumn arrivals are occasional visitors in late August or early September, the earliest being three on 5 August 1903 (Parslow[1]), but it is not until the last few days of September or the first few in October that the main arrival commences. Peak numbers are usual in the second half of October, although the greatest number on St Agnes from 1957 to 1963 was 28 on 4 October 1957. Numbers are remarkably uniform in mild winters with flocks of between 20 and 50 remaining on most of the larger islands, but during hard weather their numbers are considerably augmented. Congregations may number several hundred and the birds often arrive in company with lapwings. "Vast" numbers of both species were on the islands on 14 February 1900 (z, 1906), and in recent years in the severe weather in February 1962 and early in 1963 on St Agnes and other islands.

Most wintering birds leave the islands by March when transient flocks on return passage are also most common, especially following cold winters. Apart from March 1963, when up to 85 were recorded, the most seen on St Agnes at this season is 40 on 26 March 1957. Small parties are seen in April and early May in most years—the latest record being of one on St Agnes on 26 May 1963. As on the mainland, birds of the northern race *altifrons* are frequently indentified in the spring.

| Ringed | Recovered |
|---|---|
| Onderdendam, Groningen, Holland, full grown 23.3.'56 | shot, Bodmin Moor, February 1959 |
| Hallum, Friesland, Holland, full grown 18.4.'62 | shot, Newlyn East 20.12.'62 |
| Midnes, Iceland, adult 30.4.'53 | shot, Penzance 8.1.'54 |
| Myvatn, Iceland, nestling 5.7.'54 | shot, Bodmin Moor 28.11.'57 |

## LESSER GOLDEN PLOVER
### *Pluvialis dominica*

A single bird seen feeding in a ploughed field on St Agnes between 30 September and 10 October 1962, and another at St Just airport on 6 October 1968, are the only Cornish records of this North American wader. Breeding in northern Canada and wintering as far south as Brazil, the species migrates mainly along the Atlantic coast. One might therefore assume that it is a good candidate to attempt the Atlantic crossing, but only about eight have been recorded in Britain since 1870—perhaps due to the difficulty of identification.

The Asiatic form of the Lesser golden plover (*P. dominica fulva*), while more frequently recorded in Britain than the American species, has not so far been identified in Cornwall.

## DOTTEREL          *Eudromias morinellus*

The dotterel is a bird of the tundra and the mountains. It formerly bred extensively in northern Britain but is now largely confined to the central Highlands of Scotland.

In Cornwall it is a rare passage migrant and less commonly seen on the mainland than formerly. Clark (RI, 1908) described it as regular in spring but rare in autumn. This was either an exaggeration or many occurrences were unrecorded for only a handful of records were published. Birds from Maenporth, Bar Point, and Gyllingvase may have been those examined by Cocks from the Falmouth area between 1844 and 1849 (Cocks, MS). Another was obtained at Sancreed before 1850 (PZ).

1863    One taken on Scilly in early November (G, 6.11.'63).

1868    One taken near the Lizard about 10 September (z).

1876    An adult shot on a hillside overlooking Mount's Bay about 22 August. Rodd commented that they occurred at uncertain intervals (z).

1880    Two shot by a keeper at the Lizard Lighthouse during the small hours of 28 April (z, 1881).

1891    One of a trip shot at Pentewan in early May (RI, 1902).

1931    Two seen near Park Head on 15 September.

1938    One of a trip of eight killed north of St Kew in late March.

1968    Two remained on the cliff tops at Porthgwarra for several weeks until about 25 September. Four were also reported from Crowdy Marsh, Camelford.

Excluding the 1863 report, all on Scilly have been recorded since 1956 when three were seen on Bryher on 17 September and two on 27th and 28th. Another was seen there the following September. Since 1960 single birds have been reported by the St Agnes Observatory every autumn except in 1965. Extreme dates are 27 August 1961 and 7 October 1963. The only spring records are of two on St Mary's on 29 April 1962, and three flying north over Tresco on 21 April 1967.

## TURNSTONE          *Arenaria interpres*

So familiar is this tame little wader seen at all times of the year along the Cornish coast, where Willughby and Ray first recorded it "about Pensans" (*Ornithology*, 1678), that it is difficult to believe it is only a migrant from breeding grounds on the Scandinavian and Arctic coasts. It has never been proved to breed in this country although there are statements to the contrary. As far back as 1850, North wrote that

breeding had been suspected at Scilly. Clark (1902) wrote that its numbers had increased in recent years at Scilly, had become resident and for at least three years had bred on the sands there. Later he was more cautious speaking only of probable nesting (VCH & RI, 1908). In a letter to King (1923), Clark wrote that about 1900 a turnstone's egg "was given to me by Jackson, another was given me at Truro by a Miss Hicks from St Agnes, and a third, rather badly broken, I found in the collection of Mr. L. R. George of St Mary's. I have myself seen no actual traces of its breeding on the islands, but on the other hand I do not think these three eggs could have been introduced." Clark (z, 1906) was also reported to have handled the skins of two young birds shot on 23 July, while Jackson and King were both reported as having seen the birds nesting on the sands and to have taken the eggs. However, King wrote in *Scillonia* (1924) "I should like to protest against a statement which has been attributed to me . . . I never said that the turnstone's eggs have been found in Scilly. I know that some boatmen said this years ago, but when the case was investigated the eggs proved to be those of the ringed plover". A similar story would no doubt explain the record from the mainland for 1950, in which year on 7 May "somewhere in Cornwall", two adult turnstones with two young in down were said to have been seen.

Some non-breeding birds, mainly immatures, remain throughout the breeding season, on many stretches of coast, for example, about 40 at Marazion in 1967. The turnstone may be found on sandy beaches, particularly where the tide-line is thick with insect-infested seaweed and other jetsam, but is rarely found in appreciable numbers or for any length of time where rocks or pebbles are absent. The species has little fear of man so that it is common within harbours. An incident reported in 1955 shews at least one individual living up to his name by rolling stones to the edge of the harbour wall at Mousehole and tipping them into the sea, apparently for the simple pleasure of watching the splash.

Passage migrants and winter visitors begin to arrive in late July or early August. Turnstones are so scattered along suitable stretches of coastline that no attempt has been made to estimate the numbers present in any localities at migration time or in winter. Gatherings larger than 50 have rarely been reported but may not be uncommon for in 1967 there were about 500 at St John's Lake in late February and September, and about 200 at Looe in late September. Turnstones are rare inland. One arrived with two dunlins over Crowan reservoir in September 1962—only the dunlins settled, the turnstone circled a few times and made off towards the nearest coast to the north-west. However, grasslands adjoining the coasts are visited in cold weather. Parties have been seen probing the ground, sometimes with starlings, on golf-courses (as at Newquay), in parks and even within towns. One was seen eating bread in a bus-shelter on Penzance promenade. In the hard winter early in 1963 they survived well in most places in Cornwall, but at Bude, where conditions were more severe, many died when the beach froze, although one bird sustained himself on the entrails of a dead oystercatcher and gulls.

On the Scillies the turnstone reaches its lowest population between mid-June and mid-July, but even at this time, flocks of 20 to 40 are found on St Agnes, Annet and many other islands. On St Agnes numbers increase at the end of July with the main passage from mid-August onwards when total numbers fluctuate between 100 and 260, but as many as 300 have been noted in November. The normal wintering population is about 150 birds. Flocks of spring migrants in late April and early May number up to 200 at times and on 9 May 1963 reached 373. This annual pattern observed on St Agnes is probably typical of most islands, all of which have large populations at times of passage and in winter.

| *Ringed* | *Recovered* |
|---|---|
| St Agnes, adult 30.9.'60 | found dead, Station Dye 2 on the inland ice-cap, Greenland 28.7.'68 |
| St Agnes, first winter 30.9.'63 | shot, Kuvdlorssuak, Upernavik, Greenland 16.6.'67 |
| Midnes, Iceland, adult 25.5.'60 | controlled at St Agnes, 10.5.'61 |

## DOWITCHER LONG-BILLED/ SHORT-BILLED

*Limnodromus*

*scolopaceus/griseus*

The dowitcher is an annual vagrant to Britain from North America. It is not possible to assign many older records of 'red-breasted snipe' to either of the recently recognised forms.

1857    A probable 'long-billed' was shot by the freshwater pool on the Higher Moors of St Mary's on 3 October (Rodd, 1880. Illustrated in WLZ).

1937    One seen on a pool near Zennor on 19 October and at Marazion Marsh on 2 November.

1943    A first winter male on Tresco from 12 September was shot on the 17th. It was identified as a 'long-billed' in 1961.

1944 & '53    Single birds said to have been seen on Tresco in August but no details are available (AR).

1966 –'67    A 'long-billed' was seen on Tresco from 27 September until the end of October, and at the Hayle estuary from 30 October until 19 April, by which time it was in almost full breeding dress (R).

1968    Two 'long-billed' seen on St Mary's on 22 September.

## COMMON SNIPE

*Gallinago gallinago*

Snipe breed widely on wet moorlands, bogs and similar habitats in many areas outside the northern tundra and Mediterranean zones on both sides of the Atlantic. In Britain it breeds in most counties, though is now scarce in the south.

In Cornish the snipe was called *kyogh* (c.f. Welsh *giach*). It also possesses another Celtic name—*gavar hal* which, like its Welsh counter-part, literally means 'moor goat'. This name, and the dialect 'hatter-flitter', refers to the drumming sound produced in display flights. When Cornish was still spoken in the west of the county, the snipe was probably a widespread nester although precise information, especially from the west, is lacking.

In the Scillies the snipe has never been known to nest although birds have been heard drumming in the summer months. Birds are not known to nest in west Cornwall now. James (1808) wrote that they occurred in "great plenty" and added "I have frequently found their nests"—presumably on Goonhilly Downs not far from his home. The only other record from Kerrier was published by Montagu (1813)—"near Penryn in Cornwall there is a marsh where several breed annually and where we have taken their eggs . . ." Clark (VCH) wrote that birds bred locally throughout the county, but the only record from West Penwith refers to a nest and eggs at Tremethick Marsh, Madron sometime before 1864 (Rodd, 1864. Z, 1870). For Rodd to mention this case suggests that breeding was rare in this area. The only localities mentioned by Clark (VCH) are in the east—Goss Moor and Bodmin Moor, further noting in 1902 (RI) that nests had been found within the last five years at St Stephen-in-Brannel, near Laneast, and at St Cleer. N. Hare (PZ) in 1849 wrote of nests at Trekieve and Carkeek in St Cleer. Bodmin Moor has always been their main breeding centre; C. S. Gilbert in 1817 (*History of Cornwall*) wrote that "Almost every sportsman must recollect his springing snipe on downs even in the height of summer; and on Bodmin Downs in particular, young snipes, very recently from

the nest, have often been raised". The decrease in breeding snipe from the mid-nineteenth century is specifically mentioned by F. R. Rodd (MS), and a writer from Tregony about the same time (1870) attributes the decrease to the drier moors resulting from the gradual acclamation of land (x256/7, County Record Office). In 1868 (Rodd, 1880) young were generally scattered about the Moor between Kilmar in North Hill and Dozmary Pool. Recent records are very few; the last one published refers to young flushed at Crowdy Marsh

Common snipe

near Camelford on 5 June 1933. In 1931, Ryves mentioned snipe nesting in several places within a twelve mile radius of St Mawgan-in-Pydar (this includes Goss Moor) but never published precise information. Ryves and Quick (BB, 1946) wrote that snipe bred thinly on the moors and uplands mainly in the north of the county. Nesting may go un-noticed in places, but Bodmin Moor is the only area where it is known to have taken place sparingly in recent years. Indeed, Col. Almond[1] thinks it may be rather irregular here and at best described as rare. A bird was seen drumming and displaying other aspects of territorial behaviour south of Dozmary Pool, at Redhill Downs in 1967 and in the upper Fowey valley in 1968, but breeding was not proved.

The snipe is best known as a winter visitor. First wisps normally arrive about early September reaching a peak in the first week in October. The earliest dates are—

27 July 1963 at Scilly, 30 July 1961 at Scilly, 5 August 1964 at Scilly and the 23rd at Lelant. As many as twenty were seen at St Agnes on 18 August 1958.

The winter habitat of snipe in Cornwall has changed markedly during the past thirty or so years. Major Bolitho wrote that "before the last War farmers treated their young cattle and cows not in milk very badly, simply turning them out onto the moors in winter. Their feet cut up the wet ground making it very good for snipe. Farmers now realise the value of their cattle and do not turn them out onto the moors so that the wet places are no longer good snipe habitat."

Major Bolitho also noted that myxamatosis indirectly affected the snipe for "previously the rabbits had kept the grass short, but after the disease had virtually wiped them out there was nothing to keep the grass down in the bogs. Snipe, presumably, were then not able to run about in them and they consequently deserted a great many of their old haunts. About the same time much more winter ploughing took place in Cornwall and in a number of places snipe have moved from the bogs to ploughed fields. Thus, anyone, looking for them in their old haunts might conclude that there were not so many about as formerly."

The number wintering in Cornwall depends on the severity of the weather. One of the most outstanding seasons of the nineteenth century was 1878–79 when a total of 545 were shot at Scilly, the bag of one January day producing 93 full snipe and 14 'jacks' on St Mary's at two favourite marshy spots. By contrast, the mild weather of 1868–69 resulted in a season's bag of only fourteen at Scilly.

The heavy toll taken of snipe in very severe winters results in reduced numbers in subsequent seasons. In 1944 Dorrien-Smith reported that they were still almost non-existant at Scilly for the fourth year running; the great frosts of 1940 and 1941 had nearly wiped them out from western Europe, while the droughts in 1938 and 1939 had also taken a heavy toll. In the hard winter of 1962–63, some 90 per cent are estimated to have migrated from Cornwall (Lanarth Game Book) for the snipe that normally fed on ploughed land and the larger marsh areas left when the ground froze, comparatively small numbers remaining around springs and streams. That season the bag was 203 at Lanarth—a good total but 447 were shot in 1961–62 and 348 in 1960–61. In the early part of 1963, according to Major Bolitho, "snipe were not able to feed and suffered very greatly, losing condition rapidly and becoming so weakened that they could be caught if chased for any length of time. A great many died that winter and they still (1966–67 season) have not returned to their previous numbers." Following the hard winter, bags were reduced to 184 in 1963–64 and 102 in 1964–65. Following the winter of 1946–47, when 276 were obtained at Lanarth, the drop in numbers was even more spectacular with only 51 shot in 1947–48.

The best day's bag is almost always in January. In recent years at Lanarth they are 96 on the 4th in 1961, 79 on the 3rd in 1962, and 69 on the 7th in 1947. The best this century is 104 in January 1908. In the nineteenth century the best totals were in February, but the close season was first brought forward to the middle of that month and now commences on the 1st. Thus, the number of snipe now shot has decreased considerably, but Major Bolitho says that when out fox hunting in February it is noticeable that a lot of snipe are still about.

Most of the snipe seem to leave Cornwall in March with only small numbers remaining after the third week. No late dates have been published for the mainland, but at Scilly they include 11 May 1964, 13 May 1962 and 17 May 1963 on St Agnes, and 28 May 1965 on St Mary's.

There is little information on wintering numbers at Scilly. About twenty is probably normal at St Agnes but 70 to 100 have been present, while St Mary's and other islands with larger areas of marshland must surely hold more (Parslow[1]). Peak numbers in October-November are usually 20 to 30, but as many as 50 to 60 were seen in 1961 and 1962.

Birds breeding in Iceland, the Faeroe Islands, Orkney and Shetland are regarded by many ornithologists as a distinct sub-species although difficult to identify even in the hand. One ringed on Fair Isle, 17 October 1950 (as full grown), was shot on Bodmin Moor on 11 October 1952, and a nestling ringed at Fnjoskadalur, Iceland, 3 July 1954, killed itself against wires on Tresco, 17 February 1955. A full grown bird ringed at Utterslev Mose, near Copenhagen, Denmark on 25 August 1956 was shot near Redruth c. 12 January 1957. Seven birds ringed elsewhere in Britain have been recovered in Cornwall. A nestling ringed at Southport, Lancs., 8 June 1917, was recovered at Helston (date not known). All other records refer to adults ringed in autumn or winter in Yorkshire, Northamptonshire, Gloucestershire, Oxfordshire, Essex and Surrey. The only local recovery refers to a bird ringed on St Agnes and shot two months later on St Mary's.

The North American form—'Wilson's snipe' (*Gallinago gallinago delicata*) is doubtfully distinguishable from the European race. One supposed shot in Cornwall in 1838 (z, 1872) was regarded by Harting as a British form and the only accepted example is one shot on South Uist in the Hebrides in October 1920.

The melanistic form of the common snipe —the Sabine's snipe, which appears to be confined to Britain, especially Ireland where it was first noticed in 1822—has been obtained in Cornwall. Clark (vCH) wrote that it had been shot frequently but the only published records are—

1862   One killed at Carnanton, St Mawgan-in-Pydar about 3 January was examined by no less an ornithologist than Gould who originally regarded this variety as a separate species (z).

pre-   Bullmore reported one shot on "Mrs.
1866   Dillin's Moors", St Just-in-Penwith.

1876   One killed near Lanyon Quoit, Madron about 5 January (z).

The only more recent record is one put up in Cornwall by Michael Rogers on 29 October 1944.

## GREAT SNIPE     *Gallinago media*

A century ago the great or solitary snipe was a scarce but regular autumn visitor to Britain. Since then it has become progressively more rare, reflecting the decline of breeding numbers in Scandinavia and Russia. It has always been less common in south-west England than in eastern districts.

Unusual numbers were reported in Britain in 1868. In that year Rodd noted one from Crowdy Marsh near Camelford on 3 November (z), and two others were reported near Falmouth Moor (G, 8.10 & 15.10. '68).

Rodd (1880) noted less than a dozen individuals and while his list is evidently not comprehensive, it seems difficult to believe Clark (vCH) that between 30 and 40 had been recorded from the drier moors, mostly in the west of the county. Only two had been reported from Scilly, one from Great Ganilly in January 1877, and another between that date and 1879 (z, 1906).

The only records this century are—

1940   One said to have been seen on St Mary's on 5 January (AR).

1949   Two, thought to be this species, flushed from Tamar Lake on 22 August.

1958   One on St Agnes on 26 October.

1962   One on St Agnes on 27 and 30 April.

1963   One on St Mary's in January.

## JACK SNIPE     *Lymnocryptes minimus*

The jack snipe is a passage migrant and winter visitor to Britain from breeding localities within the forest belt from northern Scandinavia and the Baltic eastwards.

The jack snipe's Cornish name *dama kyogh* or 'snipe's mother' has been corrupted to 'dameku' in dialect. 'Hatter-flitter' is yet another local name recorded by Borlase but this more properly referred to the common snipe being a local variation of the widespread 'heather-bleater'.

While not as plentiful as the common or 'full' snipe, the 'jack' was considered by nineteenth century authors to be a common winter visitor as universally distributed as its larger cousin. F. R. Rodd (MS) wrote, "It is sometimes found, especially on first arrival, in small flocks. At Crowdy Marsh, October 1860, I killed eight out of nine without moving from one place. In March 1859 I found several Jack Snipes moulting and scarcely able to fly—no tail feathers and very few large wing feathers." Harvey (1915) described it as regular and fairly plentiful in the Land's End peninsula, but few records have been published since then. In 1931 G. H. Harvey referring to the same area wrote, "I am told by sportsmen that it occurs in small numbers . . . I do not know the bird". There is little information on its present status in Cornwall but the lack of records in game books suggests that it is now less common. Lord St Levan[1] wrote that he would put up not more than two or three in any one day, but Major Bolitho[1] wrote that "at Trengwainton (Madron) the little snipe shooting we do is with one or two guns and a keeper, probably with dogs, walking up the snipe in the bogs. The full snipe get up wild; the jack snipe sit tight and are put up by the guns or dogs. The tendency therefore, is to kill a greater proportion of the jack snipe present than of the full snipe present. While there are not as many 'jacks' as full snipe, I think there are probably more than Lord St Levan suggested . . . as he shoots driven snipe. This entails a few men walking over the ground at quite a distance from each other—enough to flush an ordinary snipe. Jack snipe sit much tighter and unless the beater almost walks on one, it would not be risen." Most recent records in CBWPS reports are of single birds, the maximum being six at Hayle on 15 January 1963. Birds are found in marshy areas throughout the county—an apparent concentration near reservoirs and estuaries indicating the movements of bird-watchers rather than birds.

Nineteenth century records from Scilly are quite spectacular. F. R. Rodd recorded (Rodd, 1880) an "immense flight" of 'jacks' and a good many full snipe on 21 December 1864, killing twenty-five of the former. "I had four Jack snipes and one full snipe on the ground at once, and killed six Jack snipes without moving from one place." 1870 proved to be an exceptional autumn with snipe and woodcocks in unusual numbers and 'jacks' actually outnumbering the full snipe by two to one in the earlier flights. The first arrived on 20 September and fourteen couples were bagged on 5 October. Other totals quoted for that year are—50 shot from 1–12 November, 11 killed on St Mary's on 26 November, 24 killed on Tresco on 2 December, and about 40 killed on St Mary's on 10 December. At least 150 were shot—mostly on St Mary's Moors (z, 1872). F. R. Rodd noted "A similar immigration . . . on the Cornish moors some years ago at the beginning of October, when on the last day of an east wind and long drought, I killed nineteen couples of Snipe, most of them Jacks, in the forenoon; The weather completely breaking up at 2 p.m. with thunder and a flood of rain from the N.W. On both these occasions it would appear that the Snipes migrated with the last of a favourable wind as if foreseeing the rain, which would open up their winter feeding grounds." Another 'good' season was that of 1878–79 when 73 jacks were killed (Rodd, 1880) and it is evident that some flights in the nineteenth century were comparable in size with those of full snipe.

Information since 1880 is very sparse, but 'jacks' are now regarded as uncommon migrants at Scilly. At St Agnes, the Observatory reports five or six annually in autumn. Most remain only a day or two, but in 1962 several remained by the Pool for at least three weeks. First flights are usual in the first half of October with further influxes sometimes in November. There were up to five on St Agnes on 26–28 November 1963 and single birds were reported throughout December 1967. Early arrival dates include 17 September 1959 on Tresco and 22 September 1964 on St Agnes. On the mainland Clark knew of one as early as 1 September (RI, 1908). Although the *Handbook* gives spring passage migrants as arriving on the south coast between late March and late April, only three single 'jacks' have been recorded between 10 March and 23 April by the St Agnes Observatory. One was seen on St Mary's on 13 May 1962. Late dates on the mainland include single birds at Hayle Kimbro near the Lizard on 10 April 1960 and at Leedstown on 18 April 1958.

# WOODCOCK    *Scolopax rusticola*

The woodcock breeds throughout much of temperate Europe. In Britain it has increased greatly this century, especially north-west of the Humber-Severn line, but remains largely absent from south-west England.

The Cornish for woodcock is *kevelek*, (pl. *kevelogas*) meaning 'little-steed' and similar to the Welsh *cyffylog*. There are few breeding records for Cornwall. The earliest is by Borlase (1758) who wrote that—"Some gentlemen, hunting in the neighbourhood of Penzance, in the summer-time 1755, flushed a woodcock; surprised at seeing such a winter bird at that season of the year, they hastened to the bush and there found a nest with two eggs in it; a gentleman, more curious than the rest, carried the eggs home; and being accidentally broken, the body of a young woodcock appeared, and encouraged him to put the other under a pigeon, and in a few days a living bird was discovered in it with its feathers on . . ."

Although Polwhele (1816) wrote that woodcocks "sometimes nested" in the county, the 1755 record was the only one published until 1843 when Couch wrote (Supplement to 1838 *Fauna*) that in the first week in June "a young woodcock was sent to Mr. C. Jackson, for preservation, that was found on the public road near Bodmin, and when discovered it was scarcely dead. As it was not of age for distant flight, it was judged to have been dropped where found, by the parents; which have been supposed to be in the habit of carrying their young to their feeding places, before they have acquired sufficient strength to convey themselves." This must be the first of the two instances of young birds in the area known to N. Hare who gives details only of the second—late June 1849 "when young had been knocked down with a stick on a marsh by the gamekeeper at Boconnoc . . . In May he several times saw a pair of adults near the same spot" (PZ). Rodd (1880) mentioned a nest of four eggs near Callington in the summer of 1853—the last definite record for the county. One August about 1948 R. J. Beswetherick[1] saw a woodcock at Venn Farm, Launcells carrying something between its legs which could have been a young bird. On the Tregothnan estate near Truro, H. Millington[1] flushed a very small young bird from a barley field in August 1966, but was unable to find a nest. There are a few other records of woodcock in summer; one was killed at Clowance in Crowan on 24 June 1905 (VCH) and single birds were seen in early August 1890 at Woods Farm, Stratton (D & M, 1892), at Penzance in 1900 (VCH) and at Trewornan on the Camel on 29 August 1962.

Woodcock are more common in Cornwall in winter than elsewhere in England, their "palatable migration" as Rodd called it, is delightfully described by Carew (1602) —"But, amongst all the rest [wild-birds], the inhabitants are most beholden to the woodcocks who (when the season of the year affordeth) flock to them in great abundance. They arrive first on the north coast, where almost every hedge serveth for a road, and every plashshoot [marsh] for springles [traps] to take them; from whence, as the moist places which supply them with food begin to freeze up, they draw towards those in the south coast, which are kept more open by the summer's nearer neighbourhood; and when the summer's heat (with the same effect from a contrary cause) drieth up those plashes, nature and necessity guide their return to the northern wetter soil again."

Remarkably large woodcock flights in west Cornwall, especially in hard weather, have attracted much comment. Robert Heath was probably the correspondent at St Mary's who told Gilbert White of Selbourne "that in the night between the 10th and 11th of this month [October, year not given but probably *c.* 1750], the wind being west, there fell such a flight of woodcocks within the walls of the garrison, that he himself shot and conveyed home twenty-six couple, besides three couple which he wounded, but did not give himself the trouble to retrieve. On the following day, the 12th, the wind continuing west, he found but few . . . some woodcock settled in the street of St Mary's and ran into the houses and outhouses." Heath also remarked that it was only easterly and northerly winds that usually took large numbers to the Scillies, and suggested that the present flight derived from Ireland.

J. A. Paris (*Guide to Mount's Bay,* 1816) found that woodcock arrived at Scilly before anywhere else in England, "most frequently with a north-east, though sometimes, with a north-west wind, and are often so exhausted as to be caught in great numbers by the inhabitants, especially near the lighthouse, the splendour of which appears to attract them, and striking against its lantern they not unfrequently fall lifeless in the gallery".

Other birds met a watery end, for Warner (*A Tour through Cornwall,* 1808) was told that in 1806 in strong north-east winds, "the poor voyagers were exhausted

before they could reach the land, and falling into the sea, were drowned, drifted on shore, and picked up, in vast numbers, by the peasantry . . . a casualty, which it should seem, not unfrequently attends the migration of the woodcock". There are no modern accounts, however, of such an occurrence, the only similar record (z, 1848) being reported "some years ago" a few miles off Land's End where the sea was strewn with hundreds of woodcock. Some of them when picked up were found to be perfectly fresh.

Flights of exceptional size are not of annual occurrence. Amongst the most notable of the last century was in 1855 with north-east winds at the end of October. Vast numbers were killed; a St Buryan farmer procured 54 in a week, while on Tresco 39 were shot in a day (z, 1856 & Rodd, 1880). The most memorable season at Scilly was in 1878–79 when 42 were taken in one day with a total bag of 415, compared with the previous highest total of 223 in 1860 (z, 1879 & 1906).

By mid-January woodcock have become scarcer in most years, but in the winter of 1881 an unusual flight occurred at the end of the month, nearly 50 couples being killed at a time when shooting would ordinarily have finished (PZ, 1885–88). Clogg (z, 1881) wrote that birds were to be seen about the streets of Polperro and local boys had been able to catch five of them with bent pins baited with worms and attached by short strings to pegs driven into the ground.

Few woodcock records are now published giving the impression that the species has become rare in the county. This is far from being the case as game-book records indicate Indeed, Major Bolitho[1] considers them to be more common now; the bags on his Trengwainton estate at Madron, shew a steadily increasing trend which cannot be accounted for only by the improvement in shotguns and cartridges.

Major Bolitho wrote that "the woodcock arrive in flights; that is there may be none about one day and a considerable quantity the next. Such flights normally occur after the October, November, and December full moons. If these periods of bright nights (for none seem to migrate in foggy weather) coincide with hard weather conditions up country, then the flight will be greater. If on the other hand, through melting snow or other reasons there is fog, the flight will be reduced. The birds that arrive on the October moon do not stay in west Cornwall; after a period of no longer than a week they continue their migration. The November and December woodcock stay in the county. On their arrival they often pitch in on the moors and on the north coast in an exhausted state and can be shot only too easily, not flying any distance when put up. After a short time they move down into the wooded, wet valleys where there is good feeding.

"In the cold winter of 1962–63 the frozen ground over the rest of England drove great quantities of woodcock down to Cornwall. The normal bag for Treng-wainton would average about 120—that season 515 were shot. I handled practically all of these and only two were not in good condition; east of Truro birds were said to be in poor shape. Woodcock are normally found in sheltered, scrubby, wooded valleys and feed in marshes; that winter they were to be found close to springs and running water where normally one would expect to find snipe. Presumably the woodcock were able to get their beaks into the ground and so retain condition, but whether they drove the snipe from their usual haunts I cannot say. A year or two after the hard winter there were fewer woodcock about, but they had returned to their previous numbers by the third winter." A note in the Lanarth Game Book suggested woodcock kept condition partly by being forced to feed for 24 hours a day to obtain sufficient nourish-ment, instead of feeding by night and sleeping by day.

West Cornwall is clearly the focal point of woodcock in the county as the game-books at Lanarth in St Keverne clearly indicate. The best day's bag normally occurs in late December, the first few days

Lelant Station on the St Ives branch line – an excellent vantage point fronting the Hayle estuary especially for watching waders at half-tide

of January, or occasionally in late November —84 on 29 November 1927. Very wet autumns make the covers too wet for the woodcock which like dry ground to rest on by day, so that game totals are poor, as in 1960–61 with 48 on 2 January and a season's total of 116. That season the November full moon fell early in the month—probably too early to give a good flight of resident birds. The poorest season this century was certainly 1936–37 with a total of only 72, 38 of them on 5 December.

The woodcock is normally seen from mid-October; early dates from the Lanarth game-book are—26 September 1956; 1 October 1953; 4 October 1960; 7 October 1959; 8 October 1945; and 12 October 1945.

One of the most outstanding seasons at Lanarth was 1920–21 when on 21 December 106 birds were shot—still the record one day bag for England and Wales. The season's total of 198, while good, was not record-breaking; compare 301 in 1948–49, when the best day's bag was 87 on 3 January. No shooting was done in the war years, but 1940 was probably exceptional for more were seen in the covers round the Lodge at Lanarth in late January than had been seen before, even in the "106 year".

Arctic conditions up-country in 1962–63 drove phenomenal numbers into the south-west. Many weak birds were reported close to houses, especially in east Cornwall—for instance at Bude—and dozens of un-protesting birds were picked up from the semi-frozen road-sides about St Columb. Others were seen feeding in open fields in the Tamar valley, on cliff tops at Bude and the Lizard peninsula between Housel Bay and Kynance. Most were seen in January with a great decrease about early February, the majority having gone by the 15th. At Scilly, birds must have come close to the 1920–21 total "for local people reported over 3,000 shot and certainly over 1,000 were killed by my knowledge" (Parslow[1]). At Lanarth 244 were shot that season—76 on 3 January—equalling the best day's bag at Antony House, at the other end of the county, on 21 January, where the birds had probably been driven from Dartmoor. Woodcock appeared in large numbers where a few are normally shot. A shoot in mid-January realized 49 in Hustyn wood and the valleys at the back of Wadebridge—"normally we are pleased to kill ten in the same area" (Lanarth game book). The season produced 100 at Boconnoc, Lostwithiel, compared with 26 in 1966–67. The record here is 233 in 1928. Major Fortescue[1] reported that at Boconnoc woodcock are never seen in such large numbers as in the more suitable wet woods and bottoms of west Cornwall, but that totals do not give a really fair picture of the numbers present, for the woods are large and infested with *Rhododendron ponticum* which makes the birds difficult to get at.

Little is known of the spring migration but it must be considerably lighter than the pronounced autumn movements. The bulk of resident birds seem to depart in late February. The latest date known to Clark (RI, 1902) was 1 March 1881, although Bullmore in 1866 wrote of one that year in Argal Moor, Budock as late as 1 April. With the shooting season ending on 31 January, late records are understandably few. The latest date is 19 March on St Mary's in 1964, and 20 March on St Agnes in 1962. Late dates on the mainland are 7 March 1959 in the Fowey valley, two at Carclew, Mylor on 17 March 1945, and one near Minster church on 13 March 1943. In other parts of Britain, migration takes place until well into April or even early May, but few records come from Cornwall at this time. In 1946 Dorrien-Smith saw a bird fly in from the south and land in a boat at East Porthcressa, St Mary's on 12 April—when flushed it continued its journey northwards. One bird was flushed (presumably near Trengwainton) on 10 April 1943, and another in the Nanven valley at dusk on 12 April 1936. The former bird was described as "apparently uninjured" for local sportsmen assumed that woodcock seen at this late date were wounded birds unable to migrate.

Birds breeding in southern England are largely sedentary, as are most Irish birds. About a third of the woodcock bred in Scotland and the north of England migrate, largely to Ireland but partly to southern England and even as far south as France and the Iberian peninsula. Considering the vast numbers shot in Cornwall, the recovery of ringed birds has been very small.

| Ringed as Young | Recovered |
|---|---|
| Netherby, Cumberland 15.5.'12 | shot, Trewarthenick, Cornelly 28.11.'12 |
| Baehomie, Perthshire 17.5.'28 | St Levan 27.12.'28 |
| Ardoch, Perthshire 2.7.'33 | shot, St Mary's 20.12.'33 |
| Rijsterbos, Friesland, Holland, 28.10.'60 | found dead, Liskeard 16.2.'63 |

## UPLAND SANDPIPER (OR PLOVER) *Bartramia longicauda*

The upland sandpiper, or Bartram's sandpiper in older literature, is an American species recorded less than twenty times in Britain.

1865 Bullmore bought one at Webber's poultry shop in Falmouth which had been shot in a turnip field at or near Goonhilly on 6 November (z).

1883 One shot near St Keverne in October (z & RI, 1907).

1903 Another found in a Falmouth poulterer's in October had been shot in the Lizard peninsula (z & RI, 1907).

1922 One shot on Tresco on 22 September (BB).

1960 One after heavy gales on St Mary's airport from 17 to 28 November.

1968 One at St Just airport near Land's End on 6 October. Two on St Mary's and Tresco from 26 September to 8 October.

## CURLEW *Numenius arquata*

The curlew nests widely in Europe outside the Mediterranean region. In the north it is replaced by the whimbrel. The breeding population in Britain has increased this century, being found in every county in England and Wales except in the south-east.

*Gelvinak* is the Cornish for curlew, a name that describes its long, curved bill. It is the most common large wader in the county and for that reason a species on which little information has been published. While the curlew is mentioned by Carew (1602) no writer gave any information on breeding until Couch (1838) wrote that "a few remain to breed in the high grounds". However, it was probably more plentiful—at least on Bodmin Moor—than this statement suggests. Rodd (1880) called it common in some years on Bodmin Moor noting that the "moor-men" searched eagerly for the young which were considered great delicacies. F. R. Rodd (MS) wrote that curlews bred on all the moors, but seldom more than one pair to each marsh. Rodd's statement is a good yardstick for measuring the present density of breeding on Bodmin Moor; a complete survey has never been undertaken, but of St Breward parish (6,800 acres) Col. Almond[1] wrote that "a breeding population would average eight to ten pairs; I believe I know each territory. Occasionally a territory is empty for a season, but usually for not more than two years in succession. While some pairs nest in the Rough Tor and Brown Willy areas, others are closer to St Breward. For example, there is usually one pair, sometimes two, on Lady Downs—Emblance Downs—King Arthur's Hall."

Clark (VCH) thought curlews bred near Kilkhampton—about 1947 or 1948, but not since, R. J. Beswetherick[1] found nests in an uncultivated fifty-acre field at Venn Farm in Launcells parish. Curlews certainly nested in fields near Tamar Lake and in Whitstone parish in the 1950's, and perhaps further south near Red Post (Treleaven[1]).

In mid-Cornwall, R. J. Salmon[1] has found birds "present every summer on many of the tin-streaming wastes where a combination of lank herbage and surface water is to be found—as at Redmoor,

Rosewarrick, Breeney Common and Bo-kiddick Moor near Lanivet". In 1939 a nest was found in a valley near Demelza, St Wenn where curlews are still found every year. On Goss Moor itself, one pair (perhaps two) frequents the westerly end south of the main A30 near St Dennis railway junction, and another pair has been seen inter-mittently over the years (but not in 1968) north of the A30 near the A.A. box. D. F. Mussen[1] wrote that curlews are wide-spread on both Bodmin and Goss moors having seen young in both these areas as well as at Lanhydrock near Bodmin and Bocon-noc near Lostwithiel in 1967 and 1968. Birds have nested on St Breock Down, as near Nine Maidens in 1944, but there are no recent records.

Birds have bred in West Penwith, Clark (VCH) giving Lady Downs near Penzance as a locality. Harvey (1915) wrote that they possibly bred on the moors and Miss Quick knew of records before the last war. N. R. Phillips[1], suspects a few pairs may still nest there. Goonhilly Downs is another breeding area cited by Clark in 1906. Of this locality A. G. Parsons[1] writes "I have found egg shells on Goonhilly Downs, and I have also seen pairs on territory on Lizard and Predannack Downs where I have also suspected breeding."

Breeding curlews take to the moors in March—actual nesting beginning in late April. As soon as the young can fly, Col. Almond (1959) has found that they come down regularly to feed in newly cut hay fields, especially in the early morning. In the late summer and early autumn, small parties regularly fly from St Breward in the direction of the Camel estuary about the time the tide starts to ebb, and return with the flood—a practice continued at night judging by their calling. Very few winter on the moors, but there is evidence of a passage in spring and autumn.

Non-breeding birds are always present on some estuaries in May and June—for example, over twenty were counted at St Clement on the Tresillian river on 23 May 1966. By July the autumn migration has started, for at St Clement the number had risen to over 200 on 1st July 1966. The size of flocks at migration time and in winter has received scant attention. Up to 500 would seem to be about normal in autumn at Hayle, about 200 at Tresillian, and 400 at Ruan Lanihorne and on the Lynher.

On Scilly, the curlew has never been known to nest but some non-breeding birds are present throughout the summer—up to fifteen in June 1962 on St Agnes. Autumn flocks normally number less than a hundred —80 in October 1961 on St Agnes where 30 to 50 is the probable average. Miss Quick[1] writes that she has never seen any notably large flocks on St Agnes—parties of a dozen or twenty being usual even on migration. Larger flocks may occur on the airport or the golf course on St Mary's, but none are known to her. The only published record of a larger flock was in 1870 when 200–300 were seen on 1 November (Rodd, 1880).

Three nestlings ringed in Cumberland, Staffordshire, and Yorkshire, were all recovered on the Camel estuary. Adults ringed at Lundy Island, Dawlish Warren, and Hayle shew only local movements. Recoveries of foreign birds are—

| Ringed as Nestlings | Recovered |
|---|---|
| Ermelo, Gelderland, Holland 24.6.'36 | Truro 11.9.'36 |
| Wijnjeterp, Friesland, Holland 5.7.'64 | shot, Camel estuary 1.9.'64 |
| Karup, Skåne, Sweden 19.6.'30 | Camel estuary 17.8.'33 |
| nr. Mariestad, Skaraborg, Sweden 10.6.'30 | St Mary's 8.8.'30 |

## WHIMBREL          *Numenius phaeopus*

The whimbrel nests in Europe to the north of, and at a greater altitude than, the curlew. In Britain, breeding is practically confined to the Shetland Islands. Birds winter as far south as the Cape of Good Hope, but a few remain in this country and in recent years one or two have been recorded annually in Cornwall—notably at Hayle and the St John's Lake area. Two were seen at Cawsand, Rame from November to April 1966.

The whimbrel is best known as a migrant. So familiar are the birds in late spring, that it has earned itself the name of 'May-bird'. 'The Seven whistler' is another popular name and Mathews (*History of St Ives*, 1892) stated that its arrival at night was regarded with apprehension by the local fishermen for whom whistling after dark was a portent of some misfortune, such as the failure of the pilchard shoals. Early in the nineteenth century the autumn migration seems to have been the more prominent, at least at Scilly, for Boyd (BB, 1930) recalled that the island fishermen knew it as the 'Harvest curlew'. During the 1840's it was sufficiently common in early autumn to merit a column to itself in the Tresco game-book, but it gradually became more scarce at that time of the year. Thus in 1843, fourteen were shot, but from 1856 to 1867 a total of only four was reached. At the end of the century two or three only were seen in autumn (z, 1906).

The spring passage occurs from mid-April onwards. Early dates include single birds at Marazion Marsh on 2 April 1961 and at Torpoint on 3 April 1964. A flock was seen moving up channel at Looe as early as 21 March 1877 (z). June records are not uncommon, as a few birds may remain in the county until caught up in the autumn migration. Thus on St Agnes birds were seen almost daily from 20 April to 11 July 1963 with a maximum of twenty in early May. The return migration, at its peak from about mid-August to mid-September, commences about mid-July. One was seen flying in from the sea at Widemouth Bay on 9 July 1962. Few remain after the first week in October—14 October 1962 at Scilly. Later dates may refer to the few wintering birds.

Even at migration time the whimbrel is largely solitary, although parties more numerous than the normal two or three are not uncommon. In 1944 twenty were counted in a flock on St Enodock golf-links —a favourite haunt—on 15 May, while at Kennack Bay near Lizard on the 3rd, parties of up to twenty were watched flying in from the south. The previous year some forty were counted at Tregorden Marsh on 11 May. Larger movements may be more common than records suggest. At Widemouth on 23 April 1966 a constant movement of flocks of 20–30 birds progressed along the coast throughout the day, one flock of 50 settling in a field near the sea at dusk. At least 300, and possibly over 400, were seen at Marazion Marsh on 28 April 1968, where a similar movement was reported on 2 May 1936 when whimbrel passed over the Marsh at the rate of 200 an hour. Several hundred were reported on St Mary's in May 1903 (z, 1906), but there are no recent reports of large movements from the islands.

| Ringed | Recovered |
|---|---|
| St Agnes, full grown 24.4.'60 | killed, Pointe de la Courbe, Charente-Maritime 24.4.'63 |

## ESKIMO (ESKIMAUX) CURLEW *Numenius borealis*

The Eskimo curlew is an American species which is now almost extinct. Lack of fear made it an easy prey and it was shot in vast numbers in the last century. There are nine or ten British records, the last authenticated one being an adult in full breeding plumage shot on Tresco by Dorrien-Smith on 10 September 1887 (z).

## BLACK-TAILED GODWIT *Limosa limosa*

The black-tailed godwit breeds in Iceland and in a belt from Holland and southern

Sweden across to eastern Asia. Formerly a common nester in eastern England, it became extinct about the 1840's until 1952, since when there has been one regular

*Black-tailed godwit*

breeding site in East Anglia with sporadic records elsewhere, including Somerset in 1963.

In Cornwall it is a migrant and winter visitor, now much more common than formerly. It was first recorded in the county by Walter Moyle (Tonkin MS) who shot two in the winter of 1715–16, but until the 1930's it remained a casual migrant, mainly in September and April, although one was shot at Swanpool on 12 December 1846 (Cocks, 1851). Clark, writing in 1902 (RI), had not recorded one since September 1893 at Helford river, while on the Scillies only five records were published between 1849 and April 1903 (Z, 1906). One was reported at Marazion Marsh from 7–21 March 1923 (BB) with the comment that it "seems to be of very casual appearance in Cornwall". However, numbers seen on passage increased in the 1920's, for in 1931 some were said to occur at Marazion and Lelant every spring and autumn. No birds wintered, for the latest date reported was 2 November

1924 and the earliest 21 February 1926 at Marazion.

Wintering birds appeared for the first time about the mid 1930's. There were 25 at Millbrook on the Lynher on 3 February 1935 and the same sized flock definitely wintered there the following year. East and mid-Cornwall remain its main winter quarters. Considerable movement occurs between adjoining creeks, so that birds will appear, for example, on the Truro and Ruan rivers when none are seen at Tresillian.

| Average winter maximum | | Maximum | | |
|---|---|---|---|---|
| Lynher | 1960–67 c. 240 | 300 | 30 September | 1967 |
| Tamar | 1960–66 c. 290 | c. 400 | 26 August | 1961 |
| St John's Lake | 3 yrs. c. 200 | 230 | 13 February | 1966 |
| Ruan River | 4 yrs. c. 220 | 400 | 23 December | 1966 |
| Tresillian | 1960–66 130 | 203 | 16 December | 1961 |

Birds do not normally winter on the Camel estuary, about 40 on 5 January 1966 at Dinham were not seen previously or subsequently. As far west as Hayle only a few are reported outside the migration periods; the first wintering bird was seen here from 30 December 1957 until well into 1958.

The autumn migration normally commences in July. Early dates include four at Cargreen on the Tamar on 9 July 1966 rising to 75 on the 30th, 8 July 1965 on the Lynher, and 3 July 1961 at Ruan Lanihorne. Unusual was one on the Camel estuary on 3 June 1953. The main departure in spring occurs in April. Late dates are 17 May 1961 at Tresillian, 14 May 1960 on the Tamar, and 12 May 1961 at Hayle. On migration, flocks appear at inland localities as well as on the estuaries. Rarely are they seen at Tamar Lake (up to nine in early September 1962) but are more common from west Cornwall with records from Drift reservoir, Hayle Kimbro and other pools on the Lizard downs. At Stithians reservoir over a hundred were seen in late March 1966 with one remaining until 10 May—few, however, were seen there in the autumn or in 1967.

On the Scillies the black-tailed godwit is almost exclusively a passage migrant, the only winter records being four in December and January 1956–57 and up to two at St Mary's in early February 1965. Small numbers occur on migration, the maximum being parties of 34 from 6 to 12 March 1966 on Tresco and 25 on St Agnes at the same time. In the autumn, twenty were seen on Tresco on 26 August 1965. All have normally departed by mid-October—the latest being 14 November 1967 on St Mary's. Spring arrivals first appear in March, as on the 2nd in 1956 and 6th in 1960 and finally leave in May—23rd in 1963 and 25th in 1965.

## BAR-TAILED GODWIT
### Limosa lapponica

The bar-tailed godwit breeds much further north than the black-tailed, nesting mainly in the tundra from north-east Scandinavia across Asia to north-west Alaska. Most birds winter in the tropics.

In Cornwall the history of the bar-tailed godwit has been less well documented than that of the black-tailed. In the nineteenth century the bar-tailed was certainly the more common of the two species (Bullmore, 1866. Rodd, 1880, etc.). It was first recorded in the county by Montagu (1813) who described a 'yarwhip' in summer plumage in a small collection at Marazion. Couch (1838) noted that at the "beginning of May 1836 numerous flocks containing many hundreds were seen by fishermen at about three leagues from land" migrating eastwards up the English Channel; one bird in advanced summer plumage was taken to Couch.

During the present century the bar-tailed godwit has become more common but the largest flocks are only half the size of those of the black-tailed. The increase has occurred mainly since about 1950, for although Harvey (1915) had recorded 70 on Penzance Eastern Green one autumn, Ryves (1948) knew of no flock larger than the 37 seen on the Camel estuary on 12 September 1943.

Apparently it was not a regular wintering bird in mainland Cornwall in the last century. Small numbers were reported wintering at Hayle by G. H. Harvey in 1931 and about 35 were seen at Millbrook on the Tamar on 16 February 1935. Few figures are published today. About a hundred were at St John's Lake in 1965–66 and 60 at Millbrook on 13 February 1966. At Hayle about a dozen is the normal winter population. In the Tresillian-Truro-Ruan estuaries, few are seen in winter although small parties are annual on migration—nineteen at Tresillian on 13 September 1960.

The largest numbers are always reported during the autumn migration which commences in July—in 1966 on the 16th at St John's Lake, 18th at Tresillian, and 23rd at Hayle. Peak numbers are usual in September but large flocks are still present in November.

| Maximum numbers | | Date |
|---|---|---|
| Camel Estuary | 250 | 14 September 1965 |
| Camel Estuary | 150 | 18 September 1963 |
| Camel Estuary | 120 | 11 September 1966 |
| Hayle Estuary | 170 | 11 September 1963 |
| Hayle Estuary | 100 | 2 November 1965 |
| St John's Lake | 150 | 7 November 1965 |

A considerable passage occurred in 1963; on the Camel only five were seen on 30 August, but in September there were 63 on 6th, 70 on 10th, 150 on 18th, 124 on 30th, 110 on 4 October and 60 still present on the 14th. At Hayle there were 120 on 8 September (with 30 at Porthkidney beach as well as a passage of 130 past St Ives on the same day) rising to 170 on 11th, 105 the following day and 80 on the 15th. Most flocks seem to move on after only a few days.

Few figures have been published for the smaller spring movements. Unusually large was a compact flock of 200 or more on Marazion beach on 4 February 1963, all but three of which had gone the next day. This flock perhaps represented the return of birds which normally winter in Britain pushed out of the country by the severe weather in the preceeding weeks. Most wintering birds and spring migrants depart in April with stragglers leaving early in May. Late dates include 15 May 1966 at Hayle, 20 May 1960 at Devoran, and 29 May 1959 at Hayle. In 1931, Harvey wrote that birds occasionally summered at Hayle and Penzance—one remained at Hayle until 24 June in 1933—but the only recent record is of one at Marazion on 3 June 1963.

The bar-tailed godwit is rarely recorded from freshwater sites, so that it is a scarce migrant at the pools on the Lizard downs where the black-tailed godwit is regular. Inland records include six at Tamar Lake on 31 May 1962, one at Crowan reservoir on 19 September 1966 and one at Stithians reservoir 31 August 1967. On several occasions since 1960 one or two have been reported with curlews on the cliff tops of the north coast, as near Park Head on 25 September 1966 and 14 on St Mawgan Airfield on 17 September 1967.

Wintering birds were reported at Scilly long before they were mentioned on the mainland. F. R. Rodd (MS) wrote that "a few years since a flock remained until April" and that "several were killed in the autumn and winter of 1870". Clark (RI, 1902) also wrote that it was fairly common at Scilly in the winter, a dozen or so probably being usual. The position seems little changed. More were seen in 1964 than in most years. In spring up to 35 were reported on most days between 19 March and 28 April, while in autumn, up to eight occurred daily from 15 August with a maximum of 30 on 1 September. In December up to sixteen on the 31st stayed until the following spring.

## GREEN SANDPIPER
*Tringa ochropus*

The green sandpiper nests in a broad belt from eastern Norway and Poland across Europe and Asia. Clark (VCH) wrote that the occurrence and behaviour of the species suggested it had bred at Trewortha Marsh in North Hill, but no nest was ever found—

hardly surprising when the only confirmed breeding records for Britain are from Westmorland (1917) and Inverness (1959).

The green sandpiper is principally a passage migrant in Cornwall. Published records are less full than for the wood sandpiper, while the picture is confused by the small number of wintering birds. March records, largely from well-known wintering haunts, may indicate the start of the very slight spring passage which is most noticeable in April.

Records between early May and mid-June are almost non-existent. Autumn passage commences at the end of June or early July, with the peak passage in August and early September. Early dates include one at Crowan reservoir on 9 June 1962 and four at Stithians reservoir on 27 June 1966. Most reports refer only to "small numbers" on the autumn migration. Single birds are most common, with frequent parties of up to four. Up to six at a time at the Abbey Pool, Tresco in early August 1964 and at Porthellick Pool, St Mary's in August and September 1967, are the most seen at Scilly, but the mainland maxima are twelve on the Camel estuary on 30 August 1942 and up to twenty at Stithians reservoir in August 1967.

Winter quarters are first occupied from about early October. Wintering was known in the nineteenth century, for D'Urban and Mathew (1892) considered it as general in south-west England and a bird was shot at Wadebridge in February 1843 (RI). Well-known wintering areas are at Trewornan and Egloshayle on the Camel, the Fal above Sett Bridge at Ruan Lanihorne, and the wet fields behind Hayle causeway. One to three birds are usual, but as many as six were seen at Devoran on 23 November 1957, and five on the Lynher on 28 December 1955. The habitat of the green sandpiper, both in winter and on migration, comprises the small channels and pools of salt, brackish and fresh water, and the shallow fringes of reservoirs. Rarely, if ever, are birds seen on the open estuary. Localities, other than those mentioned above, thus include the reservoirs at Melancoose, Argal, and Tamar Lake, Gwithian Pool, Landulph Marsh and St John's Lake.

## WOOD SANDPIPER
### *Tringa glareola*

The wood sandpiper breeds in northern Europe from the Baltic coast northwards to include part of the tundra. One pair, or more, has nested annually in northern Scotland since 1959—the first time for over a century. Clark's statement (VCH) that it may have nested in Cornwall probably refers to the statement by Rodd that a female killed near Land's End on 20 May 1840 contained the rudiments of eggs and might have bred had it remained un-molested.

The wood sandpiper, like the green sandpiper, is typically a bird of fresh and brackish waters, enjoying the shallow margins of lakes and reservoirs as well as the flooded salt-marshes and grasslands bordering estuaries. Not surprisingly, therefore, the bulk of Cornish records have come from Marazion Marsh and nearby Ponsandane, the fields behind Hayle causeway, and the Amble Marsh adjoining the Camel estuary. There are also records from other localities given under the green sandpiper.

The spring passage is much the lighter of the two and was unrecorded, for example, in 1967. The earliest date—probably the earliest in Britain—is for 8 March 1952 at Marazion. Most records fall between late April and the end of May, and consist of single birds with a maximum of four at Marazion on 14 May 1964. Records for June are few—for example one on the 8th at Marazion in 1963.

Return passage commences about early July, with the main movement throughout August until mid-September. Latest stragglers include one at Ponsandane on 3 and 4 October 1965 with another on the 10th at

Hayle, and one at Ruan Lanihorne on 12 November 1967. The sole winter record is of a bird taken in December 1837 (Rodd, 1880). This sandpiper is usually seen singly, but two or three together are reported annually, with up to half a dozen in most years. Eight were seen at Ponsandane on 27 August 1962, and eleven at Marazion Marsh on 8 September 1958—a year when there was a considerable autumn passage.

At Scilly, a few are reported in most years, mainly in autumn but also recently in May, at pools on St Agnes, St Mary's, and Tresco. The largest party consisted of nine at Periglis Pool, St Agnes on 5 July 1952—another 'good' year for wood sandpipers.

## SOLITARY (OR AMERICAN) SANDPIPER
### *Tringa solitaria*

The solitary sandpiper, similar to our green sandpiper, nests in the wooded swamps of the Canadian conifer belt and winters as far south as Brazil. About eight had been sighted in Britain up to August 1963—the second and third in Cornwall.

1882 One shot on the Lower Moors of St Mary's on 19 September (Z).

1884 One shot at Marazion Marsh in October. It passed into Vingoe's collection and realised fourteen guineas on its sale in 1889 (RI, 1907).

## COMMON SANDPIPER
### *Tringa hypoleucos*

The common sandpiper is widespread in Europe from the Mediterranean to the

*Common sandpiper*

tundra and snow-line. In Britain, breeding numbers have declined, especially since the last war in southern counties, and has disappeared completely from Cornwall. In the 1840's (PZ) it was mentioned as an annual nester on Bodmin Moor while F. R. Rodd (MS) wrote that it bred in considerable numbers in the deserted tin stream-works and wherever there are sand-banks on the Moor, as on the upper Fowey River and the shore of Dozmary Pool. Birds left the moors in July. Other localities given by Clark (VCH) are the Goss Moor and elsewhere in the china-clay district. Birds also nested beside streams and freshwater pools much further west, as at Zennor and Marazion Marsh. However, the last definite case of breeding was reported by W. H. Harvey at the Penzance reservoir in 1910 (BB, 1946). G. H. Harvey reported in 1931 that he had seen birds there as late as 12 May, but that nesting was unknown to him. Birds may have bred unobserved on the eastern moors, for bird-watching was at its lowest ebb in the county from 1910 to 1930. At the Walmsley Sanctuary on 14 May 1941, T. J. Wilcocks flushed a tame bird which he thought might have nested some-where near.

As apparently suitable breeding sites still exist in Cornwall, the decline may be due to the past climatic amelioration which has not only pushed the breeding range further north, but also been responsible for the greatly increased habit of wintering in the county. Such records were formerly very rare, but have become an annual feature since about 1955–56. Favourite localities where one or two occur, are the Trewornan and Egloshayle stretches of the Camel estuary, the upper reaches of the Fal and the Tresillian river with adjoining creeks in the Truro area. Other records have come from Hayle, the Gannel, Helford, Stithians reservoir, and the Lynher-Tamar.

The common sandpiper is a familiar passage migrant, the spring movement being by far the lighter. Birds have been reported in mid-March, as on the 14th at Hayle in 1964, but mid-April to mid-May sees the main movement. Non-breeding birds remain throughout the summer, as did up to 25 near Dinham on the Camel estuary in 1965.

The return passage normally begins about early or mid-July and lasts until mid-October, with the peak in August. Single birds and parties up to half a dozen are most common, but a noisy, compact flock of 35 was seen at Hayle on 4 August 1966. About 30 were present there on 16 July 1964, and 24 between 12 and 18 July 1953.

On Scilly a single sandpiper in 1857 (z, 1906) is the only record for the last century apart from F. R. Rodd's generalization (Rodd, 1880) that they occurred in autumn and winter, noting their arrival in 1870 in late July. Nowadays single birds and small parties are regularly reported from early April to the end of May and from mid-July to mid-October. Earliest and latest dates are 29 March 1965 and 24 October 1963 on St Mary's. The first winter record refers to a couple on St Agnes up to 21 December 1964.

# SPOTTED SANDPIPER
*Tringa macularia*

The spotted sandpiper is the North American equivalent of our common sandpiper, from which it cannot be distinguished in the field unless in breeding plumage. Indeed, it has not always been regarded as a separate species.

1924    One seen in full breeding plumage at Loe Bar near Helston on 14 June (BB).

1965    One trapped at St Agnes Observatory on 24 September was first seen the previous day and remained until 28 October (R).

1966    One on Tresco from 3 September to 1 October was trapped and ringed. Another was seen on St Agnes between 23 and 25 September (R).

1967    One on St Agnes from 6 to 21 September (R).

1968    One on St Agnes from 18 to 29 September was reported on Tresco on 1 October. Another at Porthgwarra on 28 October was found dead there on 3 November (R).

REDSHANK                *Tringa totanus*

The redshank breeds in much of temperate Europe but has decreased considerably in southern Britain in the past twenty years. South-west England is on the edge of its range. In Devon a few pairs nested on the Exe near Stoke Canon until wiped out in the winter of 1962–63.

In Cornwall the redshank is apparently more common now than in the early nineteenth century. Couch (1838) described it as rare in winter, but Gatcombe, after recording a flock of about 30 on the Lynher, wrote in 1877 (z) that "within the last few years, immense flocks have remained on our rivers during the winter . . . some were still about on 10 April. I am beginning to hope that if unmolested, some may at length be induced to nest in the neighbourhood." A pair did nest at Slapton Ley in south Devon in 1894 (the only record until 1937 on the Exe) and D'Urban and Mathew (1892) and Clark (RI, 1902) thought birds might be nesting in Cornwall. However, the only record was for a pair near Roche on Goss Moor in 1904 (VCH). Breeding may have occurred in 1968 for D. F. Musson[1] saw five adult redshanks with two young "not yet able to fly", on the mudflats of the River Fowey at St Winnow on 17 June.

The ubiquitous redshank is rarely ever completely absent from the estuaries. Although a particular estuary may appear empty at the height of the breeding season, a few are generally reported from a few localities in May and early June. First autumn arrivals are commonly seen about 15 to 25 June with numbers increasing, for example, to approximately 200 at Ruan Lanihorne and 100 at Hayle by about 20 July. The few published figures indicate a peak passage in late August and September.

Tamar. 1,200 on 2 September 1965; 1,000 on 5 September 1963 and on 18 August 1962.

Lynher. 1,000 or more on 5 September 1964.

Ruan Lanihorne. 500 on 2 September 1967.

Restronguet Creek. Over 300 on 14 September 1963.

Hayle. No figures available—200 to 300 probably usual.

Camel. The most recorded here is 80 on 8 August 1965 and 25 September 1966—probably indicative of the lack of records rather than scarcity of birds.

Observations on the Gannel by A. H. Glanville from 1959 to 1961 shewed that winter residents arrived in October. Passage migrants were reported in 1961 in July and August as well as a single bird on 7 September. No more were seen until two arrived on 8 October. On the 21st, six were present, including a partial albino which proved to be a useful marker, for its continued presence shewed that these birds were true winter residents. Another albino, perhaps the same bird, was also present in 1962.

About 200 at Tresillian are usual from November to late February, but little information is available for mid-winter totals on other estuaries, and none for the spring migration which appears comparatively light. Most redshanks depart in March but diminishing numbers remain until late April—20 April 1965 at St John's Lake, 23 April 1959 and 3 May 1961 at Scilly. Few are seen away from the coast but certainly more than published records suggest. At Stithians reservoir in 1966, one was present on 10 February, one on 24 June, and seven on 22 July.

Compared with the mainland, few redshanks are seen on the Scillies, although precise information is lacking. The maximum number published is a flock of about 25 on St Agnes from 24 to 28 November 1963, while the only winter total is ten in late December the same year on St Agnes.

Continental birds must pass through Cornwall on migration while others presumably winter, but only British birds have been recovered.

| *Ringed* | *Recovered* |
|---|---|
| Hampton in Arden, Warwickshire, nestling 22.5.'14 | shot, Landulph 29.1.'15 |
| Rockcliffe Marsh, Cumberland, nestling 17.5.'30 | found dead, Polbathick, St Germans 24.7.'30 |
| nr. Uldale, Westmorland, juvenile 15.5.'37 | found dead, Saltash 25.1.'38 |
| Wilpshire Moor, Lancashire, adult 7.5.'55 | found dead, Newlyn 3.11.'55 |
| Sandbach, Cheshire, juvenile 23.6.'63 | found dead, Newlyn 4.3.'65 |

## SPOTTED REDSHANK
*Tringa erythropus*

The spotted redshank breeds in northern Europe and Asia in a narrow belt roughly following the southern boundary of the tundra. Birds winter mainly in countries bordering the Mediterranean. The wintering of the spotted redshank in Britain is generally described as exceptional. Historic records from Cornwall are indeed very rare, the only one from the last century being a bird shot at Goonhilly and bought at Falmouth market on 3 December 1858 (Bullmore, 1866). Now they are almost commonplace, one or two have annually wintered on the Fal between Ruan Lanihorne and Ardevora since at least 1950, and on the Tresillian River since about 1956. More recently a few have been reported from the Camel, the Tamar-Lynher-St John's Lake area, and the Hayle estuary. On migration spotted redshanks are most often reported from these estuaries, less frequently at Marazion Marsh and Crowan reservoir, with rare records from such localities as Drift and Stithians reservoirs, Croft Pascoe at Goonhilly, and Tamar Lake.

Wintering birds leave about mid-March—the same time as the light spring passage commences. Early dates include 16 March 1966 at Marazion Marsh. The passage lasts until about mid-April or even early May when a few birds may be seen in their smart breeding plumage, as one on the Camel on 4 May 1965.

Since the first spotted redshank was recorded by Rodd near Land's End in early September 1840, the species had been regarded as an autumn casual with most records in August. Since the mid-1950's and especially since 1960, autumn records have increased in numbers and frequency. Ones or twos are most usual, but every year groups of four to six are reported. Larger numbers include eleven at Salter Mill on the Tamar in 1961, nine on the Camel in 1960 and at Ruan in 1966, and eight on the Camel in 1964 and 1966.

Autumn passage ordinarily commences about mid-August, but birds earlier in the month have become more frequent in the past few years. Earliest dates include 27 June 1967 at Stithians reservoir, 6 July 1967 on the Camel estuary and 22 July 1964 at Hayle. The main movement dies away from mid-September. October records certainly include passage migrants—eight at Clifton on the Tamar on 26 October 1963 were very late for such a large party—but November records normally come from the well-known wintering areas.

On the Scillies, it is an autumn migrant in ones or twos and rarely observed in spring—one was seen at St Agnes on 7 April 1967. The largest party consisted of seven at Tresco on 30 August 1964. There are no winter records from the islands.

## GREATER YELLOWLEGS
*Tringa melanoleucus*

The greater yellowlegs or 'tell-tale' is an American species found in Britain much less frequently than the lesser yellowlegs. The only Cornish records are—

1906 One shot on Tresco by Dorrien-Smith on 16 September (BB, 1907–8)—the first European record.

1927 A very tame bird was watched at close quarters on Tresco from 28 August to 3 September (BB, 1926–27).

1939 One was flushed at the Abbey Pool on Tresco and circled the pool twice before disappearing.

1950 One said to have been seen at St Anthony-in-Meneage on 26 August.

1960 One reported on the Camel estuary on 22 and 24 August (rejected R).

MARAZION MARSH, MOUNT'S BAY—This view shews part of the extensive reed beds west of the main railway line which divides the marsh in two. The whole covers only about 85 acres, but it has been one of the most closely watched localities in the south-west since the exploits of E. H. Rodd (who lived at Penzance from 1833) and the taxidermist W. S. Vingoe were recorded in the pages of the *Zoologist*. The area was the inspiration for Miss H. M. Quick's delightfully illustrated *Marsh and Shore* (1948).

Some half mile of road fronts the marsh, making observation of the open waters easy. Rarities here include Europe's first recorded American stint. Notable among its regular visiting wildfowl are garganey and shoveler.

The marsh is separated from the sea by the road and low dunes from which are obtained magnificent views of the Bay from St Michael's Mount to 'Gwavas Lake'—the sheltered waters close in to Penzance and Newlyn—noted for its grebes and divers in winter and spring. [*Photo:* D. B. BARTON]

LOE BAR AND LOE POOL, NEAR HELSTON—This massive shingle bank is a former breeding locality of the ringed plover—nesting was last proved in 1959.

To the right are the lower reaches of The Loe, the largest natural sheet of freshwater in the county. Its maximum depth is about 20′, while it extends upwards of a mile before reaching the reeds and marsh in the valley below Helston. A few mallards, moorhens and coots nest here, but these waters are better known as a refuge for wintering wildfowl, notably tufted ducks which have become common only in recent years with the construction of new, large reservoirs. The Loe is one of the localities most likely to be visited by red-necked grebe, goldeneye, scaup, and smew. The finest views of the Pool are obtained from the path on the west side through the grounds of the Penrose estate. The walk is open to the public on most days in the year except Sundays.

Divers, terns, and sea-ducks such as eiders, occur seawards of the Bar, but this stretch of Mount's Bay seems less attractive to many species than the waters off Penzance.     [*Photo:* D. B. BARTON]

# LESSER YELLOWLEGS
### *Tringa flavipes*

An annual autumn vagrant to Britain from America, the lesser yellowlegs is an impressive migrant, breeding in Alaska and northern Canada, and wintering as far south as Patagonia.

1871   One shot by Vingoe at Marazion Marsh on 12 September (z)—the second British record.

1920   Female shot at the Abbey Pool, Tresco on 7 September (BB, 1939–40).

1921   One seen on Tresco between 19 August and 17 September (BB, 1927–28).

1936   One seen at Marazion Marsh from 17 September to 11 October and subsequently on several occasions up to 19 November.

1943   One on the Scillies from 12 to 28 September.

1952   A bird at Par on 14 September, which eventually flew off south-west, may be the bird tentatively identified as a yellowlegs on Tresco on 30 September.

1954   One on the Camel estuary from 9 to 12 September was perhaps the same bird on the Tamar estuary from 24 to 27 September.

1958   One on Bryher on 11 May is the only spring record.

1964   One at Trewornan on the Camel estuary from 3 to 7 October (R).

1967   One at 'Watercress Pool' on St Mary's from 26 to 29 October (R).

1968   One on the Camel estuary on 10 November was still present in early December.

# GREENSHANK   *Tringa nebularia*

The greenshank breeds mainly in the forest belt and the edge of the tundra from Scandinavia to the Pacific. In Britain a few hundred pairs nest in parts of the Highlands and the northern Isles. In the last century parties of up to a dozen occurred at Tresco pools every autumn (z, 1906) and were not uncommon in winter (VCH). About thirty were seen in one flock at Scilly in autumn 1870 (z). On the mainland at this time it was an annual migrant, usually solitary and occasionally in twos or threes. Ryves (1948) recorded a party of thirteen on the Camel in August 1944 but winter records have only become common in the past twenty years.

The autumn passage normally commences in the latter half of July. Earliest dates are 27 June 1961 at Crowan and 29 June 1965 at Ruan Lanihorne. Peak numbers pass through in late August and early September, although in some years large parties have been recorded in early October. Whilst the greenshank is seen singly or in twos or threes on all estuaries, the largest flocks are reported from mid and east Cornwall—

Camel estuary: 30 on 8 October 1961, 22 on 22 August 1961 and 20 at the Walmsley Sanctuary on 5 October 1960. River Lynher: 31 on 6 October 1965, 22 on 16 August 1964, and 19 as late as November 1964. Landulph Marsh: 15 on 11 August 1965. Ruan Lanihorne: about 40 at Ardevora on 8 August 1968, 20 on 28 August 1966. Percuil Creek: (an area overlooked by most bird-watchers) 26 on 25 August 1957 and 25 on 4 September 1952. Tresillian River: 20 on 8 October 1961—more than three or four are very unusual here. Only two or three are usual at freshwater sites like the reservoirs at Crowan and Stithians.

Since 1960 wintering birds have been reported regularly at Hayle and occasionally at Helford, but the main wintering localities are—

River Lynher and St John's Lake where four are usual and six have been recorded. Camel estuary: normally less than half a dozen but eleven at Little Petherick Creek on 10 January 1960, and eight on 13 January 1963. Tresillian River and Ruan Lanihorne: normally two or three with six at Tresillian in December 1960.

Wintering birds leave from the end of March when the first spring migrants appear. Large numbers do not occur at this time, but more than usual were seen in 1965 with eight on the Camel on 21 March and five on 5 May. At Hayle the same year, a rather late passage occurred in May with two birds on the 6th, rising to twelve on 11th, ten on 13th, fourteen on 14th and six on the 19th. At Ruan Lanihorne a peak of seven was reached on 15 May, while two remained until the 21st. The latest departure dates are 26 May 1959 on the Camel estuary and 27 May 1957 at Hayle.

Few figures have been published for Scilly, but parties of up to four seem regular during the autumn. Twelve were counted at Tresco on 8 September 1959, eighteen at the Abbey Pool, Tresco on 19 October 1967, and twenty on the shores of Tean on 14 September 1958. During a gale on 17 October 1966, twenty-one were seen about the Abbey Pool, while another twenty were in flight in the early morning giving a total of 41. The earliest arrival date is 18 June 1964 on St Agnes.

One or two regularly winter on Scilly, but more may occur than records suggest for at least fourteen were on Tresco between 23 and 27 January 1965.

## TEREK SANDPIPER    *Tringa terek*

This sandpiper is an extremely rare vagrant to Britain from the taiga of Asia. Most of the handful of British examples have been seen in Sussex and Kent and it is remarkable that even one has reached Cornwall. This was a bird seen at Melancoose reservoir, Newquay on 13 June 1961 (R).

## KNOT                    *Calidris canutus*

The knot is a regular migrant and winter visitor to Britain from its scattered breeding grounds north of the Arctic Circle. While most are of Siberian origin, some ringed in Sussex have been recovered in Greenland. In view of Cornwall's geographical position, the Greenland form (*Calidris canutus rufa*) can be expected to occur in the county, but this has yet to be proved by ringing for the birds cannot be distinguished in the field.

The larger estuaries of the north of England commonly support flocks of 5,000 wintering birds and even larger numbers at migration time, but such assemblies are unknown in Cornwall. Thirty-five constituted the largest flock known to Ryves. This is still about the maximum as far west as the Hayle estuary, while on Scilly the largest flocks reported on St Agnes are 24 on 13 May 1967 and 45 on 4 September 1960. Since 1963 up to 100 or more have been reported on the Camel estuary, as in 1966 in January, February, and on 30 September. However, the extreme south-east of the county has proved to be the most important area with 600 or 700 regularly seen at St John's Lake where 900 were estimated on 23 November 1965. At Millbrook Lake about 1,000 were present on 10 March 1965. About 200 are normal on the Lynher.

Knots have been seen in every month of the year, but the autumn migration ordinarily commences in late August with sporadic arrivals from mid-July. Until mid-September small numbers are still in breeding plumage. In 1967 autumn arrivals were very late at St John's Lake—a single bird on 6 September remained alone until at least 21 October, but on the 23rd over 60 were present increasing to 600 by early December. Wintering birds depart before early April and knots seen from then until late May probably represent a light spring passage. Late spring stragglers are frequently in breeding plumage—as were four at Marazion Marsh on 1 June 1963, the latest date on which the species has been seen in Cornwall.

Away from the estuaries knots are rare, even at Marazion Marsh where up to five were recorded on 18 September 1967. Single birds have occurred in recent years at Tamar Lake, Dozmary Pool, and Crowan reservoir, while four were at Stithians reservoir on 6 September 1967.

| *Ringed* | *Recovered* |
|---|---|
| Dawsmere, Lincolnshire, adult 26.8.'60 | found partly eaten, St Michael's Mount 26.1.'63 |

# PURPLE SANDPIPER
### *Calidris maritima*

The purple sandpiper nests in Scandinavia and on many Arctic islands, and winters on the Atlantic coast as far south as the Mediterranean. It is not an abundant visitor to Cornwall but is well known because of its adherence to well-defined stretches of coast. The best-known colony, recorded in 1864 by Rodd, is at Penzance where birds frequent the seaweed-strewn rocks about the bathing pool. At high tide they frequently take to the ledges of the pool and the harbour pier. Occasionally they feed on the Eastern Green but rarely vacate the rocks for even a short time. This colony usually contains about twenty birds—the most reported being 49 on 8 January 1967 and 38 on 12 January 1933. Purple sandpipers are less often observed further along the coast at Newlyn, Mousehole, and Marazion.

Elsewhere in the county the species is probably more widespread than published information suggests. Only in 1963 was the small colony at Hannafore, Looe 're-discovered' after an hiatus in records since 1906 (VCH), although some of the local inhabitants were well aware of its continued existence. Small numbers have been reported from many other localities, including Bude, Trebetherick-Constantine, Newquay, Perranporth, Gwithian, and St Ives. About twenty were not uncommon in the Trebetherick-Constantine area in the 1930's, but there are no recent reports of parties this size. The rocks below the Huer's hut at Newquay were also a favourite haunt at this time from whence there is little recent information. In the nineteenth century it was common about Falmouth (Bullmore, 1866, & VCH) but none are reported here now. Sightings at localities where they are normally absent include—Treveal Cove at Zennor on 24 October 1963, Gwennap Head, St Levan on 23 September 1966, and near Dinham on the Camel on 9 October 1966.

The main influx ordinarily commences about the last week in October—earlier records appear to be of passage migrants and include one at Perranuthnoe on 8 August 1964. Winter visitors depart during April, but stragglers or late migrants are not uncommon in May—as on the 21st in 1962 and 1963, the 24th in 1930 (BB), and the 27th in 1933, all at Penzance.

The status of the purple sandpiper appears to be unchanged since the last century both on the mainland and at Scilly. On the islands most recent reports come from St Agnes. Since 1957 about 75 is a typical maximum during the spring migration in April or May with as many as 150 on 18 April 1957. In 1962, 70 were present up to

View across the bay to St Michael's Mount from Penzance – a locality well known for wintering grebes and divers and, on Battery Rocks in the foreground, purple sandpipers.

28 May, but only one was still there on 1 June. A few not uncommonly remain until about 6 June according to Miss Quick (1964). The species is probably widespread on many other rocky islands, but is hardly ever observed on St Mary's while one at Gimble Porth from 13 to 16 September 1966 was the first noticed on Tresco for three years. As on the mainland, winter visitors arrive from late October, early passage migrants including two on 22 July 1961, and single birds on 24 August 1959 and 16 September 1960.

## LITTLE STINT            *Calidris minuta*

This minute wader nests mainly near the Arctic coast of northern Finland and Siberia and winters as far south as South Africa. When on migration the little stint frequents marshes and freshwater pools as well as estuaries. Swanpool near Falmouth was formerly a favoured haunt—Couch (1838) wrote that Jackson had shot several there and once seen a flock of ten or twelve. In recent years a few have been seen at Marazion Marsh and the wet fields behind the Hayle estuary, but most are reported from the estuaries themselves, notably on the Hayle and Camel, where small numbers are annually identified feeding amongst the dunlins.

In October 1840 (D & M, 1892) about 50 were seen on the Devon side of the Tamar— an exceptionally large number. Usually found in ones and twos, the largest parties in recent years were in September 1960 with up to fifteen at Hayle, twelve at Par, and nine on the Camel estuary. Unusual were ten at Marazion Marsh on 18 September 1967. Inland records are rare—two were at Stithians reservoir on 22 September 1967. The main influx commences in the last week in August and continues throughout September when most are seen. The earliest dates are 27 July 1968 at Marazion Marsh,

when an adult in almost full breeding plumage was seen with a juvenile, and 1 August 1949 when five birds were on the Camel. Occurrences later than the second week in October are rare, but from 1960 to 1967 there have been five records between 27 December and 26 February indicating that the species has almost certainly wintered in the county.

The spring migration between mid-April and early June follows almost exclusively the east coast of England, the few Cornish records doubtless representing stints caught up in migrating parties of dunlins which move north on a broader front. The only records are of single birds on 9 March 1952 at Lelant, 1 April 1962 at Hayle, 3 April 1965 on the Camel, and 1 June 1962 at Marazion Marsh.

Small numbers annually visit Scilly in the autumn. The earliest date is 24 August 1965 on Tresco, and the latest dates on St Agnes are single birds on 18 October 1953 and from 18 to 20 November 1952. Most are seen singly—maximum numbers being up to six on Periglis beach, St Agnes from 21 to 28 September 1957, and up to four at the Abbey Pool, Tresco from 9 September to 12 October 1967. The only spring records are of single birds at St Agnes on 1 May 1960 and 1962, from 29 April to 4 May 1963, and one in breeding plumage on Samson on 2 June 1959.

## AMERICAN STINT
## (LEAST SANDPIPER)
                                *Calidris minutilla*

The American stint has wandered across the Atlantic to Britain on only about nine occasions up to 1966—four of them in 1966.

1853   The first specimen recorded in Europe was shot by W. S. Vingoe at Marazion Marsh on 10 October (z).

1890   The third British specimen was obtained by fishermen near Mousehole in September. It was bought by W. E. Bailey of

Paul in whose collection it was seen by Clark in 1902 incorrectly labelled as a little stint (z, 1907).

1962 One on St Agnes on 4 October was the second British record this century.

1965 One seen on Tresco on 24 August after a period of north-westerly gales.

1966 One on the Camel estuary near Dinham from 12 to 22 September (R).

1899 One shot near Devoran in October (VCH).

1904 One obtained at Gyllingvase marsh near Falmouth on 1 November (z, 1907).

1945 One at Scilly on 18 August.

1966 One at Burniere on the Camel estuary from 7 to 20 September.

Records of single birds at Marazion Marsh in autumn 1936 and March 1955 are not regarded as sufficiently authenticated.

## TEMMINCK'S STINT
*Calidris temminckii*

The Temminck's stint nests more widely in northern Europe than the little stint. It has bred in Scotland and once in the north of England but is an extremely rare autumn visitor to Cornwall. It has been mis-identified but all published records are given below.

1822 Two shot at Swanpool in the autumn (Couch, 1838).

1848 One shot at Marazion Marsh on 28 August (z).

1849 One, in company with little stints, shot at Marazion Marsh about 15 September (z).

1851 One obtained in the autumn—presumably at Marazion (Rodd, 1880).

1853† Rodd wrote in the *Zoologist* on 26 August that the species "appears to be by no means a rare bird in the salt marshes of this neighbourhood . . .". The previous week one had been flushed by a train passing Marazion Marsh while a few days later Vingoe observed a flock of at least twelve and shot three specimens. In spite of Rodd's comment that the bird is "invariably distinguished from the little stint by its call note which resembles that of the common cricket . . ." this record seems scarcely credible. Certainly birds were incorrectly identified even when shot, for two obtained by Pechell at Scilly on 19 September 1857 (z) were subsequently proved to be little stints (z, 1906). Others were said to have been obtained by Pechell before 1863 and others to have been shot, mostly at the pool at Newford on St Mary's before 1906, but the only specimen traced by Clark and F. R. Rodd (z, 1906) was for—

1864 When one was shot at Scilly in October.

† Incorrectly given as 1873 in Rodd's *Birds of Cornwall*.

## BAIRD'S SANDPIPER
*Calidris bairdii*

The only Cornish records of this vagrant from North America are—

1965 One on Wingletang Down, St Agnes on 25 September—the tenth British record (R).

1966 One at the Abbey Pool, Tresco from 26 August to 12 September, and presumably the same bird at St Agnes from 19 to 30 September (R). The record of one at Marazion Marsh on 20 and 21 September was rejected (R).

1967 One on Bryher from 19 to 21 August (R) and another (?) at the Abbey Pool, Tresco from 9 to 27 September (R).

## WHITE-RUMPED SANDPIPER
*Calidris fuscicollis*

The white-rumped or Bonaparte's sand-piper, called Schintz's sandpiper in the early records, is a North American species now seen annually in this country with about forty-five records between 1958 and 1967.

1848 A pair shot at Hayle on 13 October (z).

1854 One shot on St Mary's on 11 October (z).

1870 One shot on St Mary's on 10 October and another at the Lizard on the 28th. Four were also obtained in Devon, but no more were recorded in Britain until 1906.

1955 One at Par beach on 17 October.

1960 One at Constantine Bay on 18 September.

1962 One trapped on St Agnes on 2 October.

1964 One at Devoran on 19 October (R) and another on Periglis beach, St Agnes from 22 to 29 September (R).

1965   One on Tresco from 6 to 28 September was trapped (R) while another was seen at Marazion Marsh on 5 November (R).

1966   One on Tresco from 10 to 16 September (R).

1967   One at the Abbey Pool, Tresco from 6 to 20 September (R).

## PECTORAL SANDPIPER
### *Calidris melanotos*

No North American wader has appeared in such numbers in this country as the pectoral sandpiper. Only a small proportion make the crossing in spring—possibly because the weather is more settled at that time of year. The five Cornish spring records, all for May, include the first for the county and the second in Britain—a bird shot by Mitchell on Annet on 27 May 1840. Another was seen the next day (Yarrell, & Rodd, 1880).

As long ago as 1870, when five were reported from Scilly in early September (z), Rodd suggested it might be annual, its extreme rarity being due to the ease with which it is overlooked. Although a number were subsequently seen on Scilly, none was reported from the mainland after an emaciated specimen was watched at Porthgwarra on 30 April 1906 (z, 1907), until 29 August 1948 when one was seen on the Camel estuary. That year produced a miniature invasion of Britain while only slightly fewer appeared in 1950. With more intensive watching since 1950, Rodd's statement has proved correct, for up to 1968 they were not seen in only four years, while in 1962 as many as seven occurred, including three birds trapped and ringed together on St Agnes in August. Most arrive in September—earliest dates being 15 August in 1963 at Marazion and in 1967 at Ruan Lanihorne. There are few after mid-October—the latest on St Agnes on 4 November 1963.

While most are reported from Scilly which accounts for over half of all records from western Britain, there are regular reports from Marazion Marsh and Ponsandane, the Hayle and Camel estuaries, with one or two records from Crowan reservoir, Zennor, Restronguet Creek, Ruan Lanihorne, and Tamar Lake.

The closely related sharp-tailed or Siberian pectoral sandpiper, *Calidris acuminata*, is a rare vagrant to eastern England. It has not been identified in Cornwall, but one at Scilly in October 1961 may have been this species.

## DUNLIN                                    *Calidris alpina*

Five geographical forms of dunlin have been separated but none can be distinguished in the field—indeed, it may be impossible to assign a trapped bird to a particular race. Dunlins breeding in Iceland, some of which pass through or winter in Cornwall, have been assigned to the race *islandica* by a number of taxonomists, but others group them with *Calidris alpina schinzii*, the race breeding in Britain as well as parts of southern Scandinavia and the Baltic.

Cornish breeding birds are the most southerly within the normal range of the species, but as expected on the edge of its range, nesting is sporadic being confined to the vicinity of Dozmary Pool on Bodmin Moor. There is no evidence that the dunlin's foothold in the county is any more precarious now than over a century ago. N. Hare of Liskeard wrote on 6 October

*Dunlin*

1848 (PZ) that a nest had been found by a farmer's boy in the last week of May on 'Goodiver' moor near Dozmary (presumably Goodaveor in Altarnun) and that two of three eggs had been given him. The boy said the egg was a scarce one, the 'stark' only nesting occasionally and that one or two pairs are the most seen in any one year. This particular nest is the first to have been taken in the county. In 1849 Hare was unable to find any evidence of breeding. F. R. Rodd (MS) wrote that the dunlin had become "rather scarce of late years, none now breed in Trewortha Marsh.† They are confined to the large marshes round Brown Willy and to the Moors and Turf Pits to the south of Jamaica Inn (Bolventor)—they associate in small flocks during the breeding season. Moormen have often told me of Jack Snipe breeding on the moors. Dunlins have been the birds in every instance." Several nests, each with three eggs, were found between Kilmar and Dozmary Pool on 8 July 1868 on elevated tufts of coarse grass. Gatcombe found them apparently breeding at Dozmary Pool on 14 June 1874 (z) and commented on their tameness and how they approached very close in an attempt to lead him away. Clark (VCH) wrote that they occasionally bred on Goss Moor, but there is no further evidence that the species has done so outside Bodmin Moor.

Recent breeding records are few. Col.

† In fact a pair did breed there in 1870 (z).

Almond[1] wrote in 1968—"My information is that when they have nested at Dozmary, it has been quite close to the pool. I have been told of summer records of dunlins on another marsh on the Moor, but without specific evidence of nesting"—presumably Redhill Marsh where a pair holding territory and singing, was seen up to mid-June in 1968 (Musson[1]). In 1953, three or four birds in mid-June appeared as if they had nests and at least two young were seen on 3 July. A bird was heard trilling at Dozmary on 16 May 1963 and another seen on 27 May 1966, but the last definite record was in 1960 when a nest with three eggs was found on 14 May. Two days later there were four eggs, the first hatched on 3 June and the nest was empty on the 11th. The male, when incubating, was photographed and allowed approach to within three feet of the nest.

Whether the British breeding population leaves our shores completely or in part is unknown, but the large wintering flocks must belong substantially to the northern or Lapland race, *C. alpina alpina* as shewn by the recovery of ringed birds. The earliest migrants begin to frequent the estuaries in July. In 1965 six were first seen on the Camel on 1 July, but in 1966 at Hayle a party of this size was not recorded until the 31st. Waves of migrating flocks may remain for only a few days. A large influx of about 10,000 birds in breeding plumage arrived at Hayle on the night of 3–4 August 1965—

'Dozmary Pool on Bodmin Moor covers about 30 acres and is the only natural stretch of freshwater in east Cornwall. The dunlin has nested in its vicinity'

within a few days all had gone and on the 13th only about 200 in winter or immature plumage were seen.

Dunlins appear to be more common on autumn passage than in winter. Of 1,500 on the Camel estuary in early September 1964, only 5–600 remained at the end of the year. Mid-winter flocks of 1,000 or more have been reported from several localities including the Fal at Ruan Lanihorne, Restronguet Creek, Truro River, and the Camel. As many as 5,000 were estimated at St John's Lake in February 1965, about 2,000 in both winter periods in 1966, and 2,000 on the Camel in February 1967. Only a few dunlins are reported from inland localities at migration time—for example, two at Stithians reservoir on 10 August 1967 and one or two at Melancoose reservoir from 10 to 16 August 1967. There is little evidence as yet to shew any marked spring passage.

Few details have been published for Scilly. Arrival and departure dates at St Agnes are much the same as those on the mainland—birds being absent from the islands for only a couple of weeks. Earliest autumn arrivals normally appear in July. One on 21 June 1963 may have been an early migrant but some June records (up to fifteen birds between 11 April and 12 June 1963) clearly refer to spring stragglers. Migrating parties may remain for only a few days. Thus, on St Agnes only one was seen on 12 July 1950, 85 the following day, but only seven between the 14th and 17th (Parslow[1]). The size of wintering parties remains unrecorded but appears to be in tens and not hundreds. 180 at St Agnes on 13 May 1967 is the largest recorded flock in spring.

| Ringed | Recovered |
|---|---|
| Amager, Sjaelland Denmark, adult 4.8.'51 | found dead, Camel estuary, autumn 1953 |
| Midnes, Iceland, full grown 23.5.'59 | found dead, Widemouth Bay 10.8.'59 |
| Revtangen, Rogaland, Norway, full grown 30.9.'56 | shot, Camel estuary 17.11.'56 |
| Ottenby, Öland, Sweden, juv. 12.9.'66 | controlled at Hayle estuary 22.9.'66 |
| Ottenby, Öland, Sweden, adult 15.8.'49 | ring and leg bone found at Rock, Camel estuary 17.8.'55 |
| Marazion Marsh, full grown 4.9.'62 | found dead, Jersey Marine, Swansea 4.6.'64 |
| Hayle estuary, full grown 30.8.'64 | found dead, Cap Vert, Senegal 4.10.'64 (the most southerly recovery of a dunlin ringed in this country). |
| St Agnes, full grown 1.10.'60 | killed, Esnandes, Charente Maritime, France 20.10.'60 |

## CURLEW SANDPIPER
### *Calidris ferruginea*

Considering that the curlew sandpiper breeds no nearer to Britain than the eastern part of northern Siberia, it is surprising how common a passage migrant it is in Cornwall —albeit in fluctuating numbers. Small groups are found amongst the larger flocks of dunlins each autumn.

The curlew sandpiper was well known to Victorian ornithologists in the west of England, and one wonders whether it may have been more common in the nineteenth century, for the intensive watching of the past few decades has failed to reveal larger numbers than were reported seventy or more years ago. Gatcombe (z, 1878) shot three out of a flock of 50 at Wadebridge, and once saw 100 on the Lynher. These were no isolated cases for D'Urban and Mathew (1892) wrote that next to the dunlin it was the most common species to be found in the Barnstaple area of north Devon. Couch (1878) called it common in Cornwall, while Clark (RI, 1902) regarded it as frequent in the west of the county and noted a flock of 30 on the Camel in September 1900. This is the largest flock seen this century, although equalled by a party on the same estuary in 1946 when a big irruption occurred throughout Britain. The largest parties in recent years are twenty at Hayle in August 1954 and September 1967, and fifteen on the Camel in September 1963.

September is certainly the month for

curlew sandpipers, the autumn passage lasting from the last week in August until mid-October. 8 July 1956 is the earliest record, when one was seen at Porthkidney beach, Lelant in almost complete summer plumage—a rare sight in Cornwall. While there are a few records for November and December, the species cannot be said to have wintered in the county, for none have been seen in January or February. The spring passage is scarcely noticeable—the few birds seen at this time being in the nature of vagrants from the main migration route along the east coast of England. One was seen on the Camel on 18 March 1966, two on the Camel on 28 April 1960, six at Daymer Bay on 15 May 1955, one in breeding plumage at Hayle on 27 May 1930 (BB), and another in breeding plumage at Tamar Lake at the end of May 1882 (z).

While some have been reported on sandy beaches, as at Marazion and Gyllingvase, curlew sandpipers prefer the sand and mud of estuaries—especially the Camel, and to a lesser extent the Hayle. Inland records are rare but include a few from Crowan reservoir, Tory Pond at Stithians, and Tamar Lake. Birds were found at these three localities in 1959 when a considerable autumn passage occurred—a party of twelve was seen at Helford on 2 September, in contrast to the preceeding year when only one was reported from the whole county. A large influx of curlew sandpipers generally coincides with a good passage of little stints, suggesting that the two species commonly migrate in company.

At Scilly, Clark and Rodd (z, 1906) described the curlew sandpiper as a not infrequent autumn visitor. Large flocks occurred in 1870 from 1 to 15 September and were especially plentiful on Bryher. Recent records (it was virtually unrecorded before 1952) confirm that it is an annual autumn visitor in ones and twos. The earliest arrival dates are 26 August 1959 and 29 August 1966 at Tresco. The latest date is 17 October 1959—in that autumn ex-

ceptional numbers had been recorded with up to eighteen at one time on Tresco. More than usual also visited Scilly in 1967 with up to six on Tresco between 8 and 21 September, and up to ten at Porthloo, St Mary's on 23 September with as many as five remaining at Porthmellin until 11 October. The only 'spring' record is of a single bird on St Mary's on 24 February 1963.

## SANDERLING *Calidris alba*

Like the knot, the sanderling is one of the great migrants of the world, breeding north of the Arctic Circle and wintering as far south as the Capes, although some remain in Britain.

The sanderling was first recorded in Cornwall by Carew (1602). Willughby and Ray on their visit in 1662 recorded that . . . "these birds live upon the sandy shores of the Sea, and fly in flocks. We saw many of them on the Sea-coasts of Cornwall." They also said that the sanderling "was called the Curwillet about Pensance", but were mistaken on this point as 'curwillet' properly referred to the ringed plover. Borlase (1758) correctly assigned to the sanderlings the local name of 'towillees', so called from the noise they make when flying.

There is nothing in nineteenth century records to indicate that the sanderling's status differed from that at the present time. Small numbers winter in the county, normally in parties of less than a dozen. The beginning of the spring passage is difficult to time, but the peak is reached in May and records rarely extend beyond the first few days in June. Birds seen as late as 16 June could represent non-breeding birds remaining in this country.

Autumn migration commences after mid-July and continues well into September. Parties numbering a dozen or two are usual, scurrying like clockwork mice along sandy beaches or on those parts of estuaries composed of extensive sand-banks. Larger numbers have been recorded, and an estimated 1,000 in summer plumage on the Hayle estuary on 4 August 1965 is unprecedented. Inland records are rare. Single birds in August or September have been reported from Dozmary Pool (1965), Tamar Lake (1962), and Crowan reservoir (1959), while there were half a dozen at Higher Argal reservoir on 3 September 1965.

At Scilly the sanderling may be seen in any month of the year and is uncommon for only a short period from about mid-June to late July. In some years the first autumn birds do not appear until late August, as on 21st on St Agnes in 1963, compared with 28 July the previous year. Few figures have been published but maximum autumn numbers at Porthloo, St Mary's were about 200 from 29 September to 10 October 1963, and 150 on 10 October 1967. In spring, up to 83 were counted on St Agnes on 18 April 1963 and in winter about 40 on St Agnes in late December the same year.

## BUFF-BREASTED
## SANDPIPER   *Tryngites subruficollis*

This North American sandpiper has become almost an annual visitor to Britain. Since 1960 three or four have been recorded in most years with nearly twenty in 1968.

1846   One shot on the beach between Penzance and Marazion on 3 September (z).
1860   A first year bird shot on a pond near Chûn Castle, Morvah on 8 September (z).
1870   One shot by the pool on Bryher on 16 September (z).

There are no British records from 1906 to 1934.

1943   One on Scilly on 12 September.
1962   Three at St Mary's airport from 9 to 13 September.
1963   One on Porthloo beach, St Mary's on 18 September.
1967   One at St Mary's airport on 17 September and presumably the same bird on the golf course and adjoining ploughed fields up to the 30th (R).
1968   Two on St Mary's from 16 to 23 September and another at St Just airport on 1 October.

## RUFF (FEMALE REEVE)
*Philomachus pugnax*

The ruff bred regularly in parts of eastern England until about 1800, and sporadically until 1922, but does so at the present time no nearer than the Netherlands. In Cornwall it is a passage migrant and winter visitor, so that examples of males sporting their magnificent neck-feathers are unknown. Partial ruffs were recorded by Vingoe in late March 1865 (z) and by Harvey at Marazion from 7 to 18 March 1925 (BB).

In common with some other species breeding close to Britain, the ruff has a very marked spring, as well as autumn passage. In 1965 the spring passage was greater, but there is no consistent pattern and in 1958 the position was reversed. Spring passage commences about mid-March reaching a peak at the end of the month or early in April. Records fall away rapidly after mid-April with only occasional birds seen in May, as at Crowan reservoir on 2 May 1958. While most commonly reported singly, larger numbers have been seen in recent years—in 1965 there were up to 28 on the Camel estuary on 5 April, 22 at Hayle on 2 April, and 34 at Marazion on the same day.

The largest autumn flock recorded is 28 at Marazion on 12 September 1958. Early arrivals appear in late July or early August in some years—20 July 1966 at Stithians reservoir. The main passage is in September with a rapid falling off in numbers in the first few days of October. Later records may be of wintering birds. Records in winter have increased with over half a dozen birds on the Tamar and Hayle estuaries between December and February since 1962, and maxima at Hayle of eleven in late February 1964 and ten on 4 February 1967.

Ruffs have been seen on all the main estuaries where they favour the tidal gutters and salt-marsh, as well as the wet meadows adjoining the estuaries as at Hayle and the Camel. Marazion Marsh is a favourite locality, but few remain for long at inland localities like Tamar Lake or Stithians reservoir where there is a scarcity of mud at the water's edge.

Clark and Rodd (z, 1906) knew of only three occurrences of ruffs at Scilly—single immature birds in autumn 1864, on 2 September 1878 on Tresco, and in March 1885. Now, a small number are reported annually during the autumn and less frequently in the spring. Autumn migration normally commences about late August—especially early were a ruff and reeve at Periglis Pool, St Agnes on 5 July 1952. The latest dates are 17 October 1963 on Tresco, and 10 October on St Agnes in 1960 and 1961. There are no winter records but spring migrants have occurred on St Agnes as early as 18 February 1961 and 19 February 1959. The main passage is between late March and late May —later records include one on St Agnes on 8 June 1963. Most are seen in ones or twos. Although the spring passage is normally the lightest, the largest parties have been seen at this time; in 1965 up to fourteen were on St Agnes on 29 and 30 March and six on 1 April. Six were also reported on St Agnes beach on 24 to 26 May 1957. The most reported in the autumn is four at St Mary's airport on 22 September 1958.

## AVOCET  *Recurvirostra avosetta*

The avocet breeds at various localities in the Baltic and Mediterranean regions. In the last century it bred in eastern England, last doing so in Kent in 1843. A vagrant to Cornwall, it was recorded on only eight occasions up to 1938—the first being one on the Tamar before 1830 (PI).

In 1938 the story of the avocet began a new chapter. In that year a pair bred in Ireland, and a bird was seen in Cornwall at Hayle in August. The following year one was seen at Marazion in the spring, while in 1943 another was seen at Trevone in December. Not until 1944 were more nests found in Britain—in Essex for the first time in over a century. More bred in Norfolk in

Avocet

1946 and 1947. Since then it has re-established itself in Suffolk, mainly at Havergate, where up to 118 pairs have nested regularly since the late 1950's, but also at Minsmere which supports four or five pairs. A few sometimes nest elsewhere.

The normal wintering quarters are in Africa, especially in the East African Rift where flocks of over 30,000 congregate. Since the winter of 1947–48, following the first season at Havergate, a gradually increasing number has wintered on the Tamar estuary. These birds remain in a rather restricted area on the Cornish and Devon banks in the Cargreen-Landulph area. They rarely wander far so that only a few appear on the Lynher a few miles away. No other regular wintering areas exist in England. Occasionally, and for short periods, birds visit other Cornish estuaries—as Hayle in 1960 and 1965. Others have been seen at Restronguet Creek, the Camel, and Helford estuaries. Unusual were fifteen at Par beach after a gale on 2 April 1960.

It has not yet been proved that the Tamar flock comes from the British and not the Dutch colonies. However, it remains too much of a coincidence that the number of wintering birds should have increased proportionally at such a similar rate to those breeding in Suffolk, as shewn on the graph.

The arrival of the Tamar flock varies

annually. Usually, first birds arrive in the last week of October or in early November, but in 1967 three were present on 4 October. Departure takes place in March, few remaining after about the 20th. In 1967 most had gone by 5 March, but one was seen on the Devon side as late as 7 May.

The avocet remains unrecorded on Scilly.

## BLACK-WINGED STILT
### *Himantopus himantopus*

The regular migration of this species from Mediterranean Europe is not very extensive, but at irregular intervals it 'irrupts', breeding much further north than usual, including Northamptonshire in 1945. The handful of

Cornish records are presumably linked with this erratic behaviour.

| | |
|---|---|
| 1718 | Walter Moyle records how one "Himantopus of Pliny . . . was kill'd with four others at a shot . . . near Penzance . . .". |
| pre-1808 | James wrote "I never saw but one"— presumably a Cornish specimen, but gave no details. |
| 1851 | One shot at Swanpool near Falmouth (Cocks, 1851). |
| 1917 | One of two birds at Tamar Lake was found dead, stuffed and kept at a nearby cottage (BB, 1944–45). |
| 1951 | One seen on St Mary's from 12 to 16 January and at Tresco on 7 February. |
| 1958 | Two are said to have been seen at Hayle on 19 April and early the next morning. |
| 1963 | One seen at Marazion Marsh from 6 to 8 June. |

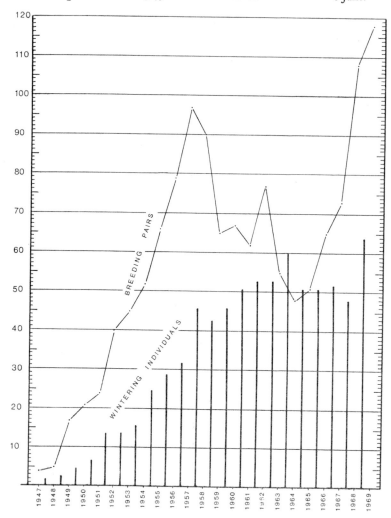

Graph comparing the increase in breeding pairs of avocets at Havergate, Suffolk, with wintering individuals on the Tamar

# GREY PHALAROPE

*Phalaropus fulicarius*

The grey phalarope has a more restricted breeding range than the red-necked, occurring mostly further north but in places overlapping on the arctic coast of Siberia and Canada. The nearest breeding areas to Britain are in Greenland and Spitzbergen. Birds winter as far south as South Africa, but mostly in the plankton-rich seas off west Africa. Migration normally takes place well out at sea but birds may easily become concentrated in mid-Atlantic by weather systems which can force vast numbers onto the shores of western Europe, producing periodic 'wrecks'.

In Cornwall it is an annual autumn visitor first reported from the mouth of the Tamar by Henry Mewburn of St Germans about December 1821. Another was shot at St John's Lake in October 1825 (PI, 1830). The first 'wreck' was in 1846 (Z) when "large numbers were obtained in the first fortnight in October . . . Almost all were emaciated and exhausted and some were found dead". Two, one taken alive, were found near Liskeard workhouse (G, 18.10.1846). Cocks (1851) reported one in full summer plumage captured alive, and four shot at Swanpool on 12 October, adding that over 30 birds had been examined by himself. 1866 was "the most memorable" year in south-west England (D & M, 1892) when a flock of 70 appeared off Tresco (Z, 1906), but no other figures were published. Another large flock appeared off Helford in October 1891 (VCH). Parties of up to twenty were seen on the Truro river in November 1904 and on 26 November 1905 (VCH), but further reports are only of a few individuals until 1948 when up to ten were seen at one time in Mount's Bay after severe gales in early December. Since then, grey phalaropes have been annual in varying numbers, mainly off west Cornwall and between Land's End and the Scillies.

Most records are for October and early November but are not uncommon from early September to early December. The earliest dates are of single birds on 10 August 1950 on the Camel estuary, on 16 August 1966 between Land's End and the Scillies, and a party of eight on 26 August 1966 near Wolf Rock. Late dates include one at Long Rock Pool, near Marazion on 12 December 1952, one in Mount's Bay on 30 December 1963 and at least five between 23 and 29 December 1967 at Padstow, Newquay, Looe, River Fal, and Kestle Mill near Newquay.

Winter and spring records are rare—only seven for January and February since 1877 when one was seen off Penzance on 25 January (Z). There have been three March records, all of single birds—on the 7th at Newquay in 1959, the 10th on the Camel estuary in 1963, and the 27th off St Ives in 1966. The only later record is of one shot at Par in May 1878 in almost complete summer plumage (Z).

In recent years large 'wrecks' have occurred in 1957, 1959, and 1960—each one being larger than that preceding it. In 1957 the invasion occurred in September—ten were first seen between Land's End and the Scillies on the 10th with the largest flock of about 25 at St Ives on the 13th. In 1959 a single bird was reported from St Agnes on 7 September, but only small numbers were seen until October when the main invasion began with up to 28 or more at St Agnes on the 9th, and maxima of twenty at St Ives on the 11th and about 30 on the 28th. All these were eclipsed by the 'carpet' of 350 close in shore off St Agnes Bay on the 23rd. The following day about 100 were counted farther out but only six remained on the 25th. Small parties were still in Mount's Bay until the end of November, with seven at Porthleven harbour until 1 December.

Even these outstanding figures were overshadowed by the 'wreck' of 1960, easily the largest ever recorded. The whole invasion was very localized, most records coming from Cornwall, Devon, Dorset,

Pembrokeshire and southern Ireland—Cornwall receiving the lion's share. Birds were first noted in Cornwall—two at Gurnard's Head and St Ives on the 4th and 5th September. On the 13th at least 200 were seen from the M.V. *Scillonian* en route to the Scillies, and 97 at St Ives on the 16th in a six and a half hours watch. While only one was seen at St Agnes on the 14th and six on the 16th, the day between witnessed a minimum of 1,000 made up of parties of 20 to 30 that extended well beyond telescope range. Small numbers continued to hug the coasts of the south-west until the end of the month, but this was only a temporary lull, for in early October great flocks were again being reported from Scilly to Dorset. On 2 October "hundreds" passed west close to St Mary's, with over 500 passing one point in a single hour that morning. The following day over 300 were seen in Crow Sound with a few found dead on the cliffs. Until at least mid-October birds were reported daily from all continually watched points in south-west England. Some of the larger numbers were two rafts of 30 each near St Mary's and over 300 south of Land's End on the 13th, and between 500 and 1,000 on the calm water of St Ives Bay on the 16th. After mid-October flocks dwindled rapidly, though as many as 120 were off St Agnes on the 25th. A few remained into December—the latest date being the 28th at St Ives. While the largest numbers were seen in west Cornwall, single birds were found as far as Cracking-ton Haven and Booby Bay and up to 30 remained off Looe until 15 October.

## RED-NECKED PHALAROPE
*Phalaropus lobatus*

The red-necked phalarope breeds in the tundra and along the arctic coast as far south as Britain where, due largely to egg collecting, it has decreased, now being found almost exclusively on the Scottish islands.

In Cornwall it is far less common than the grey phalarope, occurring as an oc-casional migrant between late September and late November, with the majority of records in October and invariably after gales from a westerly quarter.† As elsewhere in Britain, the red-necked phalarope is usually seen when the 'grey' is most common although, rather curiously, no records from Cornwall were published during the un-precedented invasion of 'greys' in 1960.

The earliest autumn reports are of single birds at Porthkidney beach, Lelant on 7 August 1968 and off St Agnes on 8 September 1959. The latest is one off St Ives on 18 December 1955. On spring passage it is frequently reported off eastern England in May and early June but the only Cornish record is of one killed off Torpoint on 7 June 1869 (z). One at Hayle on 20 February 1940 may have been an early migrant.

Most records come from the Scillies, St Ives Bay, and west of Land's End. Two were seen off Newquay on 9 December 1959, and one on the Lynher River on 14 September 1957. Inland records of storm-driven birds are rare, but birds must have escaped notice. One was shot on a pond at Treharrock, St Kew on 10 October 1872 (z), another was taken at Dozmary Pool in early September 1880 (z) and a third caught on a farmyard pond near Liskeard on 28 October 1952 was released unharmed a few days later.

Red-necked phalaropes are by no means annual visitors. There are about ten published sightings for the last century, mostly of single birds, the first being shot at Swanpool on 17 September 1859 (Bullmore, 1866). Ryves (1948) reported them in four years but since 1950 they have been seen in 1950 (one), 1952 (one), 1954 (one), 1955 (three), 1957 (five), 1958 (four), 1959 (about ten), 1962 (three), and 1965 (one). Over 60 per cent of records are of single birds—two together have been seen on three occasions, and about four, if not more, off

† Pre-1960 records involving the identification of red-necked phalaropes in flight may be suspect in some cases. Formerly 'reds' were identified by their 'blacker and whiter appearance' but such birds netted elsewhere in Britain have turned out to be grey phalaropes.

St Agnes in a flock of 20–30 'greys' on 30 October 1959. At least six to eight out of a flock of 60 phalaropes between Land's End and the Scillies on 30 October 1952, were thought to be red-necked.

Red-necked phalarope

## WILSON'S PHALAROPE
### *Phalaropus tricolor*

The Wilson's phalarope, now an annual vagrant from North America, was not added to the British list until 1954. Up to June 1966 there were twenty British records, but in 1967 a further nine were seen.

1961   One at Marazion Marsh from 15 June to 4 July (R).
1962   One at Ponsandane near Penzance from 23 to 25 August (R).
1963   One at Trewornan on the Camel estuary on 2 September (R).
       A bird at Tresco on 8 October was not authenticated (Parslow[1]).
1964   One on St Agnes on 22 and 23 June (R).
1967   One at Marazion Marsh from 6 to 11 September was also seen at Hayle on the 10th.

## STONE CURLEW
### *Burhinus oedicnemus*

The stone curlew, or thick-knee of the older literature, is rapidly becoming scarcer as a breeding bird throughout its European range. The report by Turton and Kingston (1830) that it bred in the neighbourhood of Dartmoor probably refers to the common curlew as the names were apparently confused. Today it nests only sparingly as far west as the chalklands of north Dorset.

Willughby (*Ornithology*, 1678) described a "third sort of *Godwit*, which in *Cornwall* they call the Stone-Curlew, differing from the precedent [i.e. black and bar-tailed] in that it hath a much shorter and slenderer Bill than either of them". This may have been the bird we now know as the stone curlew and described by Willughby as the *Oedicnemus* of *Bellonius*—both descriptions could be applied to the same bird. Until the last quarter of the nineteenth century the stone curlew was reported almost annually as a winter visitor in ones and twos. Thus, in 1858 Rodd reported (z) that three had come to his notice between January and 4 March, while he made repeated references in the *Zoologist* to the extreme west of the county being within their normal wintering range.

Since then the species has become progressively more fitful. In 1906 Clark (VCH) called it irregular, and by 1931 Harvey could include the bird amongst the species unknown to him in West Penwith. In 1933, however, P. D. Williams reported the amazing sight of 25 birds on 4 November near St Keverne where "previously only odd birds at long intervals had been seen". There are only six subsequent records. The dates of these are mostly earlier or later than those of the last century, clearly indicating that the species is now only a vagrant at migration time.

1938   One at Kynance on 29 April.
1946   One on Burnt Island, Scilly on 4 May. Dorrien-Smith told the observer that it had formerly been common, although up to 1906 (z) only three records are known from Scilly—December 1878, sometime in 1879, and 10 May 1890.
1949   One somewhere in Cornwall on 26 September.

1955   One at Carn Lês Boel near Land's End on 27 May.

1961   One on St Mary's on 12 May.

1962   Three at the Hayle estuary on 1 December.

## COLLARED PRATINCOLE
### *Glareola pratincola*

The pratincole is a common visitor to southern Europe, especially to Iberia and southern France, but few reach Britain— only three were recorded here from 1958 to 1967.

1811   One shot near Truro in September is the second British record (Graves, *British Ornithology*, vol. II, 1813).

1874   On 9 June Rodd saw a specimen killed a few days before by a boy coot-shooting on a pool on Lizard Downs (z).

## CREAM-COLOURED COURSER          *Cursorius cursor*

This rare straggler from the deserts of Africa and south-west Asia has been seen only once in Cornwall. W. H. Vingoe, the Penzance taxidermist, received a specimen obtained at St Mawgan-in-Pydar in December 1884 (z).

## ARCTIC SKUA
### *Stercorarius parasiticus*

The arctic skua, formerly called Richardson's skua, is the most widespread member of the family in the tundra but does nest as far south as the Scottish islands and Caithness. Most winter south of the Equator.

In Cornwall it is a passage migrant seen mainly in autumn. The 'Hagden'† described to Walter Moyle sometime before 1721 (Tonkin MS) by John Han of Gorran Haven ("Master of one of his Majesty's Ships, an

† Other names used by local fishermen were 'Lords and Captains', and 'Tom Harry'— both having been applied to other skuas.

old experienced Sailor"), refers to the arctic rather than the great skua. His picturesque, but accurate account could not be bettered today—

It is a bird about the bigness of a Mew. The Head & the Bill like it—of a dark Brown all over the Head, Neck, Back wings, & Tail; But under the Belly it is of a lighter Colour, much like a sandy, or Cinereous Sordid White. Most likely it has no other Food to live on, but the Excrements of the Smaller Gulls; For I have often seen this Fowl violently pursue these Gulls, being Swifter in motion than they, and not leave them 'till it makes them Mute: Unless happily, it then leaves this, & attacks the next. The said Hagden is so dextrous, that, when the gull has muted, He'll catch it before it can fall into the water, although it may fall from it in two or three Parcells and the Gull not 50 foot from the Sea. This bird is not Common; I never saw two of them together, always on the wing, and in the Summer-time only.

Han's statement that the species is rare, is echoed by later writers up to Ryves (1948) —the only statement to the contrary being by Couch (1838). Many arctic skuas probably occurred in the autumn of 1879 when Gatcombe (z) recorded various species off the south coast of Cornwall and Devon—one had been obtained at Mevagissey (VCH). Ryves (1948) published only three records, but since 1950 the arctic skua has shewn itself to be a regular visitor with totals of several hundred in some years. The percentage of light to dark phased birds has not been studied, but in 1966 about three-quarters of the birds seen at St Ives were thought to be light; by contrast the bulk of the 34 seen at Newquay between 30 August and 17 September were dark.

Spring records are comparatively rare but since 1961 have been reported almost annually, mostly in April when as many as nine were seen off Port Isaac bay on the 4th in 1961, and four off Gurnard's Head on the same date the following year. The earliest spring records are of one between Land's End and the Scillies on 25 March 1957, and single birds at Gyllyngvase near Falmouth and at St Ives on 31 March 1963. Occasional

HANJAGUE, ISLES OF SCILLY—Scilly comprises five large inhabited islands and about 140 smaller islands and rocks—all of granite. Typical of the many outlying rocks is Hanjague, rising to 86′ above H.W.M.T. and one of the most easterly in the archipelago.

As with many other stacks, its auk population has sadly diminished as gulls have become more common. In the middle of the nineteenth century, large numbers of guillemots and razorbills crowded its ledges. The former became scarce early this century and probably last nested about 1940. In 1967 only one pair of razorbills are thought to have nested. Razorbills and puffins are still found on Great Innisvouls and Menawethan to the south.

Large numbers of herring gulls, lesser and great black-backed gulls have replaced the auks—over a thousand of the last named nest in the Eastern Isles as a whole. A few pairs of fulmars and larger numbers of cormorants and shags are also found on Hanjague. [*Photo:* F. E. GIBSON]

TRESCO, ISLES OF SCILLY—This view shews the Abbey, with the Pool in the foreground. The former was built, for the most part, in 1841 to the design of the Lord Proprietor, Augustus Smith, a keen naturalist and sporting-gun. Many unusual birds fell to the veteran gamekeeper David Smith or to notable visitors such as Augustus Pechell, F. R. Rodd, J. H. and F. Jenkinson, forming the basis of the Abbey collection now housed in the Isles of Scilly Museum on St Mary's. Today, shooting is more moderate although the Abbey Game Book accounts for 100–200 woodcock annually (413 in 1962–3).

The Abbey Pool and Great Pool are the most important inland waters on Scilly and cover about fifty acres. The latter Pool—out of view to the right—is some half a mile long and nearly 38 acres in extent. Reeds, planted early in the 1850's, give ample cover to nesting wildfowl and rails. The present population is estimated to be (in pairs)—mallard, 25; gadwall, 12; shoveler, 2–3; mute swan, 2; water rail, a few; moorhen, 20; and coot, 12 or more. [*Photo:* F. E. GIBSON] birds are reported through to the autumn migration which normally commences in the second half of August. Peak numbers occur in September and diminish gradually after the first week in October. November records are by no means annual and the latest stragglers are single birds at St Ives on 3 and 5 December 1960.

The peak numbers counted at St Ives in any one day have been within double figures every year since 1961. The most outstanding are—

| | |
|---|---|
| 59 on 13 Sept.  1966 | 34 on 17 Sept.  1964 |
| 57 on 18 Sept.  1965 | 29 on 12 Sept.  1962 |
| 53 on  7 Sept.  1961 | 26 on 17 Aug. and 25 |
| 44 on 12(?)Sept. 1962 | plus on 4 Oct. 1963. |
| At least 38 on 12 Sept.   1957 | 25 in under three hrs. |
| | on 26 Oct. 1967. |

The largest party outside St Ives Bay is fourteen off Newquay on 15 September 1966. Birds are now regularly reported here but the only other area where they are consistently seen is between Mount's Bay and Scilly. Records from the Isles themselves were very sporadic, with records in only 5 years from 1852 to 1958. In this last year, however, the unprecedented number of 180 were counted moving west near St Agnes on 18 October. Since 1963 arctic skuas have been seen annually in autumn off St Agnes, including eight on 5 October 1966. On the mainland away from the extreme west of the county and the Newquay area, records are few but probably indicate the lack of bird-watchers in these areas. One was seen at Dodman Point on 13 September 1950, two at Par on 4 October 1961, another here on 13 September 1961, and two at Talland on 11 September 1955. In the north-east one was seen at Boscastle on 29 June 1956, and one at Widemouth Bay on 10 November 1954.

## GREAT SKUA     *Stercorarius skua*

The great skua has a largely Antarctic distribution and has been reported further south than any other species, Captain Scott having seen one at 87° 20′S. The species has also been seen even closer to the North Pole for the great skua also nests in Iceland, Orkney and Shetland. After the breeding season they wander over the open oceans, northern and southern birds mixing in mid-Atlantic.

Skuas were first mentioned in Cornish waters by Ray and Willughby in 1662 when on 30 June they were taken by St Ives boatmen to Godrevy Island and were told of "Another bird . . . here called Wagell."† Mistakenly taken to be the young of the great black-backed gull, it is described as such in Willughby's *Ornithology* under the Great Grey Gull. That the bird was definitely a skua is proved by Willughby's statement that—

> The Cornish men related to us for a certain truth, that this Bird is wont to persecute and terrifie the Sea-Swallows, and other small Gulls so long, till they mute for fear; and then catches their excrements before they fall into the water, and greedily devours them as a great dainty: This some of them affirmed themselves to have seen.

The bird described in Willughby's *Ornithology* as a skua under "Our catarracta, I suppose the Cornish Gannet . . ." clearly describes the great skua, even to the correct number of tail feathers. Willughby was hopelessly confused with his identifications, as first pointed out by Walter Moyle in a letter to Dr. Sherard dated 26 January 1719–20, in which he stated his intentions, unfulfilled by his early death the following year, to correct Willughby's errors "especially that gross one about the Cornish Gannet".

A further mystery is whether the 'wagel' is the same skua as the 'hagden' described by Walter Moyle. The differences in the descriptions are small, but that given to

† The name 'Wagell' is a mutation of the Cornish *gwagel* from *gwak*, hungry, or empty (c.f. Welsh *gwak*), and very appropriate.

K

Moyle better fits the arctic skua, and will be found under that species. Possibly the names 'wagel' and 'hagden' were used indiscriminately by fishermen to describe any skua which they doubtless identified by its piratical habits rather than its plumage. The dialect name of 'Tom Harry', which is still in use, (or 'Horry' as pronounced in east Cornwall) from O.E. *horig* meaning filthy, from the bird's feeding habits, was apparently applied to any large skua, including the pomatorphine (D & M, 1892). Perhaps 'wagel' was restricted to St Ives and Mount's Bay while 'hagden' was used at south coast ports like Looe and Mevagissey. Another local name for a skua is 'cobb' (Borlase, MS), but it was also applied to gulls, for Nance remembered it being used for a young gull at St Ives.

Couch (1838) wrote that the great skua ('skua gull') was not uncommon, while Cocks (1851) wrote much the same having noted it in Falmouth harbour and the Penryn river from which localities there are no modern records. Gatcombe (z, 1880) remarked that the 'Old Hen' had become rare off our coasts, and Clark in 1902 (RI) called it a rather casual visitor that had become rarer during the past twenty years. This apparent decrease corresponds to a known reduction of British breeding birds as a result of human persecution, but this century, with protection, there has been a marked increase, including a spread to the Scottish mainland.

In recent years great skuas have been seen annually off Cornwall in greater or lesser numbers. Since 1960 they have been reported for all months—but not in every year. The only February records are of five individual birds at St Ives in 1966, and for June, one between Scilly and Land's End on the 15th in 1964. The records over this short period shew a significant pattern of a minor spring passage centred on April, and a much larger and annual autumn migration with the bulk of records in September and October. Autumn passage often commences in the latter half of August, while stragglers are not uncommon until December. Most great skuas are seen singly and rarely more than one or two on any one day. The most notable exceptions, all at St Ives (assuming the birds did not fly in circles to be counted more than once) are—121 between 8.40 a.m. and dusk on 4 October 1967 and 20 on 5 September 1967; 29 on 12 September 1962, and 17 on 12 November 1963 and on 1 November 1965.

Outside the migration period, records must be regarded as the chance occurrence of immature and non-breeding birds which habitually range the open Atlantic. When the young leave their breeding colonies they may remain for upwards of two years at sea. South Atlantic birds may impinge on our shores, but this has yet to be proved by the measurement of captured individuals. A few have been found on land—mostly very tired or injured as one found resting on the sand at Bude on 1 April 1954 which died the following day.

A record from Bude is unusual. Most great skuas have been seen in St Ives Bay and passing west off the Island, or between Scilly and Land's End especially about the Wolf Rock. Birds are probably more common off the Eddystone than recent records indicate; three were seen there in January 1960. Within the calm waters of the Scillies, few are seen although in the past few years they have been sighted annually off St Agnes in autumn with up to five on 27 November 1966, one to five on various dates between 21 August and 23 October 1965, and eleven on 8 October 1967.

# POMARINE (OR POMATORPHINE) SKUA
*Stercorarius pomarinus*

The pomarine skua breeds much further north than the arctic skua, almost exclusively in the tundra in a narrow belt around much of the northern hemisphere but no closer to Britain than west Greenland and Novaya Zemlya.

Birds winter mainly in tropical and sub-tropical seas and are seen in Cornwall on migration in autumn. Numbers depend on the severity of Atlantic storms for ordinarily migration is well away from land. Although figures were not published, more were probably seen in the autumns of 1879 and 1891 than in any year this century. In 1879 they were abundant off the south coast of Cornwall (z) and Vingoe, the Penzance taxidermist, was offered many immatures for sale. Clark in 1906 (vCH) wrote that examples had been noted every year since 1900 between the Truro and Helford rivers. Bullmore (1866) had recorded them at Budock, and Falmouth harbour, while one was shot as far up river as Malpas in November 1890 (G, 20 November 1890)—but there are no recent records from the south coast. Indeed, there are no county records from the turn of the century until 1950 (one possibly seen off St Mary's on 26 May 1925 (AR)) when, at Newquay, one was seen on 9 September and three on 17th. One was at St Ives on 11 September 1955, but from 1958 to 1967 at least one has been seen every year except 1960. Most records come from St Ives Bay, between the Scillies and Land's End, or reported off St Agnes by the observatory watchers. The only recent record from outside this area is a light phase bird at Widemouth Bay on 21 August 1959.

About 80 per cent of sightings from 1955 to 1967 occurred between early September and late October. Extreme dates at St Ives are 14 August 1962 and 16 November 1966 (three). Reports from other months are rare —one is said to have been taken alive at Newquay in December 1850, the first dated record for the county (G, 13 December 1850), an immature was shot near The Manacles off St Keverne about 15 June 1883 (z), and one was seen near Wolf Rock on 29 May 1950.

Single birds in one day are usual, but at least twelve were amongst 200 skuas flying west during a three hour watch at Horse Point, St Agnes on 18 October 1958, and four light phase birds were identified off St Ives on 1 November 1965. In autumn 1967 more than usual were reported, the passage at St Ives lasting from 14 August to 2 November with up to nine on 28 October and four the following day. Off Sennen twelve adults (seven of them light phase) flew south-west in three hours on 26 October.

## LONG-TAILED SKUA
### *Stercorarius longicaudus*

The long-tailed skua is the smallest and rarest member of the family seen in Cornwall. It is most frequently reported from August to October, when passing from its Arctic breeding grounds, which extend to within ten degrees of the Pole, to its winter quarters deep in the south Atlantic.

Most birds are identified as adults for immatures are almost impossible to distinguish from arctic skuas. Possible immatures have been seen at St Ives in recent years. Before the 1870's there was considerable confusion for both Buffon's skua (long-tailed) and Richardson's skua (arctic) had been given the specific name *parasiticus* by equally distinguished authors. Some doubt exists as to the authenticity of early records.

pre- Couch wrote that he possessed an 'Arctic
1838 Jager' taken with a baited hook; this he distinguished from the Richardson's skua. Gould (1832–37) mentioned one shot at Mevagissey in near adult plumage.

Long-tailed skua

1874    An adult without its tail feathers was shot in early October some ten miles from the open sea, probably near Perranarworthal (z).

1877    An adult shot near the Lizard on 4 June (z).

1891    A large flock was driven onto the shores of south-west England by severe October gales—the only occasion this has happened here. How many were seen in Cornwall is not known, but at least 50 were reported around the coast from Christchurch to east Somerset (D & M, 1892). Clark (RI, 1902) wrote that numbers were reported at Polperro and Fowey. A specimen formerly at Truro Museum (D & M) may have been shot at this time or possible in the 'invasion' of October 1879 for which there are no published Cornish records.

1925    One seen three miles east of Scilly on 26 May (BB).

1961    At St Ives, one on 13 August and a light phase bird on the 19th.

1962    One off St Ives Island on 27 August.

1963    Single birds off St Agnes on 7 and 20 October.

1967    Two off St Ives Island on 3 October, and one flying south-east over the Hayle estuary on the 17th. Ohe was seen from Penninis Head, St Mary's on 16 October.

## IVORY GULL          *Pagophila eburnea*

The ivory gull is a vagrant to Britain from the Arctic where birds nest on island north of 70°. They infrequently move south of the ice-floes even in winter.

1847    An immature seen for a day or two about the Battery Rocks at Penzance after "snowy and tempestuous weather", was shot from the pier on 15 February. This is assumed to be the same bird reported at Falmouth on the 13th (z).

pre-    A bird shot at 'Quilquay' (Kiln Quay)
1866    near Trefusis Point, Mylor, was mounted and sold to a commercial traveller from Bath (Bullmore, 1966). This bird was not listed by Cocks in 1851 or by Rodd in 1864, and it is not certain that it was the gull at Falmouth in February 1847 as implied in Harting's *British Birds* (1901) and by Clark (z, 1907).

1907    Two were seen at Hayle on 24 January and one, an adult male, was shot (z).

1917    A male was obtained at Scilly in January and placed in the Abbey collection.

## GREAT BLACK-BACKED GULL
*Larus marinus*

The great black-backed gull nests on rocky coasts and islets on both sides of the north Atlantic, but no further south in Europe than Brittany. It has extended its range northwards while in Britain it has become more abundant since the beginning of the present century. The great black-backed gull was first described in Cornwall by Ray and Willughby. The bird they were told of on 30 June 1662, when on Godrevy Island in St Ives Bay, they took to be the young of the great black-backed whereas, in fact, a skua was meant (q.v. great skua). Moyle, who shot and cased one in 1716, referred to the species as the 'Great Black and White Gull' (Tonkin, MS).

In Cornwall it is now a far more common nester on Scilly than on the mainland, but was once rare in both areas. North (1850) wrote that they bred annually on Gorregan, and Smart (PZ, 1885–86) knew of a few nesting on most of the grassy islets and some rocky stacks like Mincarlo, Gorregan and Scilly Rock. In 1903 only eleven nests were found—eight on Menewethan and single nests on Great Ganilly, Little Ganinnick and Inner Innisvouls. While birds were seen frequenting the Western Isles, no nests were noticed (z, 1906). The increase in the species throughout south-west England commenced at Scilly early this century. About 1913, King (MS) wrote that he had "counted fifty nests at one time on Illiswilgig year after year with nearly as many on Menewethan, to say nothing of Annet and other islands where there are several nests every year". In 1924 the same writer (*Scillonia*) estimated a breeding population of some 300 pairs on the islands —60 adults were shot on Annet in a single day in an attempt to relieve the devastation of the shearwaters and puffins whose corpses were strewn everywhere (Wallis, BB, 1923–24). In 1933 Harrison and Hurrel estimated that between 600 and 800 pairs bred at Scilly (*Proc. Zool. Soc. Lond.*, 1933), while in the mid-1930's Bond (Parslow[1]) found them more common than herring gulls on Annet. The last extensive survey was in 1946 when the following breeding pairs were estimated—

| | | |
|---|---|---|
| Annet 100 | Ganilly 10 | Meledgan 30 (60 in 1967) |
| Guthers 6 | Mincarlo 20—30 | Rosevear 50 or more (120 in 1967 shewed a slight decrease on other recent totals). |
| St Martins 2—3 | Samson 5 | Shipman Head, Bryher 3—4 |
| White Island, St Martin's 5 | | White Island, Samson 12 |

St Helen's colony not known in 1946.

A survey in 1956 gives numbers that are certainly too low. Thus, only 50 were said to be nesting on Annet in 1956 while 150 pairs were present in 1965, and less than 100 on the Eastern Islands were about 1,000 in 1963. The north-west rocks and islands, excluding Mincarlo, contained nearly 150 nests in 1963. The Rosevear population had increased to about 120 in 1962. The total population for the islands is likely to be between 1,200 and 2,000 breeding pairs. In 1967, 520 pairs were breeding in the south-west group of islands. In 1968 one pair nested on Round Island (A. T. Beswetherick[1]).

On the Cornish mainland the great black-backed gull was apparently scarce even as a winter visitor in some years in the mid-nineteenth century. Bullmore (1866) wrote that only one had come to his notice in the winter of 1865–66 and only three the previous winter, although Couch (1838) called it not uncommon—presumably in the winter. Rodd (1880) gave no breeding localities, but Yarrell (1882–84) and Saunders (1889) spoke of a few nesting in the

county. Clark wrote that a few bred at the Lizard and at two or three places on the north coast including Perranporth (RI, 1902). A. W. H. Harvey (1915) knew of nests scattered throughout the Land's End district and during the summer of 1924, G. H. Harvey found 26 pairs between Penzance and St Ives—sixteen of them on the flat

Great black-backed gull

soil-covered top of Enys Dodnan, eight of the remaining ten pairs on isolated or semi-isolated stacks, and two on the mainland. Elsewhere a few nested near Gwithian, Portreath and Mullion (BB, 1924–25). Harrison and Hurrell (1933 *op. cit.*) estimated the total breeding population for the mainland of Cornwall at something near sixty birds. Breeding at Mullion may have been of recent origin for no early writer mentions the species there, while today this area holds the greatest concentration of great black-backed gulls in the county: of 261 nests counted in 1967, 179 were in the Mullion-Lizard area, and all but 23 of these were on Mullion Island. The only other colony for which figures are available for a number of years is Enys Dodnan at Sennen. From sixteen pairs in 1924 it built up slowly to about 20 in 1937, 28 in 1945 and 31 in 1967.

Despite the general increase in the great black-backed gull's status, numbers have declined in at least one area since the 1930's. A colony formerly existed at Bedruthan Steps—20 pairs nested there in 1931, but only six in 1953 (Davis, BS, 1956), while none were found in 1967. It is unlikely that birds were overlooked for none were found at Carnewas Rock in 1968, where there were formerly up to fifteen pairs, and none at High Cove (A. T. Beswetherick[1]). Similarly near Tintagel, Davis found twelve to fifteen pairs, mostly with young, in 1956 at Lye Rock and others at Long and Short islands, but none were seen at the former locality in 1967. Madge[1] found no breeding gulls other than herring gulls between Rame Head and Polperro in 1968, while Davis found three pairs with nests on this stretch of coast. Other nests found in 1956, but not recorded during the 1967 survey were— Polperro to Dodman, two nests and one on the west side of Dodman Point; one pair on an off-shore rock at Zone Point, St Anthony-in-Roseland; and two nests at Henna Cliff, Morwenstow.

During the autumn, numbers increase but the size of wintering flocks on estuaries and sheltered bays and the timing of their build-up and eventual dispersal, remains unknown. Flocks commonly number over a hundred —up to 120 on 15 October 1967 at the entrance to Calenick Creek, Truro, a resort made attractive by the proximity of the adjoining rubbish dump. On Tresco in 1965, 135 counted in late January were reduced to twenty by late March: in mid-September the number had risen to 108 birds.

The increase in breeding numbers since 1910 is to be regretted because the gulls cause considerable havoc amongst shear-waters and auks (see under these species). On Scilly, Miss Quick (1964) recorded seeing a gull's nest into which sixteen dried bodies were built. The decrease in the auk population—especially of the burrowing puffins—can be attributed not only to the killer instinct of the great black-backed gull, but the habit of this and other species of tearing turf from the top of grass-covered stacks in their courtship displays. This loss of grass leads to erosion by wind action and a subsequent loss of suitable ground for puffin and shearwater burrows. Unless the

numbers of gulls can be controlled, it is feared, for example, that the puffin could become extinct on the Cornish mainland within fifty years.

The only recoveries in the county of birds ringed outside Cornwall are of two from Skomer, one from Skokholm and one from Lundy Island. There is one recovery of a foreign ringed bird—

| Ringed | Recovered |
|---|---|
| Kvitsöy, Rogaland, Norway, nestling 26.6.'59 | found dead, Falmouth 21.1.'60 |

Thirty birds ringed as nestlings at Scilly and five ringed at Mullion, have been recovered. Excluding those found locally, gulls have been recovered at Cork (2); Co. Clare; Co. Wexford; Glamorgan; and Kent (2). Foreign recoveries are—

| Ringed as Nestlings | Recovered |
|---|---|
| | SPAIN |
| Annet 4.7.'67 | shot, Fuenterrabia, Guipuzcoa 6.1.'68 |
| | FRANCE |
| Annet 27.6.'62 | found dead, Pont-Aven, Finistère 23.5.'63 |
| Rosevear 22.6.'64 | found dying Ile de Sein, Finistère 2.10.'64 |
| Rosevear 22.6.'64 | found dead 2 miles N.W. of St Guénolé, Finistère 4.11.'65 |
| Annet 27.6.'64 | Penmarch, Finistère 15.10.'64 |
| Rosevear 30.6.'61 | found dead nr. St Guénolé, Finistère 21.12.'61 |
| Rosevear 29.6.'65 | killed by fishing tackle at Quiberon, Morbihan 30.8.'65 |
| Rosevear 29.6.'66 | found dead, Le Loch, Plouhinoc, Finistère 19.1.'67 |

## LESSER BLACK-BACKED GULL
*Larus fuscus*

Several sub-species of lesser black-backed gull breed around the European and Arctic coasts. The British form, *Larus fuscus graellsi*, nests on most coasts in these islands as well as in Brittany, the Faeroe Islands, and Iceland. No Cornish name is known which specifically identifies the lesser black-backed gull.

# GREAT BLACK-BACKED GULL (Plain figures)
# LESSER BLACK-BACKED GULL (Circled figures)

ESTIMATED BREEDING PAIRS — 1967

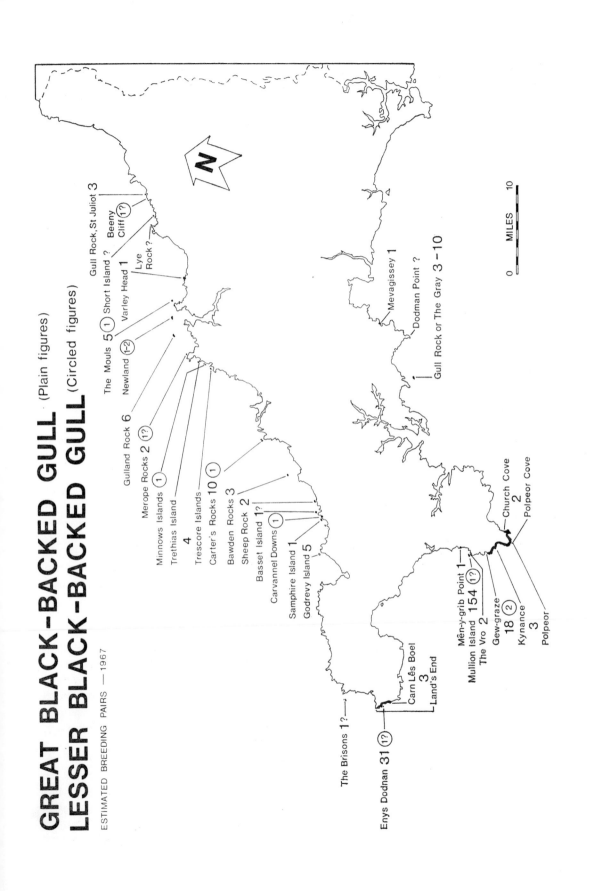

The Brisons 1?

Enys Dodnan 31 (1?)

Carn Lês Boel 3

Land's End

Mên-y-grib Point 1
Mullion Island 154 (1?)
The Vro 2
Gew-graze
18 (2)
Kynance 3
Polpeor

Church Cove
Polpeor Cove

Basset Island 1?
Carvannel Downs (1)
Samphire Island 1
Godrevy Island 5

Minnows Islands (1)
Trethias Island
4
Carter's Rocks 10 (1)
Bawden Rocks 3
Sheep Rock 2

Merope Rocks 2 (1?)

Gulland Rock 6

The Mouls 5 (1) Short Island ?
Newland (1–2) Varley Head 1
Lye Rock ?

Gull Rock, St Juliot 3
Beeny Cliff (1?)

Mevagissey 1
Dodman Point ?
Gull Rock or The Gray 3–10

0   MILES   10

The lesser black-backed gull commonly nests in large colonies but on the Cornish mainland it is the scarcest of the breeding gulls, only one or two pairs occurring at the localities shewn on the map. A few are probably overlooked but it has evidently always been rare. Few figures have been published. Holroyd Mills (z, 1903) noted only a few pairs amongst the herring gulls at Mullion Island, although Clark (RI, 1903) said it nested commonly here. In the early 1920's (BB, 1924–25) Harvey mentioned a few pairs at Gwithian and Portreath and about five or six pairs at Gunwalloe. Three pairs nested on or about Lye Rock, Tintagel in 1944 and the following year some six pairs nested on the coast about Trevose Head. Other sites known to Clark (RI, 1902 & VCH) were at Gurnards Head, Gull Rock at Veryan (commonly), and Perranporth where eggs were taken in June 1899.

In contrast to the mainland, the lesser black-backed gull is numerous on Scilly. Smart (PZ, 1885–86) found them on all the smaller Eastern Islands; Shipman Head, Bryher; Round Island; Menavawr; Scilly Rock; Maiden Bower; Mincarlo; Annet; and the Western Rocks. At Annet and the Eastern Islands eggs could be collected by the hundred. Numbers were always described in vague terms; in 1908 Frowhawk (Parslow[1]) found them the most numerous gulls on Annet, the large colony being situated in a stretch of bracken at the centre of the island. About 1936 "innumerable numbers" were on Annet when there was also a large colony on Samson (Parslow[1]). No numerical totals were published until 1946 when there was said to have been a large increase on the Scillies in general, although the Annet colony was much reduced—

| | |
|---|---|
| Annet | A few scattered pairs. |
| Gugh | At the end of May there were three colonies of 100, 60 and 40 pairs respectively. |
| Guther's | About 20 pairs. |
| St Helen's | A very large colony. |
| Gweal | Some nesting. |

| | |
|---|---|
| Samson | About 150 pairs—the colony on the west side having increased. |
| Bryher | 35 to 40 pairs on Shipman Head. |
| White Island, Samson | About 12 pairs. |
| White Island, St Martin's | A few pairs. |

The principal sites are now on St Helen's and Samson, where many hundreds nest (Hunt[1]), and on Annet with an estimated 700 to 800 pairs in 1967.

The lesser black-backed gull is most common in Cornwall as a passage migrant, but records of wintering birds have become more common on the mainland in the last twenty years. In 1965 there were two or three on the Camel estuary near Egloshayle, one at Tresillian, three on the Gannel, and one on the Tamar. About 100 were on the Tamar from mid to late December 1944 and 1945—the largest wintering numbers reported from Cornwall. Thirteen at the Hayle estuary on 22 December 1966 was an unusually large number at this date. Twenty-nine at the same place on 29 January 1966, a dozen at Hannafore near Looe, and six on the Lynher on 28 January 1967 represent early migrants. The spring migration is the most conspicuous of the two and begins early. At Scilly, where winter records are very rare, first arrivals include 6 February 1959, the 18th in 1961 and the 26th in 1963. Migrating parties often move on quickly as the fluctuating numbers from Hayle in 1965 indicate—about 285 on 12 March, 25 on 13 March, 100 plus on 21 March with another 300 at Porthkidney beach, 500 adults and 250 immatures (presumably of the same species) on 26 March, but only 40 on the 29th. In April there were some 500 on the 4th, 300 on the 5th, and 180 on the 7th. Similarly at Sennen beach in 1962 there were about 300 on 21 March where only a few were to be seen on the 29th.

Bullmore (1886), commenting on the abundance of the lesser black-backed gull in the spring, noted with distaste that they were killed in dozens "so great has become the demand for white plumes to adorn the gentler sex that this class of gulls may become extinct".

The duration and size of the autumn migration has been given less attention than the spring movement. First arrivals appear in early August, if not in late July—two were seen at Porthkidney beach on 4 August 1966. Flocks of several hundred are known to occur, but precise information is lacking. At Scilly the movement lasts into October, latest dates including 14 October 1962, and a straggler on St Agnes on 14 November 1961. Later dates on the mainland may refer to wintering birds.

Adults of the Scandinavian race, *Larus fuscus fuscus*, which winter as far south as Ghana and Nigeria, have been identified in small numbers in Cornwall, mainly between February and April. The largest party consisted of thirteen at Porthkidney beach on 2 April 1959.

While Scandinavian birds are normally conspicuous by their darker mantles, some variation exists within the British race. Up to five per cent of 400 birds on Samson in late July 1948, had darker than normal backs and accounts for the erroneous statements that Scandinavian birds had bred at Scilly, as supposedly on St Helen's in 1946.

Lesser black-backed gulls ringed at the following breeding localities have been recovered in Cornwall and Scilly—
Flanders Moss, Stirlingshire 1; Walney Island, Lancashire 1; Penmon, Anglesey 1; Skokholm, Pembs. 6; Skomer, Pembs. 1.

Only one ringed abroad has been recovered—

| Ringed | Recovered |
|---|---|
| Archipel de Molène, Finistère, nestling 7.6.'60 | found dead, Falmouth 28.8.'61 |

Thirty-eight birds ringed at Scilly have been recovered. Excluding those found within the islands, seven from the Cornish mainland, one from south Devon and another from Co. Wicklow, all recoveries have been from the Atlantic seaboard of the Continent—

| Ringed as Nestlings | Recovered |
|---|---|
| | PORTUGAL |
| Annet 21.6.'23 | Caparica, nr. Lisbon 28.9.24 |
| Rosevear 16.7.'14 | shot nr. Fao, Minho, end December 1914 |
| Annet 1.7.'24 | Lagos, Algarve 26.10.'24 |
| Samson 2.7.'59 | killed, Olhao, Algarve 12.1.'61 |
| Annet 9.7.'65 | found dead, Sines, Baixo, Alentejo 3.7.'66 |
| Annet 4.7.'66 | found dead nr. Furadouro, Beira Litoral 10.9.'66 |
| Annet 7.7.'66 | killed, Espinho, Douro Litoral 16.10.66 |
| | SPAIN |
| Annet 24.7.'24 | shot, Puerto de Sta Maria, nr. Cadiz, early March 1925 |
| Annet 22.6.'61 | killed nr. Cambados, Pontevedra 25.1.'62 |
| Annet 26.6.'62 | found alive, La Linea de la Concepcion, Cadiz 10.1.'63 |
| Annet 27.6.'62 | found exhausted, Pontevedra Bay 23.9.'64 |
| | FRANCE |
| Gugh 8.7.'24 | Guilvinec, Finistère June 1927 |
| Gugh 2.7.'25 | Ploudalmégeau, Finistère 17.9.'25 |

Godrevy Island, St Ives Bay - one of the numerous localities for nesting gulls in western Cornwall

| Gugh 8.7.'24 | shot, Aiguillon-sur-Mer, Vendée 9.5.'25 |
| Gugh 1.7.'24 | found dying, St Brevin, mouth of the Loire 20.7.'25 |
| Annet 4.7.'66 | found dead, Tréveneuc, Côtes du Nord 10.9.'66 |

## HERRING GULL    *Larus argentatus*

In Europe the herring gull nests on coasts from northern Scandinavia to Brittany and in Britain is common away from the south-east. Birds breeding in Britain, the neighbouring Continental coast, the Faeroes and Iceland, belong to the race, *Larus argentatus argenteus*. Breeding numbers have increased considerably, especially during the past quarter of a century, largely as a result of a closer association with man.

The name 'gull' is itself certainly of Celtic origin. *Gullan* (pl. *gulles*) found in Middle and in Old Cornish as *guilan* may be compared with the Welsh and Breton *gwelan* and modern French *goéland*. The Celtic name has now replaced the English 'sea-mew'. In return, English 'cob' was used within living memory, if not still, at St Ives as 'cobba' for a young gull.

The taking of gulls or their eggs is of great antiquity in Cornwall. While definite archaeological evidence is lacking, Lady Fox (*South West England*, 1964) has suggested that the ash-pits found at Trewardreva fogou, Constantine, and in the circular side-chamber at Carn Euny, Sancreed—both Iron Age sites—were for preserving gulls eggs (and perhaps auks) as done on St Kilda with gannet and auk eggs until the present century. Until bones or broken egg shells are found on a Cornish site, this can only remain a plausible suggestion.

Gulls as well as puffins were certainly taken within historic times for payment as rent, as Leland (1538) recorded at Scilly. A late sixteenth century interrogatory (L. Penna[1]) refers to the payment of a dozen gulls and other birds yearly as a rent for "the Gull Rocke next the lands called Penhale, in the parish of St Peran" to Hellwyn Manor, Crantock. The annual tithe in 1611 for Padstow's Gull Rock was two gulls (Henderson Cal. Vol. 6, RI, Truro). There are leases of 1678, 1695 and 1714 (two) referring to payments to the Manor of Trebarwith, Constantine near Padstow. For example, the ninety-nine year lease dated 10 April 1678, states that George Baron jnr. a yeoman of Trecarne, Tintagel "shall and will continually helpe fetch the gulls from the Rock called Maine Antrum and send them to the said Robert Rous" esquire of Wotton, Landrake (C. K. C. Andrews, *Devon and Cornwall Notes and Queries*, 1956). One of the two leases dated 1 December 1714 is interesting in adding that the lessee "shall and will endeavour to preserve the gulls by feeding them"—presumably on grain to make them more palatable. Carew (1602) wrote that young gulls and pewits were "fetched about Whitsuntide for the first brood, and some weeks later for the second. Some one, but not every such rock may yield yearly towards thirty dozen of gulls. They are kept tame and fed fat . . ." Both gulls and puffins were considered a delicacy in Tudor Times (see further under puffin), but at what date their harvesting lapsed in Cornwall is not known.

The herring gull has been labelled as a common nester by all past naturalists and for that reason almost no information exists on the history of breeding colonies. Curiously, the one documented colony at Rame Head has decreased in numbers contrary to the supposed general trend. Here, where there are now about half a dozen pairs, was once a large colony with birds "breeding plentifully" in 1872 and "a great many sitting in early May 1878" (z). Plenty were there about 1900 but only a few in 1932 (Madge[1]).

The 1967 census estimated 5,000 herring gulls breeding in Cornwall, excluding those on rooftops and at inland sites. The coastline

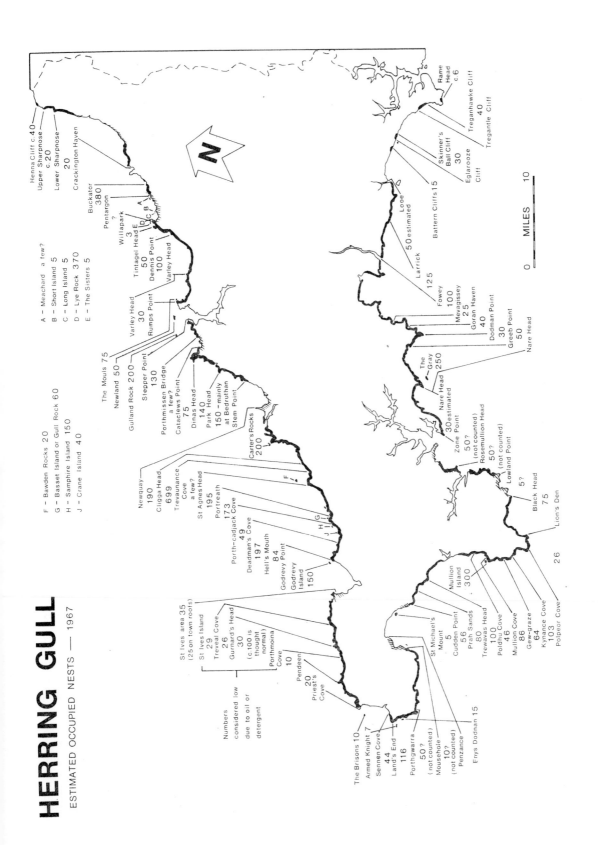

# HERRING GULL

ESTIMATED OCCUPIED NESTS — 1967

from Rame Head to Looe, being devoid of auks, was not thoroughly covered in this census, but the following year Madge[1] found four nesting areas containing approximately 90 pairs. All figures on the map for the rest of the Cornish coast may be taken as an absolute minimum. Figures between Porthleven and St Ives were especially low due to the *Torrey Canyon* disaster. Thus, only twenty nests were found between Priest's Cove and Pendeen, St Just, where the normal population was estimated by N. R. Phillips to be nearer 75 pairs.

While normally nesting on cliff ledges or on the top of off-shore stacks, less typical sites are being increasingly used, notably rooftops in seaside towns. The full extent of this habit is not known, for even in towns where it occurs widely, the nests may be extremely difficult to detect. A rooftop nest was first recorded at Port Isaac in 1910, and by the late 1920's gulls were described as being "semi-domesticated and practically parasitic on man, coming to be fed at the sound of a bell rung for the purpose" (BB, 1928–29)—probably in Newquay where nesting was first noted in the mid-1920's on the high parapet and flat tops of the dormer windows of the Atlantic Hotel. It is only since the 1940's, however, that rooftops seem to have become widely favoured—at Porth near Newquay (1943, BB), Mevagissey (1946–47), Porthleven (1946) and Polruan (1966). In Newquay numbers now nest in Henver Road despite attempts to foil the unwelcome guests. The railway station has proved a popular resort since 1959 when a nest was found on a railway handcrane and 1960 when a pair deserted a carriage after shunting operations in favour of the roof between two platforms. The eggs were taken from here and the pair moved to another glass roof. Other sites in the goods yard (now demolished) were used as well as a flower bed between the platforms, a concrete rubbish bin, and the gap between two sleepers in a siding from which two young were reared despite shunting.

In St Ives, herring gulls have nested on the roof of the Weslyan Chapel since 1952, in Richmond Place, Fore Street, and St Peter's Street since 1956 and even more widely since 1962. In Newlyn, for at least the past four or five years, pairs have bred on nearly every rooftop in Kenstella Road where the inhabitants have now constructed frames in the angle between chimney pot and roof to deter them. A few pairs nest elsewhere in the town and at Mousehole. Two pairs each reared one young on the roof of the old mill (now the Old Meade House) and a nearby barn in Gulval near Penzance in 1967, but not in 1968. In the Lizard district a pair reared two chicks in 1966 between the chimney and gutter of Glenmoor bungalow, Mullion, about a mile from the sea (*The Lizard*, 1967). In 1959, 1960 and 1961 a pair nested on the ground in front of the Poldhu Hotel, Mullion.

On the south coast a pair nested in a wallflower bed in a cliff-edge garden at Polruan in 1955, and at least twelve pairs nested in terraced gardens there in 1962. Nesting occurred in St Austell in 1958 and probably since. Unique in Britain was the attempt made to nest 30 feet above the ground in the fork of a large Scots pine tree at Porthpean House, St Austell in 1958 and 1959. At Par two pairs nested successfully on the flat walls of china-clay drying pans some fifty yards apart.

China-clay workers are familiar with the gulls as nesters in deserted clay pits, a practice first noted in 1947 at the Bloomdale Pit, Foxhole where two young were hatched about 1st July from a nest about twenty feet above the water. The same year another nest was found at a pit about three miles away. In 1948 a pair again bred at Bloomdale only a few feet above the water level and some eighteen inches inside a hole in the cliff. From 1949 birds nested at Caudletown pit, Stenalees, numbers increasing gradually to some twenty pairs in 1955 and at least forty in 1960. In 1958 one pair nested at Delabole slate quarry, two pairs in 1960, and perhaps since then, but certainly not since 1965 (Kent[1]). At Porthallow, St Keverne, "scores" are said to breed in the greenstone quarries, but exact information is lacking.

At Scilly, birds have nested on all the islands. Smart (PZ, 1885–86) noted breeding on all the smaller Eastern Isles, Annet, Shipman Head on Bryher, Round Island, Menavawr, Scilly Rock, Maiden Bower, Mincarlo, and the Western Rocks. At the first two localities, where the birds were more numerous on rough herbage, eggs could be collected by the hundred. Little has been published since. King (1924) wrote that birds had lately taken to nesting on Gugh where over 100 pairs were recorded in 1945 and "in that part of St Agnes which is cut off at high water during spring tides". Recent published reports speak only of the birds being common everywhere. The only large colony counted has been the one on Annet which has decreased since about 1960. Only 150 pairs were estimated in 1966 and 1967 compared with 400 to 500 a few years ago. On Round Island, however, only two pairs now nest (A. T. Beswetherick[1]). The total population at Scilly is about 1,000 pairs.

Wintering numbers and daily feeding movements to and from the coast have not been studied. Very large roosts are known, notably one containing "thousands" of herring, common and black-headed gulls, in Carrick Roads in the region off Penarrow Point. An inland roost at Tamar Lake in the winter of 1952–53 (Hickling, BS, 1954) comprised about 3,000 herring gulls, 750 black-headed gulls, 250 common gulls and 25 great black-backed gulls. A further study by Hickling (BS, 1960) on coastal roosts produced a number of records from south-east Cornwall—the rest of the county not being covered. At Clifton Marsh on the Tamar were under 100 herring gulls and a similar number of great black-backed amongst thousands of black-headed gulls. On the coastal cliffs between Crinnis beach and Charlestown under 1,000 herring gulls and a few great blacked-backs were noted

with a similar population between Polkerris and Fowey.

Continental birds certainly visit Cornwall but in what numbers is not known. The typical race, *Larus argentatus argentatus*, from the Baltic has been identified in the field when seen close to the British form. Two birds killed in March 1837 and described by Couch (1838) as a new species which he called 'Jackson's Gull' after the naturalist who shot them, were possibly of this form. The Karelian herring gull, *Larus argentatus omissus*, found on the Finnish and Murmansk coasts, frequently has yellow and not flesh-coloured legs. Several birds, possibly of this race, have been recorded in Cornwall—one in a field at Reskadinnick, Camborne on 20 October 1944, and one on 2 January 1950 at St Antony Creek. Only one herring gull ringed outside the British Isles has been recovered locally.

| Ringed | Recovered |
|---|---|
| Brest, Finistère, adult 17.10.'56 | found dead, Scilly 7.4.'57 |

British ringed nestlings originated at—
Anglesey, 2; Skomer, 5; Skokholm, 13; Steep Holm, 1; Lundy, 8.

All twenty-two recoveries of birds ringed on the Cornish mainland have been within the county, generally within a few miles of where ringed. Of eighteen ringed on the Scillies, the only recoveries outside the county are—

| Ringed as Nestlings | Recovered |
|---|---|
| Annet 30.6.'63 | found oiled, Great Yarmouth, Norfolk 27.2.'66 |
| | FRANCE |
| Scilly 6.7.'52 | found wounded, Piriac, Penestin, Morbihan 23.4.'54 |
| Annet 26.6.'62 | found wounded, La Barre-de-Monts, Vendée 3.12.'62 |
| Annet 12.7.'64 | caught exhausted on a fishing boat, La Turballe, Loire Atlantique *c.* 1.11.'64 |

The records support the view that most British-bred herring gulls are sedentary with some shift southwards during the winter months.

## COMMON GULL                *Larus canus*

The common gull breeds from Scandinavia and the Baltic coast across Asia to Alaska and parts of western Canada. In Britain it is largely confined to Scotland and Ireland where it has increased since the last century. The only colony in the south is a small one at Dungeness.

In Cornwall the common gull is a regular passage migrant and winter visitor. Its status seems to have changed little since the last century when all writers described it as common apart, from James (1808) who called the "winter gull" rather scarce.

Almost no numerical data have been published. It is said to have a rather patchy distribution in the county being scarce in areas which seem suitable—it certainly belies its name on the Camel estuary where R. J. Salmon[1] generally sees only twos or threes, and occasionally the odd dozen. This scarcity also applies to the beaches at Polzeath and Trebetherick. By contrast 250 have been counted on Watergate Beach near Newquay. The common gull is equally numerous on south coast estuaries. The Fowey estuary, Par Beach, and tributaries of the Fal—Truro complex are favoured localities where birds congregate in hundreds. A considerable movement occurred in south-east Cornwall in 1966 when 600 were seen at St John's Lake on 12 January and 2,400 two days later.

A few immatures remain on estuaries or beaches throughout the summer. The first adults do not return, normally, until the latter half of August—22nd at St Agnes in 1963 but not until 12 September the following year. An early date is one at Porthkidney beach, Lelant on 4 August 1966. The majority do not arrive until October and November when they disperse to feed in the fields as well as on the coast. Even in the mid-nineteenth century Bullmore (1866) commented on the frequency with which it followed the plough. In Devon and east Cornwall, if not generally throughout the county, the common gull was popularly called the "barley bird" being seen frequently about the fields late in the spring at the season of barley sowing. Flocks seemed to be especially numerous in the fields about Stithians reservoir in January 1968 when it was certainly the commonest species next to the black-headed gull. On the edge of Bodmin Moor in St Breward Parish, Col. Almond (1959) wrote that it is an irregular visitor in autumn and winter being most common in hard weather. The departure of wintering birds takes place from March to mid-April with stragglers remaining until May—21st at St Agnes in 1963.

On the Scillies it is far less common with small numbers on migration and a few, usually single birds it seems, remaining in winter. The bulk of common gulls wintering in Britain are of Scandinavian origin.

Common gulls

| Ringed as Nestlings | Recovered |
|---|---|
| Vorsö, Jutland, Denmark 20.6.'39 | Padstow 5.2.'47 |
| Jylö Island, Halland, Sweden 25.6.'21 | Cawsand 13.4.'31 |
| Hallands Väderö, Halland, Sweden 2.7.'31 | Torpoint 16.3.'32 |

| | |
|---|---|
| Knauskär, Vändelsöfjord, Halland, Sweden 23.6.'35 | Wendron 5.3.'37 |
| Knauskär, Vändelsöfjord, Halland, Sweden 17.6.'36 | Trevarno, Helston 9.1.'38 |
| Grasøyane, Herøy, Norway 10.7.'60 | Newquay 14.2.'63 |
| Hirsholm, Jutland, Denmark 25.6.'30 | "Cornwall" 16.1.'31 |
| nr. Stavanger, Rogaland, Norway 30.6.'51 | Godrevy 2.3.'52 |
| Idsal, Rogaland, Norway 20.7.'54 | Torpoint 9.11.'60 |
| Hällaryd, Blekinge, Sweden 11.7.'62 | St Ives 5.1.'63 |

The only recovery within the British Isles is—

| Ringed as Nestling | Recovered |
|---|---|
| Lough Carra, Co. Mayo, nestling 23.6.'47 | St Stephen-in-Brannel 28.1.'48 |

## GLAUCOUS GULL
### Larus hyperboreus

The glaucous gull has a circumpolar distribution breeding as near to Britain as Iceland. It is a regular visitor, mainly to the Northern Isles, but is well known in Cornwall. In the nineteenth century it was described as an occasional solitary visitor with more in only a few years, as in January 1873 and 1895 (VCH). It is now reported almost annually, 75 per cent of the birds being in immature plumage. In recent years none has been reported only in 1952, 1954, and 1956. One was seen at Mousehole on 12 September 1965 and another at Porthgwarra, St Levan on 21 September 1967, but most occur between late December and April—7 May 1967 at Marazion. An immature remained at Newlyn from 11 January to 23 August 1962. There are a few sightings away from the coast, including an immature, with other gulls, on a ploughed field near Ludgvan on 25 February 1950.

Away from the Mousehole-Marazion area and St Ives Bay where they are equally regular, glaucous gulls have been reported this century only at The Lizard on 5 May 1944, Sennen on 25 March 1934, Swanpool at Falmouth on 18 February 1937, St Mawes on 31 August 1938, and at Bude from 5 to 31 March 1941.

The glaucous is a solitary gull and only on the Scillies have there been up to three at a time. However, while it may have been overlooked, it appears to be generally rare here. Since one was shot at Pentle Bay, Tresco in 1874 (Z, 1906) it has been recorded in only ten years up to 1967. Latest dates are 16 May 1951 and 16 June 1947 at St Mary's. Three remained at Tresco until 28 May 1924 (BB). More than usual were reported in 1967—an immature at St Mary's on 20 January and 27 March, as well as an adult throughout February and March, one at New Grimsby, Tresco from January to late March and an oiled bird on 7 April, and two off the Western Rocks on 29 March.

## ICELAND GULL     Larus glaucoides

This arctic gull would more properly be called "Greenland gull" for it has never bred in Iceland. It is a winter visitor to Britain, mainly to the east coast, and in Cornwall is much scarcer than the glaucous. The first, an immature, was obtained by Jenkinson on Bryher in late May 1852 (Z), and the first from the mainland were immatures shot at Falmouth on 24 April 1863 and 6 January 1864 (Bullmore, 1866). The species appeared in at least nine other years up to the end of the century. Many, mostly immatures, were reported in January and February 1873, especially at Lamorna Cove (Z), while of the winter of 1874–75 Gatcombe wrote that more immatures and adults had occurred on the coasts of Devon and Cornwall than ever before owing to long continued gales (D & M, 1892). It was also plentiful in 1895, since when it was "not unfrequent between Truro and Penzance" according to Clark in 1902 (RI).

Records this century, mostly for late winter and early spring, are—

1914  One about three miles off Penzance on 16 April (BB).

1923  One wintered at St Mary's until at least 9 May (BB).

1928  An immature in Newlyn harbour on 29 March (CBWPS, 1931).

1944    An immature at Hayle on 3 February.

1948    One on ploughland at Porthmissen Farm, Padstow from about 29 March to 8 April.

1951    An adult at St Mary's on 28 April, and another at St Ives on 16 May.

1958    An immature at St Ives on 13 May.

1962    An immature at St Ives from 9 February to 21 March and another off Penzance on 29 May.

1965    One at Tresco on 12 February and an immature at Hayle, Marazion Marsh, and Penzance between 10 and 27 March.

1967    One flying east at Freathy, St John's on 13 May, and an immature at St Mary's on 3 November.

## MEDITERRANEAN BLACK-HEADED GULL
### Larus melanocephalus

The Mediterranean gull is regarded as a distinct species even though it has bred with the ordinary black-headed gull, as in Holland in 1934. Its normal breeding range is within the Balkans, the Black Sea area, and Asia Minor. In Britain it was thought to be a vagrant but has been reported annually since 1960, mostly on the Channel coast.

According to a MS catalogue, two birds at Peplow Hall, Shropshire were killed at Falmouth in March 1851 (BB, 1907–8). If authentic, this is the earliest British record, no other being reported until 1866 in Essex. No doubt the ready dismissal of black-headed gulls as being hardly worthy of attention resulted in the Mediterranean gull being overlooked in the past, for small numbers have been reported annually since 1960 when single birds in first summer plumage were seen at St Ives from 7 March to 10 April, 26 to 27 November, and on 10 December. In 1963 the only record was of a bird which remained at St Ives throughout most of November. In other years several were seen with a maximum of seven (unless individuals were counted more than once) in 1961. Some remain for months at a time and are only largely absent from mid-April to the end of July. None has been

seen in May and only two in June—off Godrevy Point on the 12th in 1966, and at Tresco, the only Scilly record, on the 21st in 1964. The only July record is one on the 31st in 1961 at St Ives. Spring records have gradually extended to cover an ever earlier period so that birds are present from the beginning of the year—the latest date is 14 April 1964.

Apart from the bird at Scilly, the only sighting away from the St Ives Bay–Hayle estuary area is on the Camel on 3 November 1964.

## BONAPARTE'S GULL
### Larus philadelphia

The Bonaparte's gull nests about the lakes in the forest belt of the Canadian Shield and winters as far south as Central America. About twenty were recorded in Britain up to 1968.

1865    An immature was shot by a ship's captain in Falmouth harbour on 4 January and described at length by Rodd (z & Rodd, 1880). A second specimen was shot near Penryn on 10 January (Rodd, 1880).

1890    An immature was shot by Vingoe near Newlyn on 24 October and identified by Harting (z).

1901    One seen on Marazion beach on 3 February (vCH).

1944    One shot at Scilly on 16 December.

1967    One on the Hayle estuary from 23 to 25 October (R).

1968    Single birds were at St Ives from 16 to 24 March (R) and at Newlyn on 7 November (R).

1969    One at St Ives from late February into March.

## LITTLE GULL      Larus minutus

The little gull nests near freshwater at widely scattered localities in north-west Europe and, more commonly, from the eastern shores of the Baltic into central Russia.

It was formerly regarded as rare with only

about fifteen recorded up to 1905. Couch (1838) wrote that two or three had been obtained but the earliest dated occurrence was one from Land's End on 24 December 1844 (z). Probably it was not as rare as published records suggest and its status may have changed little. Indeed, Harvey (1915) described it as not uncommon in autumn and winter. Since 1947 records have been annual and rare only from May to July with reports in each of these three months in only three years up to 1967. Peak numbers are seen each year in September and October with frequent reports throughout the winter until about early April. The majority of old records refer to immature birds, and while these still predominate adults are seen annually.

Most records are of solitary birds but at St Ives there were five adults and three immatures on 28 October 1962, eight immatures on 28 October 1959 and on 29 and 31 October 1967. The little gull is commonest in St Ives Bay where, in company with other gulls, it likes to feed at the sewer outfall off the Island. Good numbers have been reported from Mount's Bay, especially about Marazion Marsh where it has been annual since 1960. A few have been reported from Par and several other localities as far east as Tamar Lake—one on 2 August 1958—and St John's Lake—one on 4 August 1965.

The only records from Scilly are—

1905   One obtained in Christmas week (z).
1947   One at St Mary's on 18 October.
1963   Single birds at Tresco on 15 September and at Gugh on the 18th.
1967   An immature in St Mary's harbour on 25 November, one at Bar Point, St Mary's on 10 December, and another on St Agnes on 12 October.

## BLACK-HEADED GULL
### Larus ridibundus

The black-headed gull breeds widely in Europe outside the Arctic and Mediter-

ranean zones. In Britain it is commonest in the north.

Several names, variants of a common Celtic (?) root have been applied to the black-headed gull in Cornwall—'maddrick gull', 'merrick', and 'miret'. 'Skarraweet' was sometimes used for this species but more properly referred to the common tern, as does 'miret'. According to Hartley (1936) the Saltash fishermen called them 'pigeon gulls'.

*Black-headed gulls*

Cornwall is outside the normal breeding range of this gull. Carew (1602) wrote that gulls and 'pewits' bred "in little desert islands bordering on both coasts". At this date 'pewit' (originally 'puet') generally referred not to the lapwing but to the black-headed gull. By the early eighteenth century at least, its present meaning had evolved in Cornwall, although Borlase (MS) noted that its application to the plover was incorrect. Possibly Carew also used 'pewit' incorrectly, but whether he meant plover or gull the off-shore rock stacks are not a typical breeding habitat of either species, although not unknown for the gull. N. Hare had heard of a gull's nest being found on Bodmin Moor (PZ, 1846) which, if true, is hardly likely to have belonged to any species other than the black-headed gull. This is not improbable as the species was certainly more widespread in Britain early last century when it nested on the Scillies—

L

two nests were found on St Mary's in 1841, while a copy of Montagu belonging to E. H. Rodd contained marginalia (not in the owner's hand) stating that birds bred also in 1845 (z, 1906). There are no more records until 1925 (BB) when Robinson and Boyd found a nest with two eggs on 2 June (deserted on 12 July) in the middle of a colony of common terns. The first confirmed mainland record is of a nest with two eggs near Dozmary Pool on 16 May 1959. In 1967 a pair successfully reared one young at the new Stithians reservoir, building their nest on a small islet close to the main road. In 1968 the nest was deserted, possibly because great black-backed gulls ate the eggs.

The black-headed gull is a common winter visitor and passage migrant. In some areas, as the Lizard peninsula, the species is more common as a migrant, especially in autumn, and rare in the middle of winter, but comparative figures are not available for the major estuaries. There is little information on the daily flights of black-headed gulls from the coast to inland feeding sites—in winter 10,000 are said to stream up and down the Tamar. This gull is certainly the most common on many estuaries in winter—up to 1,000 have been counted at Tresillian in parties of a few dozen to 250. Figures from a few roosts were published in *Bird Study;* about 750 at Tamar Lake (1954), less than 10,000 gulls (mostly black-headed) at Clifton Marsh on the Tamar, about 1,000 at Par Harbour, and less than 1,000 at Fowey Harbour (1960). One of the largest county roosts of herring, common and black-headed gulls is in Carrick Roads below Turnaware Point, Feock.

Some non-breeding birds remain throughout the summer on estuaries, and to a lesser extent inland; most are immatures in varying states of plumage.

The arrival of autumn birds may be as early as mid-June but is usual about the beginning of July. In 1965 the first waves of migrants were at the Camel and Hayle estuaries on the first of the month, with 200 in a field at the former locality. At Stithians reservoir in 1966 a juvenile arrived on 4 July. In 1962 a large influx occurred in the Marazion-Penzance area in the week beginning 28 June and in 1967 the first birds were noted on 23 June at Falmouth. Information from the Lizard peninsula (*Lizard*, 1962) shews that the migration periods here are from July to November and the rather sparse spring passage in March and April. In other parts of Cornwall a considerable movement is said to occur from the beginning of February, but nothing has been published on its build-up or decline. In 1961 over 900 were counted on the Gannel at Newquay on 9 February—some three or four times the usual number present.

Forty-eight black-headed gulls ringed at breeding sites have been recovered in Cornwall and Scilly (mainly in autumn and winter). Only thirteen were ringed in Britain. Recovered birds came from—

ENGLAND AND WALES
Kent 6, Essex 2; Hants 2; Radnor 1; Cumberland 1; Montgomery 1; Cardigan 1.

| Ringed as Nestlings | Recovered |
|---|---|
| U.S.S.R. | |
| Babite Lake, Latvia 30.5.'63 | remains found, Lelant 27.9.'63 |
| Babite Lake, Latvia 10.6.'34 | Mousehole, January 1936 |
| Babite Lake, Latvia 23.6.'43 | Truro 12.1.'47 |
| Matsalu, Estonia 16.6.'62 | found injured, Mylor 8.1.'64 |
| Lake Juvinkas, Lithuania 6.7.'59 | Cremyll 27.11.59 |
| FINLAND | |
| Viik, nr. Helsinki 22.6.'57 | found dead, Carkeel, Saltash, Jan—March 1963 |
| Vähäjärvi, Tampere Häme 15.6.'61 | found injured, Penzance 19.1.'63 |
| Ruskis, Uusimae 4.6.'61 | sick, destroyed, Tywardreath 9.8.'62 |
| Ö Rönnskär, Helsinki 11.6.'61 | found dead, Lelant 2.1.'63 |
| Sannanlahti, Oulu 29.6.'64 | found dead nr. Newquay c. 5.3.'65 |
| SWEDEN | |
| Måkläppen Islands, Skåne 22.6.'24 | Whitsand Bay (nr. Rame) 26.1.'30 |
| Måkläppen Islands, Skåne 20.6.'27 | "Cornwall" 28.8.'31 |
| Sôdre Möckleby, Öland 18.6.'32 | River Fal 28.9.'33 |

| Ringed as Nestlings | Recovered |
|---|---|
| Askö Västerås-Baskarvö 12.6.'38 | St Mawes 17.3.'40 |
| Tysslinge, Orebro 30.5.'53 | Penzance, Oct.—Nov. 1953 |
| Gustavsberg, Uppland 28.6.'62 | found dying, Par 5.12.'63 |
| **NORWAY** | |
| Fornebu, Akershus 29.5.'56 | Saltash, February 1960 |
| **DENMARK** | |
| Thy, Jutland 12.6.'27 | Padstow 1.9.'29 |
| Vorsö, Horsens Fjord, Jutland 20.6.'35 | "Cornwall" 26.10.'36 |
| Mörköv, Jutland 2.7.'55 | released, Delabole 10.1.'56, |
| **GERMANY** | |
| Plön, Schleswig-Holstein 28.6.'50 | Newquay 4.11.'52 |
| Insel Beuchel, Mecklenburg 23.6.'57 | Saltash 1.1.'60 |
| Insel Wender, off Zingst Peninsula, Mecklenburg 8.7.'13 | "Cornwall" 7.11.'13 |
| Biengarten, nr. Höchstadt, Ober Franken 11.6.'63 | found trapped in a bouy nr. Saltash 11.1.'65 |
| Wessel, Bautzen, Sachsen 31.5.'52 | Golant 24.5.'56 |
| Wessel, Bautzen, Sachsen 16.6.'52 | Lerryn 7.8.'52 |
| Wessel, Bautzen, Sachsen 1.6.'61 | found long dead, Gannel 4.11.'62 |
| **HOLLAND** | |
| Ijdoorn Polder, Noord Holland 2.6.'59 | found dead, Gweek 9.3.'60 |
| Kijkduin, Zuid Holland, adult 6.5.'62 | found exhausted, River Camel 23.12.'67 |
| Grote Peel, nr. Nederweert, Limburg 23.5.'67 | found injured, Wendron c. 10.2.'68 |
| Plas Ravensberg, Reenwijk 28.5.'67 | found dead at a fox's earth, Liskeard 17.7.'67 |
| **BELGIUM** | |
| Kalmthout, Antwerpen 9.6.'53 | Perranporth 4.1.'54 |
| Lichtaart, Antwerpen 1.6.'55 | found injured, Penzance 16.7.'55 |
| Le Zoute, West Flanders 19.6.'62 | killed by a vehicle between Redruth and Truro 31.1.'63 |
| Brasschaat, Antwerpen, adult 23.3.'65 | found dead, Hayle c. 17.6.'65 |

## SABINE'S GULL *Xema sabini*

Sabine's gull is an arctic species breeding in the extreme north of America, parts of Greenland, and Siberia. During the winter it ranges over the north Atlantic but not much further south than the latitude of Cornwall.

In the nineteenth century about sixteen records, all of immature birds, are known from about 1860 until November 1902 when one was shot between Lostwithiel and Doublebois (z, 1907). The only examples from Scilly were one shot in autumn 1893 (z, 1906) and another, in breeding plumage, at Wolf Rock the following September (z, 1896). No more were reported from Cornwall until 1951 when one appeared at St Austell on 22 July after an easterly gale.

Since 1957 it has been seen annually in varying numbers, mostly at St Ives where a careful watch has been kept for this species. Other reports come from Scilly, Wolf Rock, and from several localities as far east as Widemouth Bay and Looe. All have been recorded in autumn, mainly between early September and mid-October after heavy westerly gales which may indicate an American origin for most of them. The earliest record is that from St Austell given above—a few have also been seen in mid-August. The latest dates are 16 October and 25 December 1967 at St Ives.

Mullion Island with Gull Rock (or The Vro) partly hidden by the mainland cliff.

While all but one of the early records are of immature birds, adults are now seen just as frequently. Indeed, in 1961, seven of the eight seen between 19 August and 8 October were adults, some in breeding plumage. About 80 per cent of records from 1957 to 1967 consist of single birds, but as many as eight have been counted on several occasions, as between 10.00 a.m. and 1.00 p.m. on 6 September 1967 at St Ives Island.

## KITTIWAKE                         *Rissa tridactyla*

The kittiwake breeds in colonies on many coasts and islands throughout the arctic, in places north of 80°, and in western Europe as far south as Brittany. About 175,000 are estimated to nest at British colonies, mostly in Scotland. The species has increased considerably this century and may represent the return to a population level existing prior to widespread persecution in the nineteenth century. In Cornwall, however, there is no record of nesting before the nineteenth century so that the county may have come within the bird's breeding range only recently.

The kittiwake was described by Willughby (*Ornithology*, 1678) as the "Ash-coloured Gull of Bellonius . . . called in Cornwall, Tarrock". The latter name is most properly applied to the young of the kittiwake, but was also used for the black-headed gulls in Cornwall and for the common and arctic terns in the Shetland Isles. In Cornwall the adult kittiwake was known as the 'kiff'—"a very like bird to the Do but no black in the tail feathers and the bill not of a black colour but all lemon or straw—a very beautiful colour bird" (Borlase, MS). This name has also been applied to the adult black-headed gull and is still used in this sense by Porthleven fishermen (Sargent, *History of Porthleven*, 2nd MS ed. 1968) and at Scilly (King, MS), while Nance said it may also have been used for terns in Newlyn. Moyle (*c.* 1718) wrote that

the tarrock was common on the Cornish coast but made no mention of breeding. The name 'Annet' has been used for the kittiwake, as by Montagu, but one cannot conclude that the island of this name in the Scillies was an ancient breeding station for its name means Little St Agnes. Indeed, there is no record of breeding there before 1965.

On the mainland Couch (1838) called the species common in autumn and winter, but unknown as a nester. Yarrell (1837–43), however, refers to nesting in "part of Cornwall" —the fourth edition also including Scilly. Lord Lilford (*British Birds*, 1885–97) found nesting stations on the south coast of Cornwall in 1852. Dresser (*The Birds of Europe*, 1871–81) refers to breeding here and on some of the granite cliffs near Land's End; Cecil Smith found them in some very perpendicular places between Land's End and the Logan Rock in May 1885 (z). Curiously neither Rodd nor Clark knew of this colony and A. W. Harvey (1915) knew of no nests anywhere in West Penwith. Not until 1923 were any discovered, or rediscovered, by G. Harvey (BB, 1924–25) who saw about 80 adults and a few young still in the nests at Carn lês Boel. The following June about 150 adults were estimated in two colonies on the island and the cliff face. Clark (VCH) did, however, note nesting in diminishing numbers at Mullion Island, Gull Rock at Veryan, and

*Gull Rock or The Gare - the only important sea-bird colony off the south coast*

in at least one south coast station between the Tamar and Fowey rivers. These colonies were unknown to G. Harvey and up to the 1940's were known only at Carn lês Boel and Morvah. The latter, first seen in 1941, but evidently established at least as early as the late 1930's, contained over 180 nests in 1944. A peak of 218 nests in 1950, fell to 142 in 1957, but the colony has probably remained fairly stable since, with 136 nests in 1967. Greeb Point, to which the colony spread from the Zawn 300 yards away in 1944 when it contained 20 nests, held about 50 nests in 1947, 120 in 1949, but was completely deserted in 1957. Only five nests were found there in 1967, when the main site had moved to Whirl Pool below Long Carn, with a further group of 15 at Brandys.

The colonies south of Land's End have become smaller mainly, it is thought, because the cliffs are now too popular with rock climbers. In 1933 between 170 and 180 pairs nested at Carn lês Boel, most of them on the off-shore stack, but by the early 1940's, more and more spread to the mainland opposite. In 1950 the colony contained 60 to 70 nests and probably does not contain more than 50 at the present time. Tol-Pedn-Penwith, probably an estension from Carn lês Boel, contained about 40 pairs in 1945, at least 58 in 1959, but only four in 1964, and eight in 1967.

Kittiwakes nested at Godrevy in 1959, but the site is not known to be occupied today†. Apart from the Morvah and Carn lês Boel colonies, the other breeding sites found during the 1967 survey were at— St Agnes, now the largest cliff colony of any species in the county with about 900 pairs in three adjoining groups on the west side of the headland. The colony was first discovered in 1948 containing 50 to 60 pairs, so probably had been in existence for several years prior to that. When Bawden Rocks off St'Agnes were first colonized is

not known, but about 150 nests were there in 1951, about 100 more than at present. A colony of three pairs was discovered in 1967 at Ralph's Cupboard, Portreath. Not recorded until 1966 is the colony at Rinsey Head where about 80 pairs now breed. The history of the Mullion colony is not known since Clark found birds there. Harvey (1924) found none, nor at nearby Gull Rock, concluding that the cliffs were too small, although many nest there today. 60–70 pairs are about normal at Mullion Island, but only about 25 bred successfully in 1965 when fifteen pairs were also sitting on Gull Rock. Little is known of the past history of Gull Rock, Veryan, since mentioned by Clark (VCH) as nesting in diminishing numbers. 100 to 150 pairs were present in 1956 and about 80 pairs in 1964. In 1967, as well as the 288 nesting pairs, another 50 sites were occupied by birds probably too young to breed.

On the Scillies, the main kittiwake colony until the middle of the last century was on Menavawr off St Helen's, where Jenkinson noted large numbers in 1852. However, they gradually forsook the rock and Smart found none here in 1883 or 1884 (PZ, 1888–89). Moving to Gorregan, highest of the Western Rocks, Jackson recorded as many as 100 nests closely packed on the south side just above the Smugglers' Hole, but from the 1870's breeding numbers diminished—three pairs in 1900 being the last record (Z, 1906. Robinson, BB, 1920–21). After an hiatus of nearly forty years, G. H. Harvey and others found about six pairs nesting on Menavawr in 1938 where a local boatman said they had been for several years. The colony was not then firmly established for Dorrien-Smith found none in 1944 (Ryves and Quick, BB, 1946). In 1945 Buxton found 20–30 nests on Gorregan and a possible 12 to 15 (at least four) on Menavawr (BB, 1946), and the following year 47 on Gorregan but none on Menavawr. However, numbers at each colony gradually increased from about 1950

† A report that 20 to 30 pairs bred at Trebarwith near Padstow in 1956 is wrong—kittiwakes have never been known to nest here (Treleaven[1]).

# KITTIWAKE

ESTIMATED OCCUPIED NESTS — 1967

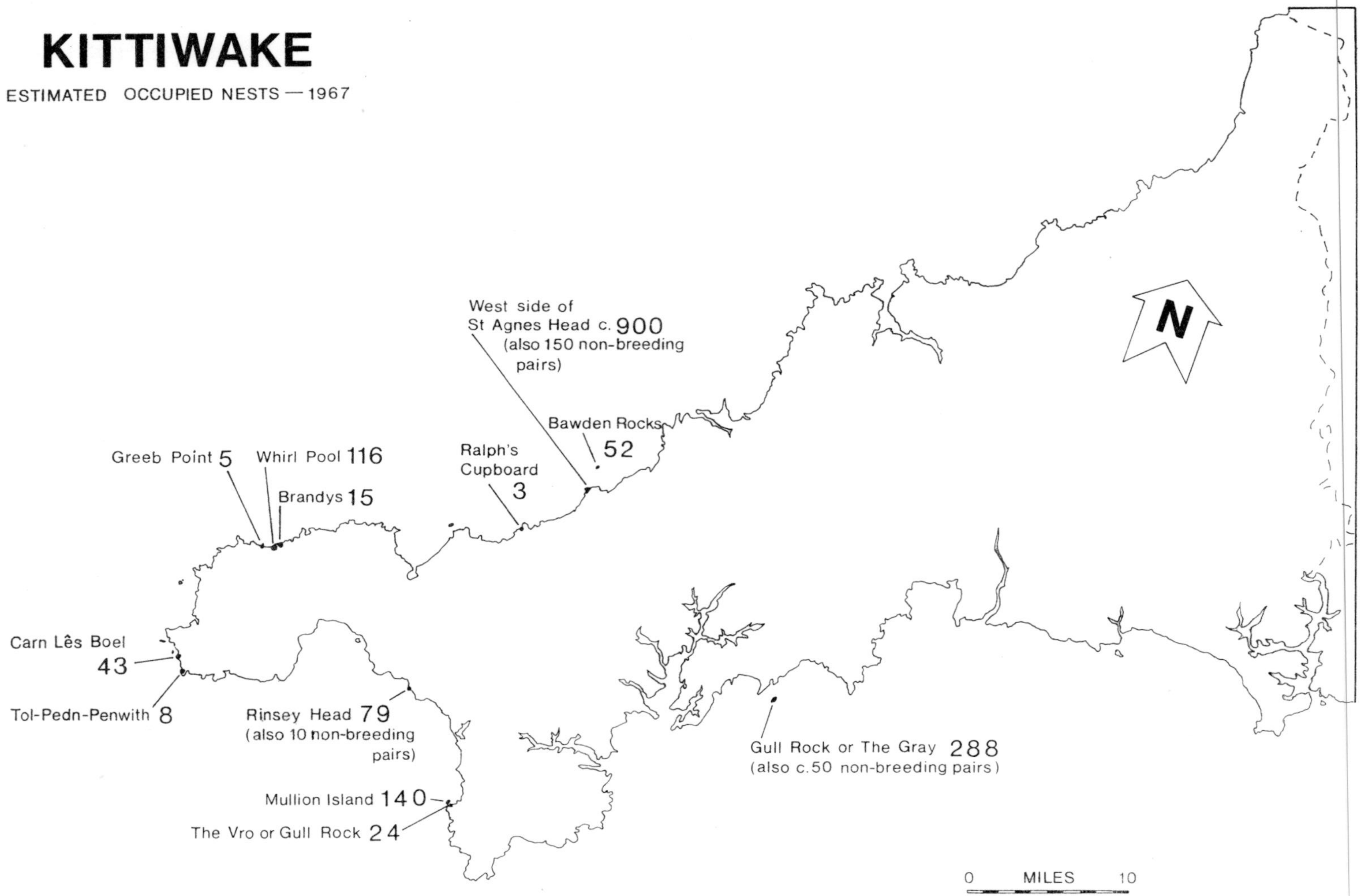

West side of
St Agnes Head c. 900
(also 150 non-breeding
pairs)

Bawden Rocks
52

Ralph's
Cupboard
3

Greeb Point 5
Whirl Pool 116
Brandys 15

Carn Lês Boel
43

Tol-Pedn-Penwith 8

Rinsey Head 79
(also 10 non-breeding
pairs)

Mullion Island 140

The Vro or Gull Rock 24

Gull Rock or The Gray 288
(also c. 50 non-breeding pairs)

N

0    MILES    10

until saturation point was reached in less than a decade. 258 nests were counted on Menavawr in 1958, over 100 in 1967 and on Gorregan about 50 in 1959 and 91 in 1961. To relieve overcrowding on Menavawr birds moved across the sound to St Helen's —about a dozen pairs nesting on the low earth cliff on the north face in 1959. The following year there were 21 nests and the colony increased to about 120 in 1967. Further colonies have been established—at the north end of Annet since 1965 and at Daymark Head with about 20 pairs in 1966 and 28 in 1967, on St Martin's since 1966 with perhaps about 20 pairs in 1967.

Kittiwakes may be seen off the Cornish coast at all times of the year. Essentially pelagic outside the breeding season, the majority rove the open Atlantic between about 40°N. and 55°N. Heavy kittiwake movements in severe weather are usually accompanied by numbers of other deep sea species such as phalaropes, petrels, and Sabine's gulls. In 1966 on 16 November at least 20,000 kittiwakes flew west past St Ives Island between 8.00 a.m. and 4.30 p.m. and a similar number was estimated on 1 November 1965 during the same hours. Movements of 1,000 an hour are recorded annually and have been known to continue for several days—as on 27 and 28 October 1959 at St Ives. Large movements have also been recorded off Towan Head, Newquay where over 3,000 passed south-west on 30 December 1965 between noon and 3.00 p.m. Birds infrequently rest on beaches but an estimated 4,000 were on Porthkidney, Lelant, during a force 7–8 north-westerly gale on 12 November 1963.

There is no evidence of a regular passage movement off Cornwall—the number of birds seen being due rather to the weather conditions. In 1957 a succession of depressions from 4 January to 11 February resulted in an unprecedented 'wreck' (McCartan, BB, 1958). Most stranded birds were recorded in the south-west—many dead and others too weak to fly. Some had died in a position which shewed that they had nose-dived into the soft ground. Post mortems indicated death through starvation. In Cornwall the first evidence of the wreck was on 4 February when two were found dead. "Unusually large numbers" were seen in the Penzance area on 7 February including fourteen in the harbour and many flying past the Battery Rocks. Over 100 were counted about Newlyn harbour. At Fowey birds became so tame that they accepted food with the herring gulls. The 1957 wreck is said to be the first in British waters, although smaller ones were known on the Continent, but a large invasion occurred in south-west England in 1877 after a severe gale in January. None were found dead, but Gatcombe reported hundreds shot when the birds became exceptionally tame (z).

| Ringed | Recovered |
|---|---|
| The Skerries, Antrim, nestling 3.7.'63 | found dead, Goran Haven 15.4.'66 |
| Puffin Island, Anglesey, nestling 2.7.'63 | found alive but weak at St Ives 4.7.'64 |
| Lundy, nestling 10.7.'57 | found dead, Camel estuary 22.5.'62 |
| Lundy, young 15.7.'51 | fell dead on a French fishing boat off the Lizard 15.5.'52 |
| Scilly, adult 22.5.'38 | found dead, St Andrews, Fife 11.8.'39 |
| St Anthony-in-Roseland, immature 13.6.'60 | found dead where ringed 18.6.'60 |
| Grand Tas de Pois, Finistère nestling 30.6.'59 | caught and released at St Ives 25.8.'59 |

BLACK TERN          *Chlidonias niger*

The black tern nests on marshes rich in reed beds throughout much of western and central Europe, but in Britain, apart from nesting at Pett Level, Sussex in 1941 and 1942, it has not done so since 1885.

In Cornwall in the last century it was described as an uncommon visitor in autumn and exceptional in spring. Clark (z, 1906) noted an increase after 1900 with annual records even in spring. A flock of 25 to 30 frequented Marazion Marsh for a few days commencing 19 April 1901 (z)— a flock still unsurpassed in size for that time of year. Despite this increase, Ryves (1948) regarded the black tern as rare, and numerous observations since 1950 have shewn it to be regular only in autumn.

The main spring migration route lies to the east of Cornwall, so that while heavy passages were noted from Somerset and the west Midlands in 1946, 1948, and 1949, none was reported in Cornwall except in the autumn when migration takes place on a broader front. An exceptional spring passage did occur in 1962 from 21 April to 18 May, mostly of solitary birds but up to ten at Marazion Marsh on 1 May. Early dates are 10 April 1903 when seven were watched at Porthellick Pool, St Mary's (z, 1906) and 12 April 1967 when two flew over Marazion Marsh.

The heavier return passage occurs between early July and mid-October. Solitary birds or parties of up to four are usual, but larger numbers are known. Parties of twenty-one, four, nine, and nineteen moved west past St Ives on 19 September 1962. Fifty were counted at Hayle on 22 September 1957, 100 flew past St Ives on 30 September 1967, while 150 were estimated to be in St Ives harbour on 29 September 1958. The latest records are of single birds at Marazion Marsh on 11 November 1954 and in St Ives Bay on 12 November 1967. One was found dead at St Mary's on 26 November 1967. Most records come from west Cornwall where birds may be seen at inland localities such as Stithians reservoir, but the species is not uncommon throughout the county.

Published records from Scilly are few but a small number are now seen annually in autumn, principally at the pools on Tresco, St Mary's, and St Agnes.

## WHITE-WINGED BLACK TERN
### Chlidonias leucopterus

Like the whiskered tern, the white-winged black tern is a marsh species with a

breeding range in Europe largely confined to the Balkans and southern Russia. Occasionally it nests beyond its normal range—as in Belgium in 1937. In recent years more have been seen in Britain than whiskered terns, but the only Cornish records are—

1882  One in full breeding plumage shot at Tresco Pool on 14 May (z).

1887  An immature shot sometime at Sennen was identified by Saunders (z).

1964  One in breeding plumage at Melancoose reservoir on 4 and 5 May (R).

1965  A bird in breeding plumage was watched at Hayle on 3 August, at Drift reservoir on the 4th and 5th, and at Marazion Marsh on the 6th (R).

## WHISKERED TERN
### Chlidonias hybrida

The whiskered tern is a marsh species with a very scattered Mediterranean and tropical distribution. The nearest regular breeding grounds to Britain are in the Loire basin—occasionally it nests further north, as in Holland in 1958.

1851  (Not 1857 as given in Rodd, 1880). An immature shot at Tresco Pool about 31 August (z).

1958  One in full breeding plumage seen about the Amble River near Wadebridge on 28 and 29 May.

1964  One in breeding plumage at Marazion Marsh on 27 May (R).

1965  Another in breeding plumage at Marazion Marsh on 19 June left early the next morning (R).

1968  A bird photographed at Ruan Lanihorne was present from 26 to 30 April (R).

## GULL-BILLED TERN
### Gelochelidon nilotica

The gull-billed tern nests at scattered localities in Europe in greatly diminished numbers—Denmark remains one of its strongholds. In 1950 (and perhaps 1949) it nested in Essex, and is now an annual visitor to south-east England.

1852   An adult shot at Tresco Pool at the end of May or beginning of June (z).

1866   The report of 27 September (G) that a fine specimen was shot in Cornwall a few days before, may have referred to the bird which Gatcombe reported killed on the Laira, Plymouth sometime between mid-September and mid-November (z).

1872   One in breeding plumage shot at St Just-in-Penwith on 11 July (z).

1965   One seen on 15 September under excellent conditions sitting on a rock off Tresco only thirty yards from the observer (rejected, R).

1967   One seen at Old Grimsby, Tresco on 3 June (R).

1968   One seen at Hayle on 18 April (R), and another at Widemouth Bay on 6 September (R).

Common terns

## CASPIAN TERN
### *Hydroprogne tschegrava*

The Caspian tern has an almost world-wide distribution. The more important European colonies flank the northern Baltic, the Black Sea and Caspian Sea. It is a rare visitor to Britain but in the ten years 1958–67, nearly forty were recorded, mainly on the east coast between May and September with most in July. The only Cornish record refers to two birds hawking over Tresco Pool on 22 July 1962.

## COMMON TERN   *Sterna hirundo*

The common tern breeds in a broad belt south of the tundra and extending to the Mediterranean in western Europe. Birds also breed extensively in eastern Canada and the Atlantic seaboard of the United States. In Britain numbers have generally decreased this century, but there is considerable fluctuation at individual colonies.

The sea-terns as a genus have been familiar to Cornish fishermen for centuries —the locals describing to Willughby and Ray in 1662 how these birds were pursued by skuas. Curiously, no counterpart of the Welsh *morwennol* (sea-swallow) survives in Cornish, however the dialect '*scarraweet*', sometimes applied wrongly to the black-headed gull, certainly derives from some form comparable to the Welsh *ysgraen*, a tern. *Miret* is another local name "extended indiscriminately to the whole genus", (Couch, 1838). An arctic tern killed on the St German's river (z, 1882) was called by the man who shot it a "pearl gull", a name commonly applied to this species in Devon and doubtless other terns. Clark wrote that the common tern bred sparingly on the Cornish coast (VCH) but the only published record refers to eggs taken at Newlyn in July 1864—"they were deposited in the sand and protected only by loose stones" (Bullmore, 1866).

The only nesting colonies at present are on Scilly. A ternery at the south end of Annet was noted by Mitchell in May 1840 (Yarrell), but the size of colonies was never recorded in the last century. About the 1850's breeding numbers were diminishing (Jenkinson MS, 1854). At this time the arctic tern was more plentiful, but by the end of the century the dwindling numbers of common terns were in excess of the depleted 'arctics' (z, 1906). Robinson wrote that in 1911 they were fairly plentiful and that in 1914 were to be seen only on Guther's (BB, 1920–21). The number of colonies and breeding birds has fluctuated considerably over the years, but the few figures from the 1920's and 1930's for better known sites like Green Island are much larger than for recent years. Boyd (BB, 1924) wrote that terns bred at four colonies and that Robinson had ringed 191 pulli on one island (Green Island?) where there were still many eggs unhatched. Terns are still widespread, not only on the smaller rocks but also on the inhabited islands—notably Tresco—but nesting is not annual here and successes are poor due to human disturbance. A colony of 50 was reported on the south shore of Tresco in May 1965 (success not indicated) while in 1955 there were only four pairs on Castle Down. The activities of rats and gulls are responsible for many failures. Many birds also nest so low down on the shore that exceptionally high spring tides may do considerable damage. Clark (z, 1906) wrote of nests being floated off and in 1942 breeding places were washed out in June, the same thing happening the following year on Green Island and Guther's. In 1952 terns had a very poor season, most birds deserting in mid-June, but the following year was one of the best.

Annet. About 60 pairs present in 1953. The main colony at the waist of the island where as many as 150 had nested in 1946, contained only ten pairs—a new site held about 50.

Tresco. None mentioned in 1953 but about 30 pairs recorded in 1962, 20 or more in 1963 and 50 in 1965.

Skirt Island off Tresco. About twelve pairs in 1953.

Green Island off Samson. At "a large colony" in 1953 most pairs were successful. About 150 pairs were reported in 1943 and 1946, but only 30 or so in 1960, 1962, and 1963.

Tean. Twenty pairs at Old Man and the same number at Yellow Carn Porth were unsuccessful in 1953. There were 32 nests in four colonies in 1951, none in 1954 or 1955.

Hedge Rock off Tean. One egg in June 1953.

Great Cheese Rock south of Tean. One successful pair 1953.

St Helen's. Two pairs seen on 10 June 1953 but no nests were found.

Guther's. About ten pairs bred unsuccessfully in 1953. In 1914 this was described as the only breeding locality, with 20 to 30 pairs "but not a full clutch among them" (Robinson, BB, 1920–21).

Great Ganilly, Eastern Isles. Some 60 eggs counted one day in May or June 1953 had gone completely two days later.

Great Ganinick, Eastern Isles. A small colony at the north end of the island in 1953 was not successful.

Hangman's Isle off Bryher. About ten pairs in 1953, but none in 1955.

Merrick Island off Bryher. About 20 pairs in 1953, none in 1955, and four in 1962.

St Agnes. At least five pairs reared young on Wingletang Down in 1953 and a few nested in 1954.

Burnt Island off St Agnes. Eight to ten nests were found in 1951 but no young were reared.

Gugh. There were four or five nests on each hilltop in 1953 but no young were seen. Four nests were found in 1952 and one in 1963.

In 1945, but not subsequently, nesting was reported from Foremans Island off Old Grimsby, Tresco, and Stony Island off Samson with 17 pairs. Isolated nests were found on Tresco and Bryher.

The spring passage, lighter than that in the autumn, is recorded annually in west Cornwall from about mid-April to the end of May. Maximum counts include 37 on 7 May 1964 at Marazion, 50 at Par on 25 May 1966, 100 at Porthkidney beach, Lelant on 8 May 1957, and over 500 off St Ives Island on 24 April 1963. Early arrival dates are 20 March 1965 at Porthkidney, and 31 March 1962 at Sennen and in 1966 at Pendower, Veryan.

A few terns remain in St Ives Bay, and probably elsewhere, throughout the summer months. A party of eighteen fishing in St Ives Bay on 8 July 1957, 100 or more at Porthkidney on the 12th in 1964 and on 17th and 20th in 1966, were all probably early autumn migrants. Several hundred common terns in a single autumn day are now reported every year. Most spectacular were 3,000 passing St Ives Island in a force 8 W.N.W. gale on 17 October 1961 and at the same locality, 500–600 on 6 September 1962, 400–500 between 8.00 a.m. and 4.00 p.m. on 17 September 1964, and 400 or more on 22 August 1965. Away from St Ives Bay only smaller numbers have been seen—59 on the Camel estuary on 18 August 1965. The sand banks of the lower reaches of the Camel are important tern resting and feeding grounds second only to Porthkidney beach. Autumn passage in recent years has been noted in small numbers as far east as Widemouth Bay and the Tamar estuary. While many may occur in early October—150 to 200 at St Ives on 4th in 1963—most have departed. Late stragglers have been seen on 2 November 1965 at Newquay, 7 November 1963 at Par, 14 November 1965 and 25 November 1963 in St Ives Bay.

Unusual, but not unknown even as far north as Scotland, are the rare winter records. A juvenile remained at St Ives until 14 December 1953, and another flew west past Hannafore, Looe on 24 December the same year. Early in 1947 one is claimed to have been seen at Perranporth standing in the snow, and one was identified at the Hayle estuary on 14 January 1940. According to Clark (VCH) common terns were often seen in winter in severe weather and occasionally, as in 1890–91, in very large flocks, but as he gives no dates, 'winter' numbers could refer to late autumn migrants.

| Ringed | Recovered |
|---|---|
| Vanajanselkä, Häme, Finland, nestling 1.7.'66 | caught on a fishing line and released St Ives c. 24.9.'66 |
| Reeuwijk, Zuid Holland, nestling 14.6.'56 | found dead, Penzance 22.8.'56 |

Six young ringed on Scilly in 1924 and 1925 were recovered where ringed within a few weeks.

## ARCTIC TERN  *Sterna paradisaea*

The arctic tern breeds mainly in the tundra, but on both sides of the Atlantic its range extends south along the coasts. In Britain the most southerly breeding station is at Scilly, and apart from sites in Brittany, the most southerly in Europe.

In Cornwall the arctic tern was formerly more abundant than the common tern. Although Yarrell (1843) had been told of only a few breeding, Rodd (1864) wrote that at Scilly "its eggs may be taken annually" and that the common tern was not so plentiful as either this species or the roseate. Up to the early 1880's it outnumbered the common tern, but by 1906 it "was sadly in the minority" (Z, 1906). By 1920 the dwindling numbers of common terns had completely taken the place of the 'arctics' (Robinson, BB, 1920–21). One pair may have bred in 1924 (Wallis, BB, 1924–25) but identification was not positive. Varying numbers of nesting arctic terns may have escaped attention from time to time, for while Ryves and Quick (BB, 1946) knew of no records, Buxton (BB, 1946) had found 31 nests on Annet on 15 June 1945—the only terns on the island. The following year Dorrien-Smith reported a very large colony on Annet; on Tean five pairs with an immature scarcely able to fly were seen in August, and thirteen nests, possibly of arctic terns on Skirt Island off Tresco seen the same month, were later destroyed. While birds have been seen since in summer, and a heavy spring migration was reported in 1952, the only recent record of nesting is in 1964 with 40 to 60 pairs on Annet. No evidence of nesting could be found the following year.

As a passage migrant the arctic tern is less often identified both on Scilly and the mainland than in the last century. Were it not for shot specimens, one might reasonably doubt the claim of Bullmore (1866) and Rodd (1880) that it was the commonest member of the family. In May 1842†, Bullmore recorded hundreds at Swanpool, Falmouth on the 1st and about the harbour on the 2nd but all had gone next day. Six, five of them males, were killed at Looe (Couch, Supplement to 1838 *Fauna*), but birds were equally common on the north coast. In 1906 Clark still described the arctic tern as a common spring and autumn migrant, but only a few are identified nowadays, mainly in the autumn. However, some are doubtless indistinguishable in the large flocks of common terns.

Between 1958 and 1967 birds were seen on only seven spring migrations—all single occurrences at Porthkidney, Lelant except in 1966 when two were seen at Hayle on the unusually early date of 8 April, and a decapitated bird was picked up in a field at Nanstallon, Bodmin on 13 May. Most are recorded from the end of April to late May. An unusual date is 30 June 1964 when one was seen at Porthkidney. On autumn migration single birds are most common but two or three together are reported every year in St Ives Bay. Maximum numbers are at least six off St Ives on 4 October 1963 and seven at Porthkidney on 5 September 1957. This latter locality has produced the bulk of mainland records, but a few occur as far east as Widemouth Bay and the Tamar. Throughout much of September 1967, ones to threes were seen between Hannafore, Looe and St John's Lake after about 45 (together with about a dozen common terns) were blown into the shelter of Caw-sand Bay on the 5th. A few have also been seen in Mount's Bay including the Lizard area. The autumn passage commences about the end of July or beginning of August, but records are too few for a peak passage period to be discerned—more have been reported in late October than in the second half of August. Early dates include one at Porth-kidney on 13 July 1964 and two at St John's Lake on 21 July 1966. Latest occurrences are at Daymer Bay on 5 November 1966 and at St Ives on 11th in 1963. Arctic terns seem to pass through the county without stopping for any length of time—hardly surprising if most winter so far away as the pack-ice of Antarctica.

## ROSEATE TERN  *Sterna dougallii*

The roseate tern has a very scattered breeding distribution throughout the world. In Britain there are a score of colonies where it is far more common than in the late nineteenth century when it became nearly extinct.

When Mitchell visited Scilly in 1840 he found the species "tolerably common", and obtained as many eggs as he required (Rodd, 1880). In 1854, Jenkinson found only a few pairs and the last recorded appearance of the birds at their former breeding haunts was in September 1867 (Z, 1906). Traditional haunts were Annet and some localities nearby, including Guthers (Z, 1870 & PZ, 1888–89). In 1908, Clark (RI) confirmed that they had been extinct for over thirty years.

The return to the islands began about 1920 in which year King (MS) recorded three or four pairs nesting on Guther's, and Green Island off Samson, while Dorrien-Smith knew of single nests in 1921 and 1923 (AR). The first published record is of a single pair amongst common terns on 26 June 1924 (BB). No further breeding was noted until 1943 when four pairs nested on Green Island and one on Guther's. Unfortunately, due to high seas, only one pair on Green

---

† Bullmore wrote 1843 but certainly intended 1842, when in early May a remarkable migration of common and arctic terns was recorded elsewhere in south-western Britain—hundreds were killed in Devon.

Island were successful. Birds again bred in 1944 (BB, 1946) but none were seen the following year. In 1947, at least two pairs probably bred on Annet and one pair on Green Island. In 1950, there was a big increase when seven nests were counted amongst those of common terns on Annet and others nested on Green Island and Guther's. A fire on Annet in 1951 reduced the breeding success to two pairs. Numbers have since fluctuated but an estimated twelve pairs in 1959 is probably the maximum for the islands while less than half is normal. Birds arrive at the islands in early May—the 5th in 1964 and 1965. An early date is 26 April 1963. Birds were last seen on Tresco on 20 September 1965 and on 21 September 1961 at St Agnes.

On the mainland the roseate tern is a passage migrant in small numbers. The only records for the last century are one shot in Mount's Bay in 1842 (VCH) and another at Swanpool, Falmouth on 1 October 1846 (Bullmore 1866). Ryves (1948) knew of no examples but since 1951 they have been recorded annually, mostly in St Ives Bay, especially at Porthkidney where they congregate on the sands with other terns. Ones or twos are usual—maximum numbers being twelve on 23 July 1966, nine on 7 August 1966, and eight on 1 August 1964. The passage commences in early July and lasts into September. Early dates are 25 June 1966 and 30 June 1964 while late dates include 18 September 1965 and an adult and immature at Hayle on 1 October 1967. Spring passage is much lighter with only one or two reported in most years during May—three on 7 May 1964. Early dates include 30 April 1967, and late dates 6 June 1966.

Away from west Cornwall there are few published records, but recent observations at St John's Lake indicate a small annual passage—in 1966 between 10 July and 14 September (five on 10 July) and in 1967 between 16 July and 6 September (maximum of eight). Three terns were at

Roseate terns

Widemouth Bay from 11 to 18 October 1966 and another as late as 21 October at Looe in 1967. Very early were others at Looe on 23 April 1966 and Falmouth on 26 April 1964.

## SOOTY TERN  *Sterna fuscata*

The sooty tern is a vagrant to Britain from the Caribbean, its nearest breeding area. Less than twenty have been recorded in Britain. Neither Cornish record is considered fully authenticated, although the descriptions given make it difficult to assign them to any other species.

1883   In the autumn of that year, David Smith watched one flying over Tresco Pool (z, 1906).

1951   One was seen and heard to call at Porthkidney beach, Lelant on 31 July.

## LITTLE TERN  *Sterna albifrons*

The little tern is found throughout coastal Europe but has become increasingly rare in Britain, breeding in just a few areas, notably in East Anglia.

Ryves and Quick (BB, 1946) wrote that it had ceased to breed in Cornwall, but there is some doubt that it ever was a regular nester here. Saunders (*Manual of British Birds*, 1889) wrote that it bred at suitable localities, perhaps deriving his statement from the early edition of Yarrell which ambiguously states that "birds visit many different places along . . . the south coast from Cornwall to Sussex". However, no writer specifically mentions breeding until Clark (RI, 1906) wrote that "The lesser tern, which has for some years been regarded as a regular spring and casual autumn bird of passage still breeds in the county. Long may the locality continue to escape observation!"

Up to 1906 the only records from Scilly are of migrants (z, 1906)—

1857   Immature shot on Guther's on 14 September.
1863   Seven (three shot) between Tresco and Samson in October.
1877   One at Great Pool, Tresco for several days in July.
1904   One on Bryher.

In a MS note of 1920, King wrote that "Frowhawk and I found one nest on Tean in 1908. One pair also bred at Pelistry (St Mary's) in 1919." In 1924 King (*Scillonia*) noted that little terns "were now so rare in Scilly that beyond mentioning the fact they do occasionally frequent the Isles there is little more to be said of them". Later in the same book he notes that he mistook a clutch of small common tern eggs for those of the little tern. This admission throws doubts on other records. Perhaps there was an over zealous attempt to add new breeding species to the county list, for it was at this time that claims were made for the breeding of turnstones on the Scillies.

On the mainland a light spring passage is nowadays recorded almost annually between mid-April and mid-May—15 April to 21 May off Marazion in 1966. One was seen at Par on 9 April 1964 and another as late as 3 June 1964 off Marazion. Most spring sightings are of single birds, but four were seen at Padstow on 26 April 1965.

The return passage commenced as early as 3 July 1965, but most pass through during August. Rarely since 1950 has the largest daily count in any one year not reached double figures. Maximum numbers in St Ives Bay are 44 on 8 August 1951, about 40 on 17 August 1954, and 30 on 2 August 1963. Records mainly come from St Ives Bay where, along with other terns, they favour the broad sands at Porthkidney beach. In recent years increased records have come from the Camel estuary and Par Bay. Eleven were seen at Carlyon Bay on 29 August 1966 and up to seven at Padstow on 10 August 1965. Most autumn movements are over by about 20 September. Later records include two on the Camel estuary on 19 October 1967 and two off Torpoint ferry on 16 October 1967.

On Scilly the little tern is now a scarce migrant, mainly in autumn. After Clark's account given above, the only published records have been since 1952. All refer to one or two birds between mid-August and early October—9 October 1965 at St Mary's. The largest party is eight off St Agnes on 14 August 1959. Spring records are of single birds on 2 May 1953 at St Mary's and 3 May 1962 at St Agnes.

# SANDWICH TERN
*Sterna sandvicensis*

The sandwich tern nests in scattered localities along the western seaboard of Europe as far north as the southern Baltic. In Britain most nest in Ireland and northern Britain.

On the Scillies it was common in the early nineteenth century, over a hundred nests being recorded in 1841. Forty of them were regularly found in a large stretch of bracken on the north side of Annet (z, 1906). In 1879 there were "heaps of sandwich terns on their eggs and nests with eggs" on Guther's (z) but numbers were gradually diminishing, the species finally disappearing from its favourite nesting ground on Annet about 1885 (RI, 1908). Saunders (*Manual of British Birds*, 1889) wrote that a recent exploration of the islands had failed to find any evidence of breeding, but sporadic nesting did continue. In 1903 two pairs began to build on Guther's only to desert within five weeks, but at least one brood was successfully hatched "in a less frequented spot" (z, 1906). Clark (RI, 1908) wrote that a nest was seen again in 1905—the last record for the islands. In 1911 Robinson saw four sandwich terns on White Island (Samson ?) at the end of May but found no evidence of nesting.

Today the sandwich tern is a passage migrant in small numbers. Early arrivals are seen from mid-March—11 March 1965 at Hayle—with the heaviest passage in April, a party of forty at Porthkidney beach on 12 April 1963 being the most notable. Few are seen after the first week in May until the return passage commences in late July. Unusually early were forty at St John's Lake on 9 July 1965. Parties of this size are now of annual occurrence on the mainland in late August and September but four on several occasions in late September 1963 is the most at Scilly. 1964 saw a good passage with fifty in St Ives Bay on 6 September, eighty on the 20th with a few stragglers remaining until 24 October. Most have gone by this date, but some remained in St Ives Bay until 12 November 1963 and 28 November 1960. The latest occurrence on the Scilly Isles is 13 October 1963 at St Agnes.

to large 'wrecks' on British and Continental coasts.

Cornish records go back to 1823 when Henry Mewburn of St Germans sent Thomas Bewick a bird which had been caught at Treskelly, a mile and a half from the sea, on 5th October. Published nineteenth century records are few, although the species was apparently not uncommon for Rodd (1880) wrote that "during the winter months this small sea-bird comes to us from the north in little parties of ten or a dozen, which soon get broken up and dispersed, and single individuals find their way into our harbours and estuaries".

The largest British wreck was probably that of January 1895, but Cornwall does not seem to have been affected in that year. February and March 1900, however, saw another large wreck and one little auk was picked up dead on St Agnes "in midwinter" (z, 1906)—the first record for Scilly. There have been only ten subsequent records for the Scillies up to 1967 when single birds were seen at St Agnes on 11 October and 2 November. Many may have been unrecorded for Dorrien-Smith (BB, 1952) wrote that in 1950 there were "some about in January *as usual*". The islands apparently escaped the large wreck of February 1950.

Since 1946 there has been at least one record on the mainland for all years except 1947, 1956 and 1961, but the little auk is easily overlooked unless it passes close inshore. The most notable year is 1950 when, in February, large numbers were wrecked on the coasts of south-west Ireland,

## LITTLE AUK           *Plotus alle*

The little auk is one of the most northerly birds breeding in parts of Greenland and several islands including Spitzbergen and Novya Zemlya. In winter it wanders widely over the north Atlantic, being the victim in some years of extremely adverse weather conditions which lead, as with phalaropes,

Little Auk

south-west England and northern France. In England, most were recorded in Cornwall—at least 70, but total estimates have been put at several hundred. Severe gales blew from 8 to 17 February. On the 11th, many were blown inland near Bude, while on the 12th four were seen at Holywell Bay, Cubert. The following day single birds were reported from Hayle, Tregorden Marsh on the Camel, and the Helford River. One was seen off Penzance harbour on the 16th and six were found dead on Prah Sands the next day. During March the remains of about 40 were counted between Loe Bar and Poldhu Cove, Mullion.

Almost every year small parties, or single birds, are seen flying west at St Ives Island—especially in November and December. Similar observations have been made from other headlands in west Cornwall—Godrevy, Pendeen, and Gwennap. Fifteen were reported from St Ives on 12 November 1963 and at least thirteen on 27 November 1965. One or two are sometimes seen resting on the sea in St Ives Bay and more rarely in Mount's Bay. Early records are of one flying west off Pendeen on 4 October 1965 and two on the 8th, with another off Godrevy Point on the same day. Late records include two flying west off St Ives Island on 12 March 1966 and one at Whitsand Bay, St John's on 31 March 1965. Between early April and early October the only little auks reported are two blown over Park Head in a north-westerly gale on 21 April 1952, and single birds off Newquay on 4 June and 10 July 1947.

## GUILLEMOT                    *Uria aalge*

The guillemot has a similar, but more widespread, European breeding range to the razorbill from north-west Iberia to Finland. In Britain it is usually the more abundant where the two species occur in the same colonies. Birds nesting in this country belong to the southern form *Uria aalge albionis*.

In Cornwall, guillemots breed at fewer localities than razorbills, although the total populations on the mainland are roughly similar†. Little is known of the history of their colonies. Clark wrote (VCH) of nesting on the south coast somewhere between the Tamar and Fowey rivers and on the north coast as far east as the Devon border, but there are no colonies here now. In 1952, at least sixteen birds were seen at High Point, Dodman on 30 May, but there are no other records from this cliff. Further west at the turn of the century a few guillemots bred west of Kynance, and small colonies existed at Tolpedn Penwith and Carn lês Boel. At the latter up to a hundred birds were seen in 1942, but only a few young were reared and none were reported in 1943 or since, although it is not known exactly when the colony died out. A colony at Morvah, estimated to contain fifty sitting birds in 1942, had dropped to a maximum of twenty in 1944 and only a few in 1947 and 1948. More nest here now—forty is regarded as about the usual maximum although only seventeen occupied nests were counted in 1967, perhaps due to the effect of the *Torrey Canyon* disaster. At Porthmissen near Padstow, where some 70 birds were on breeding ledges in 1937, there were only four birds ten years later, rising gradually to over twenty in 1965. In 1944, a small colony was noticed on the mainland cliffs under the Ladies' Window at Trevalga. It still existed in the early 1950's (Treleaven[1]), but in 1967 the only nesting birds were seen off-shore on Long and Short islands. On the latter island, the birds pack themselves on two small ledges at the north end.

While there has been a general decrease in the guillemot population, the decline is thought to have been slower than for the razorbill and some observers maintain that remaining colonies are holding their own at a reduced level.

† Fuller details on this and provincial names are given under razorbill.

On the Scillies, guillemots are said to be outnumbered by razorbills by about twenty-five to one, and never to have been so abundant. Even so, the guillemot formerly nested in great profusion becoming scarce late in the last century. The populous centres given by various authors were at Mincarlo, Gorregan, Rosevean, Menavawr, Hanjague, and Scilly Rock. Smart (PZ, 1885–86) noted only the last three localities and put the population at no more than thirty pairs. Clark and Rodd (z, 1906) noted small numbers on Menavawr and possibly on Hanjague but found it nowhere prominent. Only one broken egg was found on Scilly Rock in 1903 while "on Gorregan one of its recent strongholds, only three eggs were discovered while on Mincarlo, where King says there were nine or ten nests in 1900, no trace of it could be found". Clark in 1908 (RI) wrote that for the last three years the only nesting sites were on Menavawr and Hanjague. The population has not strengthened at any time since. Birds seem to have shifted their stations periodically and numbers have fluctuated for King (MS, 1912–28) reported nesting on Gorregan and Mincarlo as well as Menavawr and Hanjague. Robinson in 1920 wrote that they were almost confined to Gorregan and Rosevean with a few pairs on Menawethan. "Fair numbers" were maintained in 1911, but the species had become "very scarce" in 1914 due to destruction by gulls. Herring gulls smashed eggs not five yards from where Robinson stood on Rosevean in 1914 (BB, 1920–21). In 1938, Harvey found a few on Mincarlo where there had been many with eggs in June 1923 (Wallis, MS), and numerous on Menavawr on the top of which they, and razorbills, were thick under the great boulders. In 1946 and 1947, nesting was noted on Menavawr and Gorregan where the colonies were "too large to estimate", on Mincarlo and on a few of the Eastern Islands. At present about 25 pairs nest on the ledges on Menavawr, eight on Scilly Rock, and seventeen on Gorregan,

but are probably extinct at Mincarlo and Hanjague. Hunt[1] (1967) wrote that more now nest under boulders, a habit not mentioned before 1923 and which may be a recently developed protection against gulls.

Guillemots

Both guillemots and razorbills nest in passages and channels between the rounded boulders of the outer rocks . . . "They are still communal and up to twenty birds may crowd together down a long tunnel, each standing over its egg or chick" (Quick, 1964). Six or seven were found dead together in one burrow on Gorregan on 12 June 1952.

Guillemots' eggs were found in Cornwall as early as 23 April in 1932, but mid-May to early June is the normal time for laying. All young have generally left by the last week in July.

The large movements off the Cornish coast in autumn are further detailed under razorbill. The main passage is in October with small numbers from July. Observations at St Ives suggest that a large proportion of identifiable guillemots belong to the northern form *Uria aalge aalge*, the typical race breeding in northern Europe including north and east Scotland. In 1961 most of the guillemots that passed St Ives Island on

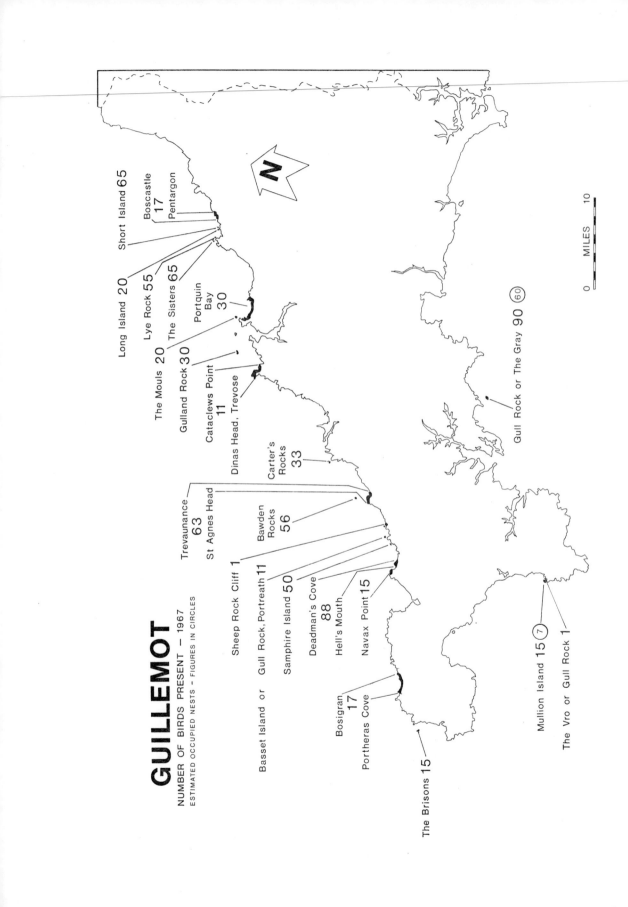

# GUILLEMOT

NUMBER OF BIRDS PRESENT – 1967
ESTIMATED OCCUPIED NESTS – FIGURES IN CIRCLES

N

0     MILES    10

Short Island 65
Boscastle 17
Pentargon
Long Island 20
Lye Rock 55
The Sisters 65
Portquin Bay 30
The Mouls 20
Gulland Rock 30
Cataclews Point 11
Dinas Head, Trevose
Carter's Rocks 33
Trevaunance 63
St Agnes Head
Bawden Rocks 56
Sheep Rock Cliff 1
Gull Rock, Portreath 11
Basset Island or
Samphire Island 50
Deadman's Cove 88
Hell's Mouth
Navax Point 15
Bosigran 17
Portheras Cove
The Brisons 15
Mullion Island 15 (7)
The Vro or Gull Rock 1
Gull Rock or The Gray 90 (60)

17 October and all those identifiable on 20 October, belonged to the northern form, but examination of over 1,000 wings from birds washed ashore after the *Torrey Canyon* disaster, shewed the proportion of the two forms to be about equal. Curiously, the northern form is generally considered to be resident, or to disperse in winter over very short distances. A few dead northern guillemots had previously been picked up in Cornwall in autumn and winter.

A few guillemots shelter in bays throughout the winter, although less commonly than razorbills. Guillemots may return to nesting ledges as early as January and February—at Hells Mount near Godrevy, over forty on 6 January 1964 and sixty on 11 February 1965—but it is not clear whether they remain on the ledges until the breeding season, for in other parts of Britain these early visits have been only temporary.

The bridled guillemot is a rare variety in Cornwall. Two were identified on nesting ledges on Gorregan in 1949, and three on Menavawr in 1958. No doubt some are overlooked for the last published mainland records are of single birds at the now extinct colony on Carn lês Boel in 1931, 1933 and 1941. The percentage in Cornwall is certainly less than one, compared with about twenty in the Northern Isles and there is some indication that bridled birds are becoming rarer in Britain, especially in the south.

All ringed guillemots recovered in Cornwall—mainly on the north coast during the winter or, more frequently, during the migration periods—were marked as young or adults at the following British breeding colonies—Isle of May, 1; Farne Islands, 2; Rathlin Island, 3; Great Saltee, 1; Isle of Man, 1; Calf of Man, 1; Bardsey Island, 1; Grassholm, 1; Skokholm, 4; Skomer, 4; Lundy Island, 16.

The only recoveries of locally ringed birds, excluding eleven recovered within the county and ex-*Torrey Canyon* victims released and recovered on the Cornish coast, are—

| Ringed | Recovered |
|---|---|
| | FRANCE |
| Scilly Rock, adult 31.6.'60 | found exhausted, Fort-Bloqué Morbihan 23.8.'60 |
| Menavawr, adult 4.7.'58 | found dying, Rade de Brest, Finistère 18.4.'64 |
| | SPAIN |
| Gorregan, nestling 29.6.'61 | shot off Pasajes, Guipuzcoa, 7.11.'61 |
| Menavawr, nestling 4.7.'58 | caught by a fishing hook near Pasajes, Guipuzcoa, 20.11.'58 |

## ARCTIC (BRÜNNICH'S) GUILLEMOT
*Uria lomvia*

The arctic guillemot breeds on widely separated stretches of coastline and as near to Britain as Iceland. It rarely moves south in winter, even to north British waters. Bullmore (1866) wrote that one had been shot by George Copeland at Rosemullion Head, Mawnan in 1858, but as no further details were supplied, the record is not generally regarded as acceptable.

## BLACK GUILLEMOT
*Cepphus grylle*

The black guillemot nests on many rocky cliffs, on islands like Spitzbergen and Iceland, and on the mainland on both sides of the north Atlantic including Scandinavia. In the British Isles it breeds on most Irish coasts and in Scotland, except the east and south. Some former haunts, as in North Wales, have been abandoned.

In winter, those breeding furthest north move to the edge of the pack-ice, but British birds are mainly sedentary, wintering off their immediate breeding areas. This accounts for the rarity of the black guillemot in Cornish waters. It was first described as a Cornish species by Walter Moyle (Tonkin MS) under the name of 'Greenland Dove' or

*Black guillemots*

'Sea Turtle', which he 'shot and cased' in 1718. Tonkin added that "This being a Rare Bird in these Parts, where it is seldome seen, I will (if I can procure the Bird) give a Description of it, that in Willughby being imperfect, as I believe he had never seen it himself". The species is not mentioned again until 1838 when Couch wrote that it had occurred in Cornwall in winter plumage. The only subsequent records are—

pre- One obtained "some years since" in
1850 Mount's Bay (PZ).
pre- One obtained at Gyllyngvase, Falmouth
1851 (Cocks, 1851).
1873 One shot at Falmouth on 27 January (Z).
1905 One picked up dead at St Anthony lighthouse on 12 March (RI, 1906).

Harvey (1915) said it had been obtained in the Penzance-Land's End area but gave no details.

1930 One seen diving for food off Sennen Cove on 7 and 8 November (BB).
1947 The only example reported from Scilly was seen about St Mary's and the Eastern Islands from 4 March to 4 June.
1948 One off Polurrian Cove, Mullion on 13 January.
1949 Two in winter plumage off Trevose Head on 16 September.
1956 One in St Ives harbour on 11 April and another off Park Head, St Merryn on the 18th.
1962 A bird in near breeding plumage remained in Sennen Cove from 21 March to 8 April.
1963 A bird in winter plumage seen about a mile off Land's end on 9 October.

# PUFFIN                 *Fratercula arctica*

Puffins breed on the north Atlantic sea-board from New England to Spitzbergen and as far south as Brittany. In this country the principal colonies are in the north and west, but breeding numbers have shewn a marked decrease, especially in the south, during the present century. Lundy, which derives its name from the Old Norse—*Unde* (puffin) and *ey* (island), contained incredible numbers at the end of the last century, about 3,500 pairs in 1939 and only 93 pairs in 1962. Birds breeding in Britain, as well as the Faeroes, southern Scandinavia and Brittany, belong to the southern form *Fratercula arctica grabae*.

The puffin, popularly regarded as a veritable buffoon of birds because of its human bearing, has attracted more attention than most other species of common seabirds. In Cornwall, it has inherited a host of popular synonyms. 'Brilley' or 'bully' was used in Mousehole, a name probably derived from the Cornish *eden bylly* (mackerel bird) which correctly referred to the Manx shearwater. 'Bully' was widely used on the east coast, as well as in Cornwall, for birds and fishes which are short and thick-set. The Cornish *popa* (pl. *popys*) was Anglicised to 'pope' or even 'popey duck', a name recorded by Ray (1662) and still used at St Ives†. *Nath* (pl. *nathas*) was used in north Cornwall and north Devon at least until the nineteenth century—"puffins, or naths, abound about Boscastle and in the parish of St Gennys" (Bray, *Tamar and Tavy*, 1836). The name probably survives in Nathaga rocks in Gwithian parish. In west Cornwall, as at Porthleven, the puffin was called a 'Londoner', possibly so named from its visitor-like custom of standing upon the cliffs in crowds and gazing vacantly seawards, or perhaps from the likeness of its plumage to the black-and-white evening-dress of hotel guests. 'Lundy parrot', and 'Welsh parrot', were names used in north Cornwall and north Devon.

† This name was also loosely applied to the razorbill.

Most appropriate, however, is the name 'Scilly parrot', for on these islands the species formerly nested in tens of thousands. Scilly furnishes the earliest reference to the puffin in Britain. An inquisition of 30 November 29 Edward I—that is A.D. 1300, lists—

> Fee farms pertaining to the gate of the castle of Launceveton [Launceston] to be received by the Lands of divers tenants viz . . . SULLY, 6s. 8d. [half a mark] from [i.e. in lieu of] 300 puffons rent.

Six years later, Edward I granted the castle of Ennor—the old name for St Mary's—to Randulph de Blancminster, or Randulph de Albo Monasterio, in return for finding twelve armed men, keeping the peace and paying yearly at the gates of Launceston Castle at Michaelmas (29th September) a rent called 'waiternfee' (watching fee) of three hundred puffins or six and eight pence. By 1440 the rent was fifty puffins or six and eightpence. Bowley (*The Fortunate Isles*, 1938) wrote that the rent was paid annually up to the time of Edward VI (1547–1553) but always in the form of money. Payment must originally have been in puffins, presumably before 1300 A.D. An item in the Descriptive Catalogue of Ancient Deeds at the Public Record Office, dated 10 Edward III, refers to the subletting of the castle at a rent of 13s. 4d. in default of which a payment of 150 puffins was persecuted.

The farming of puffins is certainly of much greater antiquity than 1300 A.D., for their bones (as well as those of razorbills and guillemots) were discovered during the excavation of the Romano-British site at Nor-Nour, Scilly. The remains of the razorbill outnumbered all others. Dr. F. A. Turk (RI, 1967) who examined them suggests that all these species were also taken so that their oil could be used in lamps "as is that of gannets, storm petrels and fulmars, of which bird species the oil is sometimes burnt in the carcass to provide a light, and it is not impossible that some of the un-identifiable burned bird bones from Nor-

Nour belonged to these kinds".

On the mainland rent was partly paid in puffins in at least one instance. Stephen Hoskyn of Penzance paid Thomas Bouryng in 1494 or 1495 (?)—

> xij pofyns sufficiently savyed for manys mete or ij d. for every pofyn . . . payable at the feast of the purification of our lady yerely. And that the said Stephyn and hys heyrs shall cary the said pofyns to the said Thomas and hys heyrs to Salcomb or Bourynggeslegh in the county of Devonshire . . . at the cost of the said Stephyn (Toy, *History of Helston*, 1936).

The distance which these birds were carried indicates what a delicacy they were. Concerning their eating, Carew (1602) observed that "The Puffin hatched in holes of the cliffe whose young ones are thence ferretted out, being exceeding fat, kept salted, and reputed for fish as coming nearest thereto in their taste". Montagu (1813) recorded exactly this practice on the Isle of Man where "The young are fit to take in August when great numbers are killed and barrelled with salt, which the inhabitants boil and eat with potatoes".

Puffin

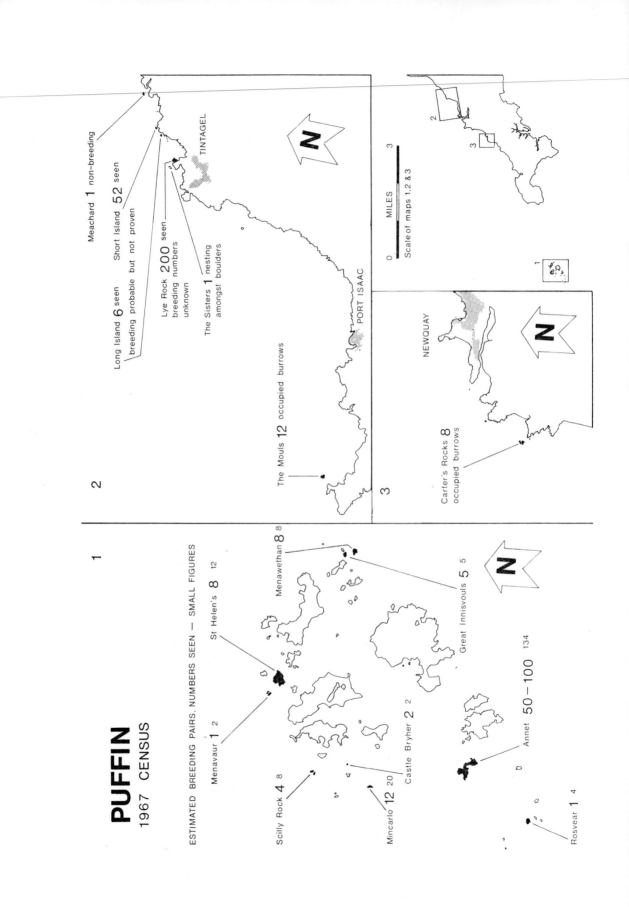

PUFFIN
1967 CENSUS

ESTIMATED BREEDING PAIRS. NUMBERS SEEN — SMALL FIGURES

St Helen's 8 12

Menawethan 8 8

Menavaur 1 2

Great Innisvouls 5 5

N

Scilly Rock 4 8

Mincarlo 12 20

Castle Bryher 2 2

Annet 50 – 100 134

Rosvear 1 4

1

2

Meachard 1 non-breeding

Short Island 52 seen

Long Island 6 seen
breeding probable but not proven

Lye Rock 200 seen
breeding numbers
unknown

The Sisters 1 nesting
amongst boulders

TINTAGEL

PORT ISAAC

The Mouls 12 occupied burrows

N

0      MILES      3

Scale of maps 1, 2 & 3

3

NEWQUAY

Carter's Rocks 8
occupied burrows

N

Young gulls were kept alive and fattened on terrestrial food to make their flesh more palatable, but Carew makes no mention of this practice being directed towards the puffin, and the resulting dish would seem hardly palatable to the modern tongue. Ligons (*History of Barbadoes*, 1673) spoke of the ill taste of puffins "which we have from the isles of Scilly" adding "this kind of food is only for servants". The Pope permitted the eating of puffins during Lent and it was far from an unpopular dish in the sixteenth century. "There was nothing that Tudor persons would not eat" wrote A. L. Rowse (*Tudor Cornwall*, 1941) quoting letters from the time of Henry VIII from St Aubyn to Lady Lisle—letters accompanied to Calais by presents of puffins and gulls "which Bosworthogga or John Keigwin will deliver". Oliver Goldsmith (1728–74) remarked that the flesh of the puffin, although excessively rank, is when pickled and spiced, much admired by those who are fond of high eating. At what date the taking of puffins or other sea-birds on Scilly ceased, is not recorded. Probably it was no more than a memory to the islanders in 1756 when Borlase wrote (*Observations* etc. *of Scilly*) that puffins must have been taken "for the sake of their feathers, I suppose, rather than their flesh . . .". His reference in *The Natural History* (1758) to the salting of puffins is acknowledged as a direct quote from Carew, and nowhere does he suggest it was practiced in his own day. One might reasonably suppose that the islanders would have supplemented their diet with bird flesh in times of extreme hardship, were the practice still known to them. At the beginning of the last century poverty was at its most extreme, especially on the smaller islands, and the greater part of the inhabitants had very little barley-bread or potatoes, some living almost exclusively on limpets and fresh water. But *A Report detailing the Extreme Miseries of the Off-Islands of Scilly* (G. Smith, 1818) which involved interviews with every family, did not reveal a single instance of the eating of birds—not even on Annet where distress was greatest.

It is hardly likely that puffin farming seriously affected the numbers of breeding birds. In the mediæval period puffins bred on some, if not all, of the islands now inhabited, for William of Worcester (*c.* 1475 described "Rascow" (Tresco) as an island "cum cuniculis et avibus vocatis pophyns". The dramatic fall in the population has largely materialized within the lifetime of many people still living. As recently as 1908 Frohawk found amazing numbers on Annet, and estimated 100,000 birds to be present (Parslow[1]). In 1899 King wrote (*Cornish Magazine*) that Annet could scarcely be called *terra firma*, it being so riddled with burrows that the roofs would cave in every few paces. On other islands like Scilly Rock and Menavawr, where the ground is too hard for burrowing, nesting takes place in crevices in the bare rock.

During the first decade of this century the number of great black-backed gulls nesting on Scilly began to increase to the detrement or young puffins and shearwaters which provide a ready-made larder for this voracious gull, which seems, above all, to be responsible for the dramatic decrease of puffins. While King in 1924 (*Scillonia*) still found thousands at Annet disporting themselves off-shore in a "puffin playground", Wallis, in the same year (BB), wrote of the tremendous devastation—"forty corpses within forty feet linear". By 1945 no more than twenty pairs were seen about Annet, and the following year none may have nested for only one bird was seen there. At Menavawr a few pairs remained where many had nested until the 1930's. None was seen at Gorregan, but small numbers remained at Haycocks, Melledgan, and Mincarlo, while other rock-stacks probably contained a few pairs. Since 1947, a small but gradually increased colony of between 60 and 100 pairs has been maintained on Annet—more birds than on the other islands combined, as shewn on the map. Round Island no longer contains breeding puffins, probably because of the lighthouse cats. While some still nested there in 1906 (z) few have probably done so since 1887 when the lighthouse was built. At that time the island was thick with birds which even overflowed onto St Helen's (PZ, 1888–89). *The Cornish Telegraph* (16 August 1888) records that puffins, the only inhabitants, "are very tame and were wont to walk in and out of the kitchen of the workmen who built the tower. It is interesting to speculate how far they will be dispossessed after the permanent occupation of the islet by the lightkeepers."

Puffins are now far less common on the mainland than formerly. Ray (1662) and Borlase (MS) recorded them at Godrevy Island where they may have bred until the lighthouse was built in 1860. In the nineteenth century Rodd (PZ, 1850 etc.) wrote that they were "occasionally on the Land's End cliffs", suggesting a few pairs nested there, but none were known to do so by Harvey (1915). Some may have gone undetected on off-shore islets, for in 1957 three were seen at nesting ledges on the Brisons off Cape Cornwall.

In the Lizard peninsula, puffins were said to be locally common as far east as Falmouth (VCH)—presumably in rabbit burrows. Marginalia, evidently written in the late nineteenth century, in a copy of L'Estrange's "*Yachting Round the West of England*" (1865) in the County Library at Truro, informs us that the anonymous reader "took nine at one scramble at the Lizard", and that "sixty dozen were taken off one rock at Mullion". This was certainly Gull Rock where, according to Harvey (*History of Mullyon*, 1875) and Johns (WLZ, 1874), they bred commonly with gulls and cormorants each holding "their appointed portions of the rock, in a happy truce that had been reached five years before after a dreadful war of twelve hours duration, the din of which reached even to the Church Town".

No puffins are now known to nest on the south coast of Cornwall. In 1967 eight burrows which could have belonged to puffins were found on Gull Rock, Veryan, but only one bird was seen on the sea half a mile away. In June 1951 eggs were found there and a Portloe fisherman told the author in 1968 that a few had bred there up to about ten years or so ago while he remembered large flocks of the 'sea parrots' about the rock in the 1920's.

It is impossible to determine breeding numbers with any accuracy without landing, an operation not undertaken in 1967 as it would have meant distributing the razor-bills and guillemots, as well as the puffins, whose eggs would soon have fallen foul of the gulls. A maximum count on three visits to Lye Rock gave 200 birds on the sea below the burrows, but it is not possible to say whether this represented 200 pairs; only two occupied burrows could be counted from the mainland. Even if this number were nesting in 1967 it represents a tremendous decrease since the end of the last century. Cecil Smith found thousands there in 1885 (z) and in the 1940's 3,000 or more could be seen. Both Long and Short islands lack turf and have suffered considerable soil erosion. Proof of breeding is lacking, but small numbers almost certainly nest among the boulders. One bird was seen incubating amongst the boulders on The Sisters west of Lye Rock; another was seen at Meachard Island off Boscastle, but there was no proof of breeding. On the mainland birds unsuccessfully bred at Willapark, west of Tintagel, in 1942. Until about 1950 a few nested on the mainland at the Rumps, but since then they have been confined to The Mouls.

Puffins may have nested at Porthmissen, Trevone Bay near Padstow, but W. S. Watts who closely watched the area never proved to his own satisfaction that any nested, even though he counted as many as a hundred in the vicinity in 1950. On Carter's Rocks, Hollywell Bay, eight occupied burrows with one bird sitting were counted in 1967. A possible nesting site is Gulland Rock, Padstow, but only one bird was seen here.

Evidence from islands like The Mouls and Carter's Rocks demonstrates that the decrease in puffins has been due, at least in part, to the destruction of their habitat. Erosion has left insufficient soil for the puffins to burrow into. Gulls are responsible, for by stripping the islands of grass little remains to hold the soil in place except a few stems of mallow. On Carter's Rocks, where no turf now remains, humans have also contributed by removing material for use as garden manure, the few puffins burrowing in the last remaining soil which is only a foot deep in places.

Puffins desert their breeding ledges in July, sometimes vacating them completely by the middle of the month, although a few may be present in mid-August. At this time of the year, small migrating parties can be seen moving west at places like St Ives although few are recorded here in spite of intensive watching—a party of fourteen on 12 July 1964 was unusually large. A small number, rarely with more than ten in a flock, are sometimes seen off north and south coasts between October and March when most southern puffins are ranging over the Continental shelf as far south as the North African coast. Exact movements are not known but some Scottish birds have been recovered off Newfoundland. While some birds in Cornish waters may be southern puffins driven inshore by adverse weather conditions, some are known to belong to the northern race *Fratercula arctica arctica* as R. B. Treleaven has identified the corpses of oiled birds washed up near Bude. Birds begin returning to their breeding sites about mid-March, along with other auks, but are not at full strength until mid-May.

Lye Rock, Tintagel –
the most important puffin
colony off the Cornish mainland

Ringing records refer to four birds from Skokholm and one from Skomer found dead on the north Cornish coast (4) and at Gunwalloe (1). An adult ringed at Rouzic, Sept Iles, Côtes du Nord on 6 July 1934 was controlled breeding at Annet in May 1936.

## RAZORBILL                           *Alca torda*

The razorbill is a north Atlantic auk, nesting in Europe from north Finland to Brittany. Birds breeding in Britain, Iceland, the Faeroes and Brittany belong to the form *Alca torda islandica*, but the northern form (*Alca torda torda*) is not distinguishable in the field.

Razorbills and guillemots were described in Cornwall by Willughby and Ray (1662) at Godrevy Island where they found the razorbill less common than the 'guillems' or 'kidduns' of which "many scores of young ones lie dead here". 'Kiddun' seems to have been applied only to the guillemot, but the name 'murre' was applied to both species although mainly to the guillemot in east Cornwall and to the razorbill in the west. Carew (1602) wrote of 'murres' and their suitability as food, and no doubt both razorbills and guillemots were eaten. Until about thirty years ago guillemots—as well as puffins—were eaten by the Farne islanders, and their eggs were preserved in a mixture of salt, water and peat ash.

Most razorbills are found on two stretches of the north coast—Beeny Cliff to Trevose Head and Holywell Bay to Godrevy. A smaller concentration occurs between the Land's End and Bosigran, Zennor. The only other localities are at Mullion and Gull Rock, Veryan. In 1952 a previously un-recorded colony of some twelve birds was found at High Cliff, Dodman, but there are no subsequent records. In 1957 a chick was being fed close to the shore off Downderry, St Germans, on 6 July, but no colony has been found in south-east Cornwall since Clark wrote in 1906 (VCH) that birds nested

somewhere between the Tamar and Fowey rivers. Large numbers nested early this century at Gull Rock, Veryan (VCH). Johns (WLZ) described them as numerous in the Lizard peninsula in the nineteenth century and large numbers still nested up to 1906 west of Kynance (VCH) where they are now confined to Mullion Island and nearby Gull Rock. The colony at Godrevy Island (described in 1662) may have been extinct for many years, but A. C. Thomas[1] (1967) wrote that birds formerly nested on the north facing cliff of the main island and were seen there in 1959 and possibly in 1960. Cecil Smith, on his tour of May 1885 (Z), found a good many nesting near Land's End, presumably at Carn lês Boel where there were only three or four pairs in the 1930's. Two pairs were seen here in 1942 but none since about 1950. On the north Cornish coast colonies formerly extended as far east as Gull Rock at Marsland Mouth, but none are now known east of Beeny Cliff, St Juliot. A colony that has shewn a considerable decrease is at Navax Point, Gwithian, where about a hundred birds were said to be nesting in 1941, compared with only twenty in 1967. Figures published for many north coast localities are of limited use, however, for the number of birds present in an area may be far greater than the number actually breeding. Thus, at Trevone, 200–250 birds were seen in 1946 and 1947 when only six and two chicks were counted respectively.

Published works, as Ryves (1948), des-cribe the razorbill as far more common than the guillemot in Cornwall—a situation that is the reverse of most other places in the British Isles apart from Ireland. The 1967 census, however, shewed that the two species nest in similar numbers in the county —between 720 and 740 pairs each. The razorbill is the more adaptable and will nest not only on high cliffs but also on a boulder-strewn shore so that it is found at more localities than the guillemot as the maps indicate. However, where the two species nest in the same colony, the guillemot is

# RAZORBILL

NUMBER OF BIRDS PRESENT — 1967
Apparently occupied nests — figures in circles

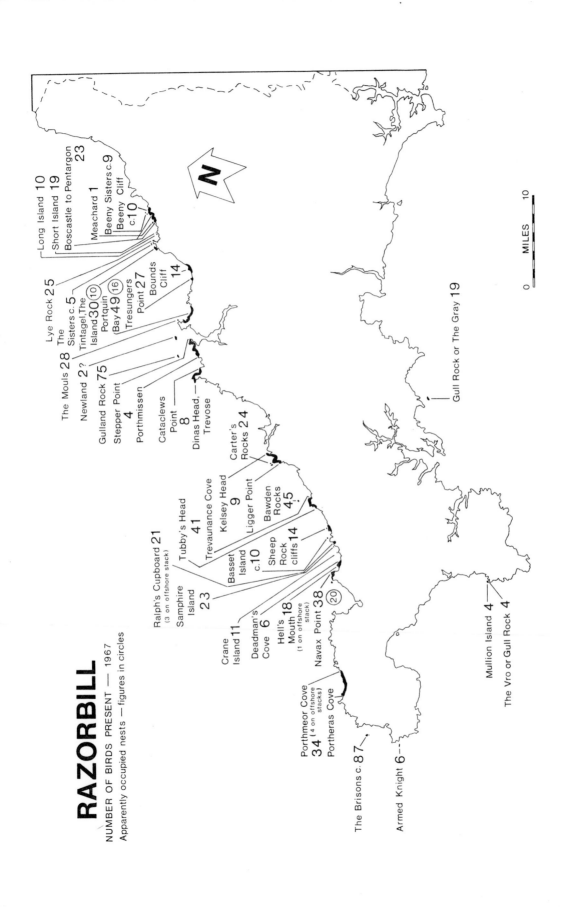

N

Long Island 10
Short Island 19
Boscastle to Pentargon 23
Meachard 1
Beeny Sisters c.9
Beeny Cliff c.10

Lye Rock 25
The Sisters c. 5
Tintagel, The Island 30 (10)
Portquin (Bay 49 (16)
Tresungers Point 27
Bounds Cliff 14

The Mouls 28
Newland 2?
Gulland Rock 75
Stepper Point 4
Porthmissen
Cataclews Point 8
Dinas Head, Trevose

Carter's Rocks 24

Trevaunance Cove
Kelsey Head 9
Ligger Point
Bawden Rocks 4.5

Tubby's Head 41
Basset Island c.10
Sheep Rock cliffs 14

Ralph's Cupboard 21
(3 on offshore stack)
Samphire Island 23

Crane Island 11
Deadman's Cove 6
Hell's Mouth 18
Navax Point 38

(1 on offshore stack)
20

Porthmeor Cove 34
(4 on offshore stacks)
Portheras Cove

The Brisons c. 87

Armed Knight 6

Gull Rock or The Gray 19

Mullion Island 4
The Vro or Gull Rock 4

0          MILES          10

# RAZORBILL

ESTIMATED BREEDING PAIRS — 1967

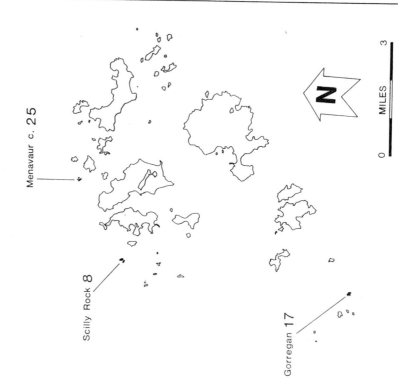

Haniague 1
Menavaur c. 100
Menawethan 6
Great Innisvouls 10
Little Innisvouls 1
Shipman Head 1
Scilly Rock 30
Maiden Bower 3
Illiswilgig 7
Mincarlo 60
Castle Bryher 20
Melledgan 20
Annet 9
Rosvear 8
Gorregan 29
Rosvean 15

# GUILLEMOT

ESTIMATED BREEDING PAIRS — 1967

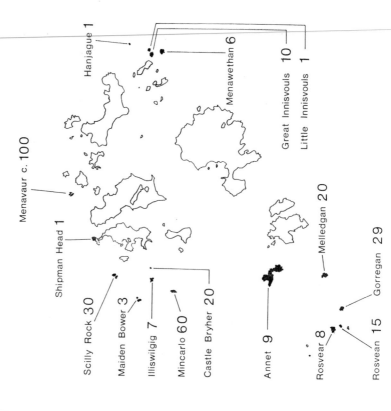

Menavaur c. 25
Scilly Rock 8
Gorregan 17

N

0 MILES 3

usually more abundant—

| 1967—number of nests: | Razorbill | | Guillemot |
|---|---|---|---|
| Gull Rock, Veryan | 19 | .. | 60 |
| Samphire Island | 23 | .. | 60 |
| The Sisters & Lye Rock | 30 | .. | 50 |

At only a few localities were razorbills more common—

| Gulland Rock, Padstow | 75 | .. | 30 |
|---|---|---|---|
| West Penwith area | 127 | .. | 32 |

A surprisingly low total of guillemots at The Brisons—ten to fifteen nests (about 100 in 1957) compared with 87 for the razorbill—may have been due to oil pollution, but it is curious that both species were not affected to a similar extent by the *Torrey Canyon* disaster.

Few nineteenth century records give any indication of breeding numbers on Scilly. It was certainly far more common than the guillemot. Smart wrote that it bred "in countless numbers" but only on rocks—Hanjague, Menavawr and all the Western Rocks, in greater or lesser numbers (PZ, 1885–86 & 1888–89). Clark and Rodd (Z, 1906) also noted "extraordinary numbers" especially on the Western Rocks and those to the north and west of Bryher. On 2 May 1903 on the eastern half of Scilly Rock, forty-one eggs were found in less than half-an-hour. Hundreds, if not thousands, were still nesting on Rosevear up to 1914–15 (Robinson, BB). King estimated that razorbills outnumbered guillemots by about twenty to one—the lack of steep cliffs making the islands largely unattractive to guillemots while the razorbills were content with the shelter afforded by the countless boulders and large detached rocks. In 1946 (BB) the razorbill was still described as 'abundant' although this must surely have been an exaggeration compared with numbers forty years previously. In late May 1961 only 75 birds were seen about all the islands.

During the autumn large movements of both razorbills and guillemots are noted off the Cornish coast. N. R. Phillips[1] (1968), working at St Ives, considers razorbills to comprise the greatest numbers of identifiable auks. Similarly, A. G. Parsons working at Godrevy in 1958, saw almost all razorbills, using as his criterion for identification the silhouette of the bird—the razorbill's shorter beak and neck giving the bird a distinctive 'dumpy' look compared with the guillemot.

As the two species are not normally distinguishable unless close to land, the movements are considered together here. It is impossible to assess accurately the numbers of migrating birds, but some 200 an hour pass St Ives Island for hours on end, especially during north-westerly gales. Smaller movements are visible from shore irrespective of wind direction. In north-westerly gales, peak counts at St Ives include *c.* 50,000 in eight-and-a-half hours on 1 November 1965, 20,000 or more in eight hours on 16 November 1966, about 7,000 in two hours on 2 November 1967, and 4,000 in two hours on 20 December 1965. While most movements have been watched from St Ives and other headlands in west Cornwall, large passages have been seen at Newquay and Port Isaac.

Small numbers of razorbills remain close off-shore throughout the winter in the sheltered waters of St Ives Bay, Mount's Bay and Veryan Bay. Birds do not congregate off their breeding stations in any numbers until March. Few dates have been published for the earliest settling on nesting ledges—six on 12 March 1933 at the now extinct colony of Carn lês Boel, while at Trevone none were seen until 25 March in 1945. Eggs are laid in early May—unusually

Razorbill

early were those seen on 24 April 1933 (BB). In contrast, some young are still being fed up to the end of July in some years.

Adults or young razorbills ringed at the following British breeding colonies, outside Cornwall, have been recovered in the county—most of them picked up dead on the north coast—
Rathlin Island, 1; Isle of Man, 1; Calf of Man, 1; Skokholm, 10; Skomer, 2; Lundy Island, 7.

Recoveries of locally ringed birds, excluding six found within the county or off the south Devon coast are—

| Ringed | Recovered |
|---|---|
| Menavawr, nestling 4.7.'58 | found dead, Siouville, Manche, Normandy 20.6.'64 |
| Annet, adult 31.6.'60 | found dead, Muzillac, Morbihan, Brittany 17.9.'66 |
| Annet, nestling 22.6.'61 | shot at Skottning Lighthouse, Hordaland, Norway c. 5.10.'62 |
| Annet, adult 9.7.'61 | found dead nr. Katwijk aan Zee, Zuid Holland 7.2.'65 |
| The Mouls, St Minver, adult 23.6.'49 | found dead, Little Haven, Pembs. 27.8.'51 |

A nestling ringed at Kandalaksha, Murmansk, U.S.S.R. on 22 July 1956 was caught and released at Fowey on 3 February 1957 where it was found dead on the 15th. A number of razorbills washed up on the north Cornish coast have been identified by R. B. Treleaven as belonging to the northern race *Alca torda torda*.

# INDEX OF SPECIES

[Only the main references are given]